BMW
MOTORCYCLES

Darwin Holmstrom and Brian J. Nelson

motorbooks

ACKNOWLEDGEMENTS AND DEDICATIONS

I want to thank David Percival of Andover, Maine, who made available his amazing collection of rare motorcycles; Evan Bell and Brian Bell from Irv Seaver's BMW in Anaheim, California, for opening up their shop to me; Bob Henig from Bob's BMW in Jessup, Maryland—the coffee's always on at Bob's shop, which is a virtual BMW Museum; Erich Bley of Bley Engineering for being considerate enough to let me photograph his rare and exotic race bikes; Henry Fuchs from the Otis Chandler Museum; and all the other BMW owners and shops who let me photograph their bikes.

—Brian J. Nelson, 2009

Many people made this book possible—too many to list here—but I want everyone involved to know I appreciate their hard work. However, the contributions of several people cannot go unmentioned. I want to thank my editors Lee Klancher and Jeff Zuehlke, as well as Ken Fund, president and CEO of Quayside, Motorbooks parent company, our publisher Zack Miller, and the hard-working Deborah Turenne, just because she has a thankless job and deserves a thank you. I especially want to thank Brian J. Nelson for being my partner on this project. Brian is without question one of the finest photographers working in motorsports today and I am fortunate to have worked with him on this project. Most of all I want to thank Patricia Johnson, who is still the reason I get up in the morning. I want to dedicate this book to Brian, Kristen, and Alison Toay.

—Darwin Holmstrom 2009

First published in 2009 by Motorbooks, an imprint of MBI Publishing Company, 400 First Avenue North, Suite 300, Minneapolis, MN 55401 USA

Motorbooks titles are also available at discounts in bulk quantity for industrial or sales-promotional use. For details write to Special Sales Manager at MBI Publishing Company, 400 First Avenue North, Suite 300, Minneapolis, MN 55401 USA.

To find out more about our books, visit us online at www.motorbooks.com.

On the Front Cover:
The BMW R1200GS Adventure. ©*Henry von Wartenberg*

On the Frontispiece: With its simple, angular lines, the R68 ranks as one of the most elegant BMW motorcycles.

On the title page: This striking two-tone paint job was available on the Special Edition version of the K1100RS, produced for the 1995 model year.

On the back cover, top: In 1960, the R69S took over the R69's spot as BMW's top dog. Its 594cc engine pumped out 42 horsepower.

On the back cover, bottom: The HP2: an uncompromising, sporting, and exceptionally light off-road boxer.

Library of Congress Cataloging-in-Publication Data

Holmstrom, Darwin.
  BMW motorcycles / by Darwin Holmstrom ; photographs by Brian J. Nelson. — New ed.
    p. cm.
  Includes index.
  ISBN 978-0-7603-3748-6 (pbk. : alk. paper)
  1. BMW motorcycle—History. I. Nelson, Brian J., 1965– II. Title.
  TL448.B18H65 2009
  629.227'5—dc22
                                    2009015471

Editors: Lee Klancher and Jeffrey Zuehlke
Layout by Katie Sonmor
Cover designed by Brenda C. Canales

Printed in China

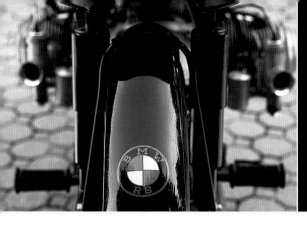

CONTENTS

INTRODUCTION: "GRIND THEM INTO DUST"   7

CHAPTER 1   CHILDREN OF WAR: BMW'S EARLY BIKES   11

CHAPTER 2   THE GREAT DEPRESSION AND THE THIRD REICH   29

CHAPTER 3   AFTER THE WAR   51

CHAPTER 4   LIVING IN THE MODERN WORLD   73

CHAPTER 5   FLYING BRICKS AND THE REVENGE OF THE AIRHEADS   97

CHAPTER 6   FROM MONOLEVERS TO PARALEVERS   119

CHAPTER 7   THE OILHEAD   141

CHAPTER 8: NEW LIFE IN A NEW MILLENIUM   168

            INDEX   192

"GRIND THEM INTO DUST"

Some time back a tuner who specializes in European twin-cylinder motorcycles said something profound to me. He was making sweeping (but amusing) generalizations about the types of people who ride certain brands of motorcycles. When the subject turned to BMW motorcycles, he became serious. "BMW riders are … different," he said.

"How so?" I asked.

He thought about this for a bit, then said, "They want to go out and ride their motorcycles until they grind them into dust."

His description made perfect sense to me. I understand the impulse to get on a bike at the crack of dawn and not get off until the odometer reads 1,000 miles more than when I started riding. I have ground more than one motorcycle into dust.

But not a BMW. The motorcycles produced by *Bayerische Motoren Werke* are not easily ground to dust, a trait that makes them the bikes of choice for many long-distance riders. Every year, more and more people discover just how hard it is to wear out a BMW.

Today most motorcyclists know about the legendary quality BMW builds into every one of its motorcycles, but riders were not always so

ABOVE: The blue-and-white BMW rondelle, designed to represent a spinning airplane propeller against a Bavarian blue sky, has graced some of the finest motorcycles ever made, including this RS54 Rennsport.

LEFT: Eighty years of BMW innovation, from the R32 (bottom left) introduced in 1923, to the 2002 R1150RT (top left).

BMW's two most magnificent racing motorcycles: the RS54 Rennsport of 1954 and the most legendary BMW of all time, the supercharged prewar Kompressor.

familiar with the German marque, especially in the United States. In the not too distant past, BMW motorcycles were exotic commodities here, motorcycles so rare that author Robert Persig felt the need to explain what they were and where they came from in his book *Zen and the Art of Motorcycle Maintenance*. He also explained why people were willing to pay a bit more for a BMW. "The BMW," Persig wrote, "is famous for not giving mechanical problems on the road."

I knew nothing about BMW's iconic status when I first saw one. I was standing in my uncle's driveway alongside U.S. Highway 59 in extreme northwestern Minnesota, and I heard an odd-sounding engine winding out, coming toward me from the north at a fast clip. What most struck me as the bike rode past was an impression of quality. The simple black paint, the heavy Earles fork, the art deco saddlebags, and the dense, boxer engine all hinted at an elegance missing from the small-displacement Japanese motorcycles my older cousins rode or the chopped Harleys and Triumphs that sometimes passed by on the highway.

Being a kid, I didn't articulate these thoughts at the time. Most likely I went back to whatever I was doing, probably some worthwhile activity like throwing rocks at my uncle's mailbox. It would be several years before I even thought about BMW motorcycles again.

The late 1960s and early 1970s marked a time when a lot of motorcyclists didn't give much thought to the simple but rugged

motorcycles coming out of Berlin. This was an era when four-cylinder Japanese motorcycles occupied the thoughts of any right-thinking motorcyclist. Honda's new CB750 four-cylinder was much faster than any oddball twin-cylinder 600 from Germany, and it cost much less to buy. Later even more grandiose equipment from the Far East, such as Kawasaki's mind-boggling Z1, filled our collective conscious. Why bother dreaming of lesser bikes?

But BMW wasn't standing still. It introduced the /5 series in 1969, marking the most major update of the basic boxer twin motor since the introduction of the R5 back in 1936. That series found its ultimate expression in the 898-cc R90S, a bike that brought BMW back to motorcycling's mainstream. On March 5, 1976, at the Daytona International Speedway, Steve McLaughlin won the first official AMA Superbike race ever held, and he won it aboard a BMW R90S. Prior to that race, many motorcyclists dismissed BMWs the way they dismissed Harley-Davidsons of that period. Both companies used archaic technology; both featured twin-cylinder engines with two-valve cylinder heads operated by, of all things, *pushrods*. Yet in Daytona that year, McLaughlin and second-place finisher Reg Pridmore soundly trounced the sophisticated Japanese four-cylinder competition, and Pridmore went on to win the AMA Superbike Championship.

Unlike earlier BMWs, the R90S motorcycles that Pridmore and McLaughlin rode were beautiful machines. The /2 has a mechanical purposefulness in its appearance, but the R90S has style; many riders found it every bit as sexy as the finicky sportbikes being built in Italy. Here was a BMW that inspired more than mere respect. It inspired lust.

Lust sells more bikes than respect, and BMW's presence in the United States began to increase after the introduction of the /5 series. As BMW introduced increasingly modern machines like the /6, /7, RS, and RT models, spotting them became a more common experience. The bikes were still relatively rare compared to Japanese motorcycles, but the people who bought these bikes rode them, and I began to encounter BMW riders in the most isolated parts of America. I met them in Moose Jaw, Saskatchewan, and Walden, Colorado. I met them in Stanley, Idaho, and Warsaw, North Dakota. If I was lucky, I got a chance to talk to some of these riders for a few minutes, before they rode off to whatever far-flung place they were headed to next. Often I'd just see them in my rear-view mirrors as they rode up behind me on the plains of Montana or in the fields of Minnesota. They'd wave as they'd pass, and then I'd watch them disappear into the horizon ahead of me. I knew nothing about these riders, but they became my heroes.

The introduction of the multicylinder K bikes in the 1980s made BMW motorcycles more popular among a wider range of riders. Though the K bikes proved not to be the replacements for the beloved boxers that their designers had envisioned, they developed a loyal following that continues to this day. The introduction of the giant dual-sport GS series did more than the K bikes to increase the BMW's popularity, but it was the advent of the oil-head Boxers in the 1990s that really made BMW take off in the United States. By the turn of the century, BMW was selling almost as many motorcycles in the U.S. market as all other European manufacturers combined.

Now there are more BMW riders than ever before, exploring the farthest reaches of the earth—trying to grind their motorcycles into dust. Thanks to the high standards to which BMW motorcycles are built, and have been built since the firm produced its first motorcycle in 1923, the vast majority of these riders are still failing.

ABOVE: Many BMW fans don't just own BMW motorcycles— they live them. This is the museum section of Bob's BMW in Jessup, Maryland.

LEFT: For a motorcycle that is comfortable enough for cross-country touring, the R1100S gets around a racetrack rather quickly.

CHAPTER 1

CHILDREN OF WAR:

BMW'S EARLY BIKES

In 1914, Europe exploded in war, ostensibly over the murder of Archduke Franz Ferdinand, heir to the throne of Austria and Hungary. Nineteen-year-old Serbian student Gavrilo Princip shot Ferdinand in Sarajevo on June 29 of that year, stepping out of a crowd and firing what came to be known as the first shots of World War I.

In reality, the war was caused by diplomatic incompetence, territorial greed, hubris, and the fact that most of Europe was governed by an isolated class of royalty inbred to the point of hemophilia. Regardless of its causes, World War I had a tremendous impact on engineering practices, accelerating the pace of technological development, as war always does. The quest for more powerful, reliable, and efficient military equipment translated to more powerful, reliable, and efficient civilian machinery after the war ended.

World War I changed the course of one engineering company rather dramatically. The terms of the Versailles Treaty, which went into effect June 28, 1919, prohibited *Bayerische Motoren Werke* (Bavarian Motor Works, or BMW) from manufacturing aircraft engines. This presented a problem for the Munich-based company, since aircraft engines provided the main portion of its income.

ABOVE: The heart of Max Friz' innovative design: the longitudinal boxer twin.

LEFT: The bike that started it all: the R32 of 1923.

Flat, horizontally opposed twin longitudinally mounted across the frame, shaft drive, elegant style. Sometimes you get it right the first time.

CORPORATE ROOTS

To understand why the terms of the Versailles Treaty proved so devastating to BMW, one needs to understand what the company became at the end of the war.

The immediate (and temporary) need to supply a military fighting a war forged BMW into the company it was in 1919. The firm's roots date back to 1911, when Gustav Otto, son of Nikolaus Otto, inventor of the Otto cycle four-stroke engine, opened an aircraft factory in Munich. On March 7, 1916, Otto joined forces with Karl Rapp, owner of an aircraft engine manufacturing plant, to create the *Bayerische Flugzeugwerke GmbH* (BFW, or Bavarian Airplane Works). On July 29, 1917, Franz Josef "Karl" Popp joined the company. The name was changed from *Bayerische Flugzeugwerke GmbH* to *Bayerische Motoren Werke GmbH*, with Popp acting as managing director of the new company. In 1918, the company went public and became known as BMW AG.

The Versailles Treaty severely limited BMW's future. The company's devotion to aircraft, particularly the devotion of

company engineer Max Friz, made the situation even worse. Friz joined Rapp Motorenwerke in 1914 as chief design engineer and became one of the directors of BFW. Friz' passion was airplanes. He often referred to automobiles as "stupid conveyances," and thought even less highly of motorcycles. During the war he had designed a 185-horsepower overhead-cam, inline six-cylinder aircraft engine. When mounted in the Fokker D. VII, Germany's finest World War I fighter plane and perhaps the finest aircraft of its day, this potent engine outperformed a similar engine built by Mercedes and earned BMW a reputation for quality it has maintained to the present day.

Though the Versailles Treaty prohibited BMW from developing aircraft engines, Friz refused to give up his passion. In 1919, he modified his six-cylinder engine, mounted it in a biplane, and proceeded to set a new (and illegal) world altitude record, flying to 32,000 feet. The Allied Control Commission retaliated by confiscating all of BMW's plans and documents related to aircraft, effectively forcing BMW out of the airplane business.

This nearly wiped out the struggling company, and by 1921 BMW's staff had fallen from a wartime high of 3,500 to just a skeleton crew. BMW stayed in business thanks in part to the help of Viennese banker Camillo Castiglioni, who became BMW's major shareholder. With Castiglioni's cash, BMW built such mundane items as agricultural equipment, truck and boat engines, and air brakes for railroad cars. It wasn't as exciting as building aircraft engines, but it helped pay the bills and kept the factory doors open.

BUILDING A BETTER "STUPID CONVEYANCE"

BMW was pulled into the motorcycle market as a subcontractor in 1922. The postwar German economy was in shambles and most people couldn't afford automobiles, though some could afford less expensive forms of personal transportation such as motorcycles. The Otto factory, still doing business as BFW, built a motorcycle called the "Flink," which used a 148-cc two-stroke engine designed by Curt Hanfland. Otto contracted BMW to build a four-stroke engine for the Helios, a larger motorcycle Otto intended to produce. Designed by Martin Stolle, the resultant M2B15 engine resembled the motor used in the British Douglas motorcycle. With a perfectly square bore and stroke of 68 millimeters, the 486-cc side-valve boxer twin developed a tick at less than 6.5 horsepower. Like the Douglas, the engine was mounted in the frame with its cylinders facing fore and aft.

BMW purchased the struggling Otto firm, BFW, outright about the time series production of the Helios began in 1922. This put BMW in the motorcycle business completely. The company also manufactured the M2B15 engine for other motorcycle companies. The boxer engine wound up in motorcycles with names such as Bison, Corona, Heller, Heninger, Scheid, SMW, and Victoria. In spite of its popularity, the M2B15 wasn't a particularly good engine. Nor was the Helios a particularly good motorcycle.

Otis Chandler owns this original unrestored R32.

ABOVE: The shaft-drive design graced every motorcycle BMW built up until the 1994 F650.

BELOW: It's a long way from the crude leaf-spring front suspension of the R32 to the sophisticated Telelever systems used on today's BMW motorcycles.

Karl Popp felt BMW could produce a better machine and asked Max Friz to design an improved boxer-powered motorcycle. By all accounts Friz was no more enamored of motorcycles than he had ever been, but he accepted the assignment and began working on BMW's first motorcycle design. Though legally bound to abandon the pursuit of aircraft engineering, Friz was able to mount a small token of his real passion on his motorcycle. Like every BMW vehicle ever built, the R32, Friz' very first motorcycle, bore BMW's corporate insignia, a small blue-and-white badge representing a spinning propeller that pays tribute to the company's aeronautical roots.

GROUND ZERO: THE R32

Friz approached designing a better stupid conveyance with the same thoroughness and dedication to quality he used when designing aircraft powerplants. Although Friz' assistant Martin Stolle, designer of the original M2B15 engine, left BMW to design motorcycle engines at rival manufacturer Victoria in 1921, Stolle was instrumental in early stages of the motorcycle project. Friz retained Franz Bieber to assist in turning his ideas and sketches into metallic reality, and to test the finished product. Friz and crew unveiled their creation, the R32, at the Paris Motorcycle Salon in 1923.

BMW-SPEAK

Prior to introducing the three- and four-cylinder K series bikes in the 1980s, BMW used the letter *R* as a prefix for all its motorcycle model designations. R stands for "Rad," a German slang term referring to motorcycles. Rad comes from the word *Motorrad*, which in German means "Motorcycle," or more precisely, "Motorbike." Thus Rad means "bike."

The R32 proved to be the hit of the 1923 Paris motorcycle show, but not because it broke new technological ground. It was a technically advanced machine, to be certain, but the technology Friz employed had all been used before.

The M2B32 boxer engine powering the R32 featured the same perfectly square 68-by-68-millimeter bore and stroke measurements as the M2B15 powerplant upon which it was based. Like its predecessor, the new engine, which Friz designed in a mere four weeks according to legend, used side-valve cylinder heads, as did many other motorcycles in 1923. Given the questionable quality of the fuel available at the time, the decision to use side-valve technology was understandable, but even in 1923 it was clear that overhead valves offered much greater performance. Most likely Friz and crew chose side valves to keep costs down. Although still using a pedestrian side-valve design, Friz' decision to use aluminum alloy cylinder heads set the M2B32 engine apart from most of its peers. These were based on cylinder heads developed in 1922 by Rudolph Schleicher, the BMW engineer who would replace Friz as chief designer when Friz turned his attention to designing aircraft engines once the terms of the Treaty of Versailles were eased.

The new engine also featured an advanced wet-sump recirculating oiling system that force fed oil to the engine through a geared oil pump. Recirculating oiling systems were considered high tech in 1923, when many manufacturers still used total-loss oiling systems that required riders to pump oil into an engine at regular intervals. BMW used this same basic system until the last /2 models were built in 1969, testifying to the advanced nature of the design.

A single carburetor mounted on top of the engine provided fuel to the combustion chambers. This rather sophisticated unit of BMW's own design, which featured two slides within the carburetor body, one for each cylinder, capitalized on BMW's aircraft engine experience.

The most unique aspect of Friz' design was his placement of the engine. Like the Helios, most motorcycles using boxer-type motors, such as the Douglas and Harley-Davidson's Model W Sport Twin, featured engines with the cylinders running fore and aft. Friz recognized the problems inherent in such arrangements—long wheelbases and inadequate cooling of the rear cylinders—and rotated the entire engine 90 degrees, so the pistons jutted out into the cooling airflow. This had been done before. England's Sopwith built a motorcycle, the ABC, with cylinders laid out in this fashion.

This orientation of the engine allowed Friz to bolt the three-speed transmission solidly to the crankcase, which housed the clutch and flywheel. This tidy arrangement, known as unit construction, allowed Friz to design a compact chassis in which to house the drivetrain and simplified the manufacturing process. It also eliminated the problematic primary drive system, which usually consisted of a chain connecting the crankshaft to the clutch, a system that requires periodic maintenance. Although not the first unit-construction drivetrain, it was very advanced for 1923. Automobiles used unit-construction drivetrains, but on motorcycles they were still fairly rare and would be for some years to come. British rival Triumph didn't adopted a unit-construction for its twin-cylinder motorcycles for another four decades. Even today a few companies like Harley-Davidson, Buell, Royal Enfield, and some third world manufacturers with unpronounceable names still use non-unit construction.

Rotating the engine also made it easier for Friz to design a shaft-driven final drive system for the R32. His use of shaft drive provided the bike with another major advantage over its competition. While shaft drive had been used on motorcycles as far back as 1907, when Glenn Curtiss employed a driveshaft on his record-setting V-8, most motorcycle manufacturers of the day used chain final drive systems. BMW's shaft-drive system greatly eased tire changes, an important consideration back in a time when roads were primitive and punctured tires an everyday occurrence.

The original R32 displayed at the 1923 Paris Salon had a rigid connection between the transmission output shaft and the driveshaft, though this was updated after the first 50 production bikes had been built. Later R32s featured a Hardy flexible

disc coupling to compensate for the motion created by the twisting of the frame on rough roads.

A magneto-type ignition provided spark to the cylinder heads and also provided electricity for the lighting system, which was still considered a state-of-the-art feature at that time. In an early example or marketing speak, BMW called its magneto system a "High Tension Ignition."

None of these features in themselves were unique to the R32. What was unique was Friz' incorporation of all this technology in one package. Taken as a whole, the R32 was arguably the most advanced mass-produced motorcycles of its day. It was expensive compared to the competition, but no other motorcycle offered the features and overall quality that BMW offered. This obvious quality and technological advancement was what caused such enthusiasm at the Paris show. Visitors knew they were seeing a very special motorcycle, but what they didn't know was that they were looking into the future. In this simple but elegant motorcycle, they saw the foundation of every motorcycle BMW would build for the next 60 years.

HITTING THE STREETS

BMW produced a small number of R32s in 1923 and began full-scale production in 1924. The R32 proved as popular in the real world as it had been at the Paris Salon. BMW understood the needs of its customers, and tailored the R32 to meet those needs. Because the ability to haul a sidecar was important

That brake system, which consists of a block of wood pressed against a dummy rim, was as useless as it looks.

15

ABOVE: Valve adjustment on the side-valve R32 engine could not have been any simpler.

RIGHT: BMW relied on its aircraft engine expertise when designing the sophisticated twin-slide carburetor used on the R32.

R32's 8.5 horsepower, but back in 1923, the R32 was considered, if not fast, at least adequate. It attained a top speed of 55 miles per hour and could cruise all day long at 40 miles per hour. Given the crude state of both the highway system and suspension technology, this was as fast as any sane German cared to ride. Besides, with solo gearing the R32 could achieve nearly 80 miles per gallon when ridden in a conservative manner. In post-World War I Germany, this was a more important consideration for many riders than outright performance.

Like the roads of the time, the suspension of the R32 seems primitive by today's standards, but in all fairness, the suspension of the R32 was state of the art for the era. The rear suspension was standard practice for the day, which is to say it was nonexistent. The rigid rear frame contained no provision for damping road imperfections. The only thing protecting the rider's spinal column from the potholes that littered the mostly unpaved roads were the small springs under the saddle and the thin layer of padding within it. The front suspension was more advanced and was similar in design and function to the front fork used by America's Indian Motocycle Company. The fork was not attached directly to the axles but rather to short trailing arms that ran back to the axles. The axles were directly connected to a leaf spring that protruded over the front fender by a U-shaped rod that ran from one side of the axle, up over the fender to the spring, then back to the other side of the axle. One can see hints of BMW's future suspension systems in this elegantly simple design.

The R32 may not have been fast, but it was rugged and reliable. Most bikes that used BMW's M2B15 engine mounted the motors in weak frames composed of spindly tubes, frames designed primarily to be cheaply produced. Strength was not a high priority. Friz placed a higher premium on durability than the cost-conscious assemblers building motorcycles around BMW engines. He designed a duplex frame with twin tubes running from the steering head back over the fuel tank, down to the rear wheel, then back under the engine and up to rejoin the steering head. With its additional bracing, the frame was sturdy but heavy. The R32 weighed 264 pounds, light by modern standards, but heavy compared to its contemporaries, especially considering the bike had only 8.5 ponies to motivate it.

There were motorcycles available with significantly more power than BMW's claimed 8.5 horsepower in 1923. Where the M2B32 powerplant differed from its contemporaries was in its smooth power delivery. This was a time when most motorcycles used large displacement singles and V-twins, engines that shook hard enough to crack frames and break engine castings. The smoothness of the boxer twin allowed the rider to operate the machine for extended periods without being beaten into

to many customers, and would remain an important consideration throughout much of the 20th century, BMW offered the R32 with two final drive ratios: 1:4.4 for solo bikes and 1:5.36 for sidecar rigs.

With a compression ratio of 5.0:1, the M2B32 engine produced 8.5 horsepower at 3,300 rpm, a significant improvement over the M2B15. The new engine may have been faster than the unit it replaced, but it was still rather mild compared to other motorcycles of the period and seems almost pathetic by 21st-century standards. Today we have 50-cc two-stroke scooter engines that can be tweaked to produce more than twice the

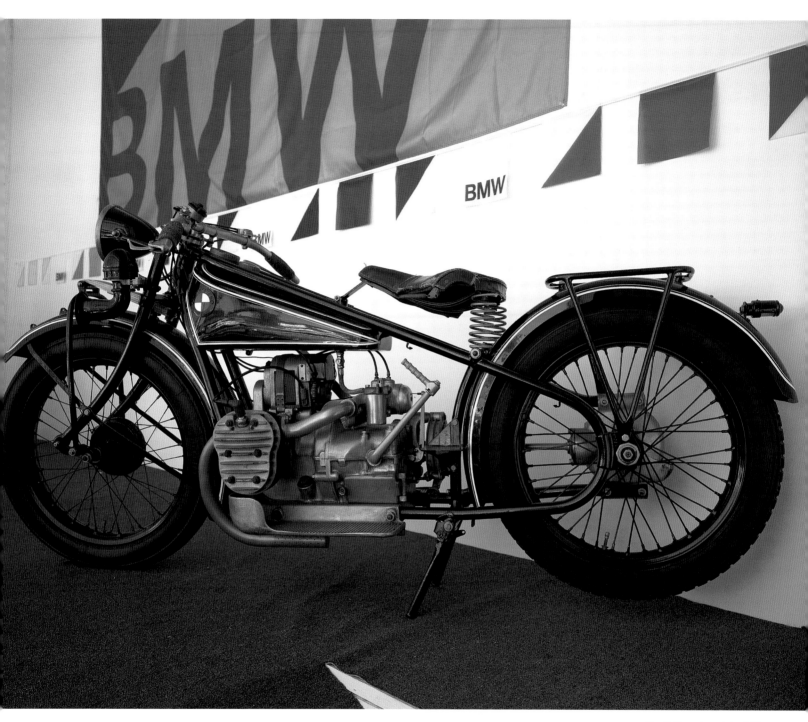

The R42 replaced the R32 in 1926.

BMW motorcycles would retain their hand-shifted transmissions long after most other European manufacturers switched to foot-shifted transmissions.

submission by excessive vibration, a quality as appreciated by riders then as it is now. Besides, the R32 could still go fast enough to tax its inadequate braking system.

The brakes proved to be the only serious flaw with the original design. The front brake mimicked the technology of the rear suspension; that is, it did not exist. A V-block brake that pressed against a dummy rim mounted to the rear wheel provided all the braking forces available, which, when combined with the bicycle-sized tires, was not much force at all. The system was outdated even in 1923.

BMW began a program of steady improvement almost as soon as the R32 became available to the general public. The Series 2 R32, introduced in 1924, used a mechanically operated

expanding shoe front brake. In 1925, BMW increased engine capacity to 494 cc. At that time the heads were upgraded to a split design, allowing for easier access to the valves for maintenance and repair. By the time the R32 was replaced in 1926, BMW had sold 3,090 examples of the model.

EXIT FRIZ, ENTER SCHLEICHER

The absolute prohibition against the production of aircraft engines imposed by the Versailles Treaty ended on May 5, 1922. This meant Max Friz was free to return to his original passion: designing and building aircraft engines. That's exactly what he did in 1923, leaving future motorcycle development in the hands of Rudolf Schleicher, who remained with the company until 1960. Unlike Friz, Schleicher considered motorcycles anything but stupid conveyances. An avid motorcyclist, Schleicher not only rode motorcycles as transportation, but he also rode them in competition, racing with some success in cross-country events. Under his reign competition began to play a larger role in the development of BMW motorcycles.

Under test rider Franz Bieber, the R32 achieved some success in competition. This success didn't come on road courses, where the admittedly underpowered was seriously outclassed by the competition, but in time-distance events, a form of competition that places more emphasis on ruggedness and reliability than on outright performance. Success in time-distance events was one thing, but Schleicher had grander plans for competition. While the R32 may have been powerful enough for road use, Schleicher and his colleagues realized they would need a higher performing motorcycle to achieve significant success in road racing.

THE NEXT STEP: THE R37

As his first full-scale project, Schleicher chose to develop a competition version of the R32, which was no surprise, given his interest in racing. Schleicher decided to use a more efficient overhead-valve system on his first complete motorcycle design, the R37. Otherwise, the R37 was much the same as the R32, which was sold alongside its higher-performing sibling. The pushrod-operated overhead valves were fully enclosed, a major improvement over the exposed valve gear then common on many overhead-valve motorcycles of the period. The exposed systems were vulnerable to the elements and to road debris, and they either featured inadequate top-end lubrication, or else they sprayed their riders with oil. Neither option was acceptable for a BMW motorcycle.

As with the R32, Schleicher constructed the R37 cylinder heads from lightweight aluminum alloy. He machined the cylinders from solid billet steel to create a sturdy but heavy package. Weight of the new machine increased to 295 pounds. Fortunately horsepower also increased, thanks to the overhead valves and an increase in compression to 6.2:1. A new carburetor featured three slides rather than the two-slide setup of the R32. The R37 was rated at 16 horsepower, almost double the 8.5 ponies of the original R32. This was enough to give the bike a top speed of 70 miles per hour. Fuel consumption deteriorated a bit but was still an impressive 71 miles per gallon. To emphasize the racing intent of the bike, the electric lighting system was removed.

Schleicher's team tested the R37 in 1924, and BMW introduced a production model in 1925. The high price of this prestigious machine kept it out of reach of the average German motorcyclist, and the bike was not a success in the marketplace. The company sold just 175 copies during the two-year production run of the R37.

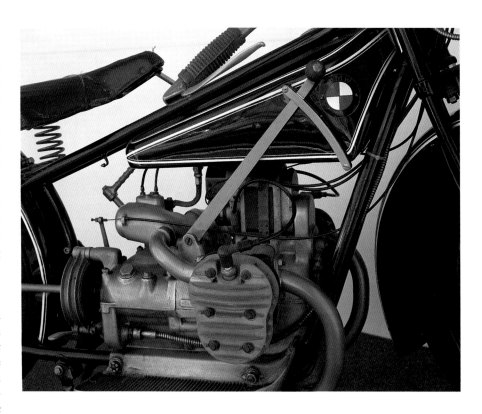

COMPETITION

The road-going machine might not have found showroom success, but the racing version of the R37 stomped its competition in road races and trials events all across Europe. BMW built 10 racing machines that featured a shorter wheelbase than the road-going version and nickel-plated steel forks.

The competition bike met with immediate success. Franz Beiber won the 1924 German 500-cc championship and in 1925 won nearly 100 road races, both at home and abroad. An R37 won the German Grand Prix that year, but the bike's crowning achievement came the following year. In 1926, Rudolf Schleicher himself rode an R37 to victory in one of the most prestigious motorcycle competitions of the era, the International Six Days Trials. Schleicher competed in that year's event, held in Wales, as a privateer, without factory backing. He even had to use his personal vacation leave to get time off to compete. Like any privateer, Schleicher had to be resourceful. Unable to procure any trials tires, he was forced to compete using street tires. Even with this handicap, he managed to beat the best riders in the world, winning that year's top gold medal. This was the first time a German had ever won the event.

The new M43 engine in the R42 pumped out 50 percent more power than its predecessor, and ran cooler, thanks to the cross-section cooling fins that replaced the radial fins used on the R32's engine.

ONE-LUNGERS

In 1925, BMW's third year of motorcycle production, the company introduced its third model, the R39. The first two models, the R32 and R37 boxer twins, were expensive, luxurious motorcycles, the latter so much so that few people could afford to purchase an example. While more successful than the R37, the R32 still cost too much for it to see the kind of sales numbers BMW management envisioned. The company's third bike, a single-cylinder model, was targeted at customers who couldn't afford the more exclusive models.

To create a single, BMW engineers basically lopped off one cylinder from the existing twin. Fortunately, company designers chose to lop an overhead-valve cylinder off of the more potent R37 powerplant rather than dismembering the side-valve R32 unit. Design work began in the spring of 1924, and the prototype was ready to show at the Berlin Motor Show

in December of that same year. Measuring the same 68-by-68-millimeter bore and stroke as its twin-cylinder brethren, the single retained the same basic layout as those machines: longitudinal crankshaft, wet-sump oiling, single-disc dry clutch, unit construction engine and transmission, and shaft final drive. In single-cylinder form, the R39 displaced 247-cc, weighed 242 pounds, and could achieve a top speed of 60 miles per hour. The single received upgraded brakes, with a mechanical drum brake up front and a transmission brake replacing the dummy-rim setup out back. This system represented a definite improvement, but braking continued to be a weak area with BMW production motorcycles.

The smallest BMW cranked out 6.5 horsepower, making it at least a match for the more expensive R32 boxer. Released late in the summer of 1925, the R39 soon joined the R37 at racetrack podiums in Germany and across Europe. Initial

sales of road-going versions were strong, too, but fell off in 1926. Part of the reason was the bike's price, which was much higher than BMW executives had predicted. When fully equipped, the price of the single was only 50 German marks less than a similarly equipped R32 twin. Apparently it didn't cost that much less to manufacture a motorcycle with one fewer cylinders.

With the introduction of the R39, BMW set a pattern that would continue until the 1960s. The company would offer three types of motorcycles: touring models, as represented by the R32; sporting models, as represented by the R37; and proletarian singles, as represented by the R39.

BMW NOMENCLATURE

Throughout most of its history, BMW has been one of the world's most consistent manufacturers when it comes to giving its motorcycle models logical designations. The twin-cylinder bikes have always began with the prefix *R*, which you may recall stands for "Rad," or "Bike," and have been followed by a numeric code related to engine size. The R2 is a 200-cc (actually a 198-cc) single, for example, while the R65 is a 650-cc twin and the R1150R is a 1,150-cc (actually a 1,130-cc) machine. As BMW's model line-up increased in number and became more specialized in purpose, the R bikes took on descriptive suffixes like S for sporting models, GS for *Geländestrasse* (which is the German term denoting a dual-sport type motorcycle), and R for unfaired roadsters like the R100R and R1150R. BMW's only deviations from this formula in modern times were the three- and four-cylinder K-series bikes introduced in the 1980s and the F650, introduced in the mid-1990s. In the former case, K seems to have been some sort of internal code, and F stood for the unfortunate term *Funduro*, which apparently doesn't sound foolish to German ears.

BMW has remained remarkably consistent in its naming over the years, unlike brands such as Harley-Davidson, which uses an utterly bewildering alphabet soup in its model designations. For example, the top-of-the-line Harley touring model for 2002 was called the FLHTCUI Ultra Classic Electra Glide. Although the system BMW has used for most of its history is logical, in the early years it seemed to be as haphazard as the system Harley currently uses. The R was always a part of the nomenclature, but after that the system seemed to fall apart. Prior to the introduction of the R2 single in 1931 and the R5 twin in 1936, BMW seemed to have even less logic in its alphanumeric model designation system than Harley-Davidson has today.

STEADY IMPROVEMENT

Almost as soon as the first motorcycles began rolling off the assembly line, BMW began the process of evolutionary improvements to its basic design, a process it has continued until this day. As good as the initial BMW motorcycle offerings were, there was room for improvement. Early bikes consumed excessive amounts of oil because of rapidly wearing cylinder bores, a problem BMW solved by replacing stock cylinder liners with specially hardened units. One problem that proved more difficult to remedy involved loosening tolerances on the complex alloy barrel and crankcase unit on the singles. This problem proved so vexing it brought single-cylinder production to a halt in 1926, after only 885 R39 models had been constructed.

In 1926, the R42 replaced the R32. Although still using the side-valve design, the R42 powerplant—designated the M43—pumped out an impressive 50 percent more horsepower than the original M2B32 unit. The fact that it had a lower 4.9:1 compression ratio made its 12 horsepower even more impressive. Top speed was a bit lower than on the R32, probably due to a 13-pound increase in weight, but the new bike achieved an astounding 94 miles per gallon. In addition to improved performance, the new M43 engine provided improved appearance. The new engine abandoned the spiked radial cooling fins of the original M2B32 engine in favor of the same cross-section cooling fins used on the overhead-valve R37, making the new motor a much more modern-looking unit. Perhaps the greatest selling point of the R42 was its price, which was considerably less than the R32. Here was a BMW that average Germans could afford, and BMW sold 7,000 R42s between 1926 and 1928.

A year after introducing the R42, BMW began selling an overhead-valve version of the bike, the R47. Given the designation M51, the overhead-valve engine produced 18 horsepower at 4,000 rpm. The R47 abandoned the tricky three-slide carburetor of the R37 in favor of a less finicky two-slide unit, and it traded its billet steel cylinders for better cooling (and cheaper to produce) cast-iron units. The R47 used the same frame as the new R42, which had been altered to provide better weight distribution. Both the R42 and R47 received the upgraded brakes introduced on the R39. Like the R42, the R47 cost much less than the model it replaced, and sales were up roughly 1,000 percent, with BMW selling 1720 R47 machines during its single year of production.

LONGER STROKE

In 1928, BMW finally abandoned the perfectly square 68-by-68-millimeter bore and stroke it had used since Martin Stolle designed the M2B15, BMW's first motorcycle engine. That year BMW replaced the R42 with the R52. This 487-cc

machine featured a longer stroke than previous models (78-millimeter versus 68-millimeter) but a narrower bore (63-millimeter versus 68-millimeter). This engine produced the same 12 horsepower as the R42, but probably produced a bit more torque, an especially desirable quality for a sidecar-equipped motorcycle. Versions destined for sidecar use also received double-disc dry clutches rather than the single-disc dry clutches used on solo machines. The most important improvement involved the front suspension, which now featured a shock absorber.

The sporting version of this motorcycle, the R57, retained the traditional square bore and stroke ratio of 68-by-68-millimeter, but otherwise was basically an overhead-valve version of the R52. Detail changes to both bikes included revised shift levers, which now were mounted directly to the transmission instead of the engine cases, and a revised kickstart mechanism. All bikes now came with a magneto generator as standard equipment. Bosch electric lights were listed as optional in factory literature, but all bikes produced from 1928 on came equipped with lighting. These bikes marked the end of the first

BMW was an early leader in offering reliable electrical lighting on its motorcycles.

23

ABOVE: The small taillight of the R42 would probably not pass muster with too many transportation departments today.

RIGHT: Though their physical presence was huge, the aural presence of BMW's early horns was negligible.

era of BMW. The R52 would be the last 500-cc side-valve twin BMW would ever produce, and it would be years before the company produced another overhead-valve road-going twin in the 500-cc class.

Instead, BMW began to focus on larger-displacement road machines and produced a pair of 750-cc-class machines for sale to the general public in 1928. These were the side-valve R62 and overhead-valve R63. BMW had campaigned 750-cc race bikes since 1926, bikes that often trounced their liter-class competition, so road-going 750-cc machines seemed inevitable.

Neither machine looked much different than its respective 500-cc predecessor, and the side-valve model really was just the 500-cc machine with a larger engine, but the overhead-valve model had some significant changes. The R62 and R63 differed far more from each other than had previous BMWs. For starters, the side-valve touring version featured a square bore-and-stroke ratio of 78-by-78-millimeters, giving a capacity of 745 cc, while the sporting overhead-valve version featured an over-square ratio of 83–by-63-millimeters, giving a capacity of 734 cc. Moving back and forth inside those shallow holes were a pair of alloy pistons. Previously BMW had used cast-iron

The addition of a small front brake greatly improved the stopping power of BMW's motorcycles.

RIGHT: Like all BMW motorcycles built before World War II, the levers on the R42 pivoted from the outside, rather than the inside.

LEFT: By 1926, the feeble dummy-rim brake had been replaced by a slightly less feeble driveshaft brake.

pistons. The side-valve version produced 18 horsepower, while the overhead-valve version produced 24, making it the fastest production BMW yet. It was also the most expensive BMW yet, costing far more than the side-valve version.

THE KOMPRESSORS

Starting in 1926, racing BMWs began sporting small humps over their transmissions. These cylindrical protrusions contained small air compressors that force fed air into the combustion chamber; that is, they were superchargers. A shaft connected to the crankshaft powered the supercharger, which blew air through the carburetors. These blown BMWs, first in 500-cc form and later in 750-cc form, soon dominated European road racing, decimating all competition. A blown 500-cc BMW cranked out 55 horsepower, and a blown 750-cc machine produced an astounding 75 horsepower. These bikes were giant slayers, humbling 1,000-cc machines from other companies.

BMW used superchargers built by the Swiss firm Zoller. These were vane-type units geared to run at 5,200 rpm to the engine's 6,000 rpm, providing a boost of 1.2 atmospheres. Compression was reduced to a mere 6.0:1, but the Kompressor still nearly doubled the output of a nonboosted engine. The rest of the bike itself was fairly conventional. Like all previous BMW motorcycles (and unlike most of the company's competition) the machine used shaft drive. Combined with the less-than-cutting-edge suspension, this contributed to handling that was distinctly sub-par when compared to the competition.

BMW turned to supercharging because its bikes did not handle as well as the competition, especially the motorcycles coming from England. BMW figured if they couldn't beat the Brits in the corners, they'd overpower them in the straights. This strategy worked for a while, but by the end of the 1920s the competition was starting to catch up. Bursts of speed on the straights were no longer enough to keep ahead of the more nimble bikes produced by other marques, and BMW temporarily shelved its Kompressor race bikes.

BMW had grown immensely since Max Friz produced his first motorcycle in a desperate attempt to save the company. By 1928 BMW had built more than 25,000 motorcycles, mostly side-valve boxers. The company had grown from just a handful of employees in the devastating years following World War I to 3,860 employees in 1929, exceeding its wartime record of 3,500. The company once again manufactured aircraft engines, and in 1928 produced the Dixi, BMW's first automobile. The R62 and R63 marked the last iteration of Friz' original design. Radical new motorcycle models were already under development.

ERNST HENNE

In the years between World Wars I and II, the public became fascinated with the concept of absolute speed, and the men who set speed records became worldwide heroes. During this period BMW's Ernst Henne earned a place as the fastest motorcycle rider on earth. Henne joined BMW's works racing team in 1926. He soon became one of the marque's top riders, winning many races, including Italy's prestigious Targa Florio in 1928, but it was his record-setting land speed runs that earned him his greatest fame.

In the late 1920s English motorcycles using potent JAP (J. A. Prestwich) 1,000-cc V-twin engines—machines like the fabled Brough Superiors—dominated the land-speed record books. Prior to that, American motorcycles held most such records, primarily because of the strength of their 61-cubic inch V-twin engines. It seemed the way to break speed records was through exercising brute V-twin force. But Henne and BMW felt it might be possible to break existing records using advanced technology rather than larger engines.

According to legend, Henne stumbled into the land-speed record game by chance. While honeymooning in Paris he read about an Englishman with the thoroughly French-sounding name of Bert Le Vack achieving 129.05 miles per hour aboard a JAP-powered Brough Superior. Henne believed he could do better, and over the summer he worked with BMW engineers to mount a Zoller Supercharger to the company's new short-stroke 734-cc-boxer engine. On September 19, 1929, Henne set out to break the world's record on the completed machine. The motorcycle itself was naked. It featured no streamlining bodywork, but Henne himself was fully faired. He wore a dapper riding suit that featured a streamlined helmet and a streamlined tail cone. The outfit didn't do much to help the bike's stability, but it looked spiffy, and certainly didn't hurt Henne's effort, because he set a new record of 134.75 miles per hour. This was the first time either a German motorcycle or a supercharged motorcycle had held the world's speed record.

Because of a bureaucratic snafu with the sanctioning body, Henne was forced to redo his record attempt. This time his front axle came loose at around 130 miles per hour. Miraculously Henne managed to bring the bike to a stop without crashing, though legend has it he did soil his jaunty streamlined riding suit.

But such experiences didn't deter Henne from continuing to set records. The top-speed race was on, and others tried to improve on Henne's record. The British continued to develop their 1,000-cc engines, finally adopting superchargers themselves, and later the Italians got into the act with supercharged multicylinder machines. Yet each time a record was broken, Henne and BMW came back to retake their crown. BMW motorcycles set at least 76 speed records between 1929 and 1936, with Ernst Henne earning the lion's share of those records.

On November 28, 1937, Henne set a record of 173.88 miles per hour aboard a supercharged, 500-cc, overhead cam BMW Gran Prix machine with streamlined bodywork. Henne's record would stand for 14 years. A few riders tried to challenge this record. Englishman Eric Fernihough, who had held the record briefly when he achieved 169.78 miles per hour aboard a motorcycle powered by a supercharged 1,000-cc JAP engine, tried to regain the crown in April 1938, but he crashed while traveling nearly 180 miles per hour and was killed.

By this time, BMW was putting all its resources into winning the 500-cc Gran Prix championship and was losing interest in setting absolute speed records. The company had already proven it could defeat the brute strength of the big British bikes by using advanced technology, and Henne had proven he had the courage and skill to ride the shrieking, supercharged beasts BMW built, and ride them faster than any man on the planet.

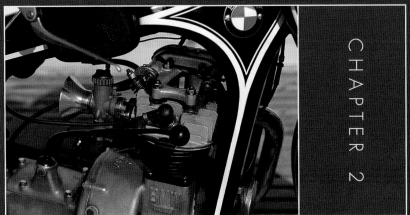

CHAPTER 2

THE GREAT DEPRESSION AND THE THIRD REICH

By the late 1920s, BMW produced some of the highest-quality motor-cycles ever built. It's aircraft-engine manufacturing operations were in full swing, the fledgling automobile production business was taking off, and the company's employment roster was at a record level. Given the situation, BMW could have been excused if it had put all its efforts into preserving the status quo. Few expected radical change in the company's motorcycle line, but the company's next generation of motorcycles surprised fans of the marque and competitors alike. Despite the success of the original design, BMW abandoned Friz' tubular frame in favor of what the company called the "star-frame" concept. The star frame was a pressed-steel exoskeleton-type frame unlike anything the world had seen before.

Frame weakness had been a problem on previous models, primarily due to the fact that joints were brazed rather than welded. The frame around the rear axle had been a particularly weak spot on Friz' tubular frame design, a problem exacerbated by using the motorcycles to haul sidecars. As weight increased, so did frame problems, especially on heavy models like the R62. BMW needed stronger frames, especially if it wanted to secure military contracts, where sidecar use was an important consideration. But strength alone might not account entirely for the

ABOVE: The most notable difference between the 1931 Series 1 R2 shown here and the later versions was that the Series 1 featured exposed valve gear.

LEFT: The side-valve R16 and the overhead valve R17, both introduced in 1935, were the world's first production motorcycles to use telescopic forks.

The R2 brought BMW's pressed-steel frame concept to its single cylinder lineup. Shown here is a 1932 Series 2 model.

switch. BMW undoubtedly wanted to strengthen the chassis, but competition BMW models from this period retained tubular frames, although the competition frames were welded rather than brazed. Since the demands of competition were more taxing on the frame than normal road use, this indicates BMW knew how to build a tubular frame of sufficient strength for even *Wehrmacht* duty. Likely the switch to the Star frame was a cost-saving measure as much as an attempt to address frame weakness. Regardless of the reason for the switch, the new frames were strong, and the Star-framed bikes held up well, even when subjected to strenuous sidecar use with the German military.

BMW launched its 750-cc Star bikes in November 1928, at the London Motorcycle Show in Olympia. The R11 replaced the R62, and the R16 replaced the R63. Other than the frame, very little changed mechanically. The R11 retained the square ratio 18-horsepower side-valve engine, while the

short-stroke overhead-valve engine used in the new R16 was rated at 25 horsepower, thanks to a slight increase in compression. Performance of the side-valve model was down significantly because of a drastic increase in weight. Using the star frame, the R11 gained 15 pounds compared to the R62 it replaced. Performance of the overhead-valve bike remained strong, despite the fact that the R16 weighed 22 pounds more than the R63, indicating BMW might have consciously detuned the R11 in an attempt to differentiate it from the more-expensive R16.

Although introduced in late 1928, BMW manufactured few bikes with pressed steel frames until well into the following year, due in part to problems encountered with the new fork. The new fork design retained the same basic trailing link architecture as in the past, but now the girders were made of pressed steel, like the frame. The new bike had strong initial sales, but sales dropped off as the world sunk into the economic depression caused by the

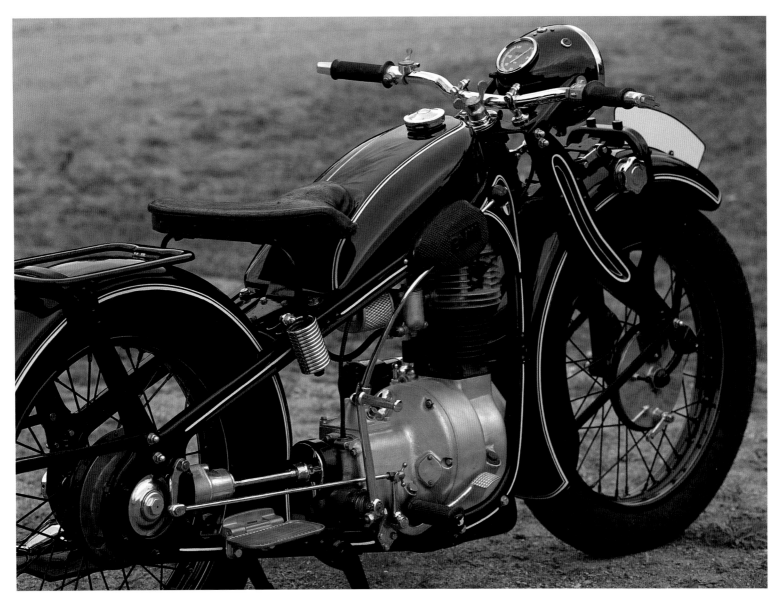

American stock market crash of 1929. Still BMW continued to develop its motorcycles, and the R11 and R16 received numerous improvements before being superceded by the R12 and R17 in 1935. One of the most significant changes to the overhead-valve R16 was the use of two needle-jet carburetors manufactured under license from the British firm Amal. First used in 1932, these carburetors increased power output from 25 horsepower to 33 horsepower. In 1934, the R11 also received a pair of Amal carburetors, bringing its power output up to 20 horsepower.

RETURN OF THE THUMPER

BMW resurrected its single-cylinder motorcycle concept in 1931, building a single that, like the R11 and R16, used a pressed-steel frame. With this bike, the R2, BMW capitalized on a new German law excluding people who rode motorcycles of 200-cc or less from paying road taxes or obtaining driver's licenses. The German government passed this law in an attempt to stimulate the economy and pull the country out of its economic depression, and in so doing, created a new market for small-displacement singles. The R2 was BMW's entry into that

BMW designed the 398cc R4 to be a more technologically sophisticated alternative to the 500cc side-valve twins.

The knurled knob on the fork's leaf spring is a friction damper, making this an early adjustable suspension.

market, and the company put every effort into keeping the cost of the new single as low as possible in order to keep the price at a more competitive level. The most noticeable result of this emphasis on cost control was that the new single featured exposed valve gear. Less obvious was the use of thinner gauge steel in the frame and fork, which helped keep down both cost and weight.

One area where BMW engineers didn't skimp was in the design of the crankcase. The R2 was the first BMW to use the tunnel-style one-piece crankcase design that would be used on all air-cooled BMW engines until the last R80GS was produced in the late 1990s. The R2 set the pattern for every single-cylinder engine BMW produced until the company ceased producing the R27 in 1966. BMW also chose to introduce an improved rear brake system on the R2. On this model engineers did away with the feeble transmission brake, replacing it with an expanding mechanical drum rear brake similar to the brake used up front. The bike was also the first BMW to feature an air filter.

The R2 was the BMW for which a lot of people had been waiting. Performance was good for the class. The engine's 6 horsepower propelled the 242-pound machine to a top speed of around 55 miles per hour, and the bike returned 100 miles per gallon from every gallon of gas. This might have been an important selling point for a less-expensive motorcycle in economically devastated Germany, but the high price of the machine probably negated any real savings. The R2 was an expensive motorcycle compared to the 200-cc two-stroke competition from companies like DKW, but it was inexpensive for a BMW. The R2 cost half the price of the company's least expensive twin, and BMW sold 4,260 copies before modifying the design in 1932. While the first version had been relatively trouble-free,

BMW added an enclosing valve cover for the second series and also began using an Amal type carburetor, increasing horsepower by more than 30 percent.

In 1932, the same year BMW upgraded the R2, the company introduced a second single-cylinder model, the R4. Other than receiving a strengthened fork and larger fenders, the 398-cc R4 was basically an over-bored R2. This bike was meant to fill the market niche left vacant after the demise of the side-valve R52 500-cc twin, which had been phased out in 1929. Performance of the new single was roughly similar to the earlier twin.

A year after the introduction of the R4, Germany experienced a political upheaval that would send the entire world spinning into chaos, but an event that would, in the short term, prove profitable for BMW: the rise of Adolf Hitler and his National Socialist Party. Hitler and his Third Reich rode a wave of racism, nationalism, and general hysteria to power, and much of his appeal rested in his promise to restore Germany's military might to what it had been prior to the Treaty of Versailles. To be mighty, militaries need equipment, and the rugged R4 was just

LEFT: This is the view of the R4 preferred by the more-than 15,000 people who purchased the machine.

BELOW: The gray paint, rubber footrests, and single carburetor signify this R12 was produced for the German Wehrmacht.

Sales to the German military helped BMW sell more than 36,000 side-valve R12 models, and made this the best-selling prewar BMW motorcycle.

the sort of equipment the German *Wehrmacht* would need: simple, reliable, and effective. The R4 proved popular with the military and police forces, though it was less popular with civilians. Not that civilian popularity mattered much. R4 production reached more than 15,000 machines before the model was replaced by the R35 in 1937, thanks to strong military sales.

BMW built one other single-cylinder machine during this period, the R3. Essentially a 305-cc version of the R4, BMW introduced the R3 in 1936, intending it for markets where 300-cc machines were preferred to 200-cc or 250-cc motorcycles. Apparently these were very small markets, because in its single year of production, BMW built just 740 R3s.

ADOLF HITLER, THE THIRD REICH, AND THE *WEHRMACHT*

The Great Depression hit Germany especially hard. The country hadn't completely recovered from the aftermath of World War I, and when the U.S. stock market crashed in 1929, dragging the world economy down with it, many German companies were driven out of business. More than 17,000 German firms went out of business in 1931 alone. BMW wasn't doing so well itself, but thanks to its diversified product line, the company avoided joining its many competitors in insolvency. By the time Adolf Hitler came to power, BMW had returned to profitability. By the end of 1933, BMW production reached

record levels and the company employed nearly 5,000 people. By 1935, the workforce reached more than 11,000 employees.

Sales of the R2 totaled more than 15,000 between 1930 and 1936, the highest sales numbers yet achieved by a single model of BMW motorcycle. This helped the company weather the depression. Even though the R4 model was less popular with civilians, its strong military sales helped ensure the firm's survival.

BMW undoubtedly benefited from the military build-up instigated by the Nazi regime, but other aspects of the new government benefited the company as well. The Third Reich devoted huge sums of money into building high-speed roads—Germany's famous *Autobahnen*—and wherever there are high-speed roads, there are high-speed vehicles. Being in the business of building high-speed vehicles of both the two- and four-wheel variety, BMW was well situated to capitalize on this Nazi extravagance.

TELESCOPIC FORKS

In 1935, BMW introduced the first production motorcycles ever to use telescopic forks with hydraulic damping: the R12 and R17. The side-valve R12 replaced the R11, and the overhead-valve R17 replaced the R16. The new models were the most technologically advanced road-going motorcycles yet produced by BMW, a company famous for producing technologically advanced motorcycles. The new bikes featured an extra cog in their gearboxes, bringing the total number of gears up to four. BMW watchers expected this change, since the R4 had been using a four-speed transmission since 1933.

BMW AND THE NATIONAL SOCIALISTS

Simply put, the Nazi Party was very good for business for BMW, at least in the early years of the Reich. While it is easy to pass moral judgment on such a relationship in hindsight, given what we know of the barbarous Nazi regime, the situation becomes less clear cut if one imagines what it must have been like to be a BMW executive in the 1930s. It's conceivable that most Germans, BMW brass included, had no idea what was in store as the Nazis rose to power in 1933. The events that would occur over the following dozen years were so unspeakably horrible that most people could not have imagined them in advance. With that in mind, it's easy to see how German businesses looked forward to a new administration taking charge of Germany with something approaching optimism. Things were once again moving forward, and business was looking up.

What wasn't as expected was the radical new front suspension. The new fork incorporated hydraulic shock absorbers and helical compression springs, not all that different from the hydraulic fork designs used on motorcycles throughout the rest of the 20th century. Telescopic forks had been tried in the past, but this was the first time internal oil damping had been used to tame the rocking motion inherent in such a design.

BMW's telescopic fork first appeared on the R7 show bike in 1934. Created by Alfred Boening, who would later co-design the R75 *Wehrmacht* sidecar rig along with Alex von Falkenhausen, the R7 design exercise proved pressed-steel frames did not have to be ugly. In fact, judging from the R7, pressed-steel frames could be extremely stylish. Stylish, but impractical: the art-deco steel frame may have looked ultra hip,

LEFT: BMW's shaft drive proved ideal in the rugged conditions encountered by the Wehrmacht.

BELOW: The 33-horsepower R17 was one of the most expensive motorcycles available prior to World War II. This model is extremely rare today.

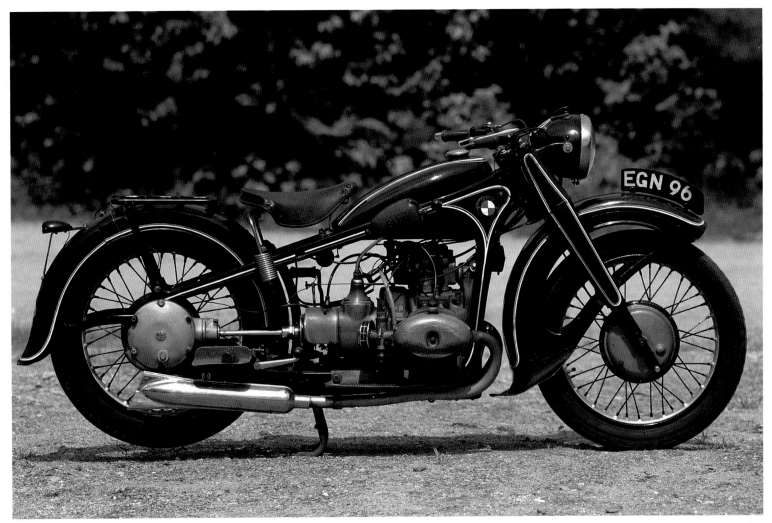

but it must have been extremely heavy. Though the Bauhaus frame never saw the light of day, many of the advanced features of the R7 did find their way to production models, like the deeply valenced fenders, the sprung saddle, and most important, the hydraulically damped telescopic fork.

The new fork allowed the fitting of a smaller 19-inch wheel. This made steering feel much lighter, since the smaller wheel had less gyroscopic force for the rider to overcome. The new wheel sizes also allowed the bikes to use the same tires as their competitors from England, both on the street and on the track. The engines were largely unchanged, but so were their prices. Both the R12 and R17 cost the same as the models they replaced.

If the new models fell short in any area, it was in their retention of the hand-shift setup. By now most other European motorcycle manufacturers had switched to foot-shifted transmissions, although the Americans still used hand-operated shifters on their large-displacement V-twin motorcycles. Shifting a BMW by hand was a cumbersome process that undoubtedly contributed to at least a few accidents. To shift gears, the rider first closed the throttle, then moved his hand to the shift lever, pulled in the clutch, selected the desired gear, then released the clutch as he was placing both hands back on the handlebar. This was challenging enough on the slow-revving

side-valve R12; on the R17, which could achieve a top speed of nearly 90 miles per hour, the experience must have approached the level of sheer terror at times.

THE R5

At the 1936 Berlin Motor Show, BMW launched its most sporting motorcycle to date, the R5. With the engine powering the R5, BMW reverted to its original, perfectly square bore-and-stroke dimensions of 68 millimeters by 68 millimeters, giving a capacity of 494 cc. Other than its measurements, this engine was about as different from the M2B32 as an air-cooled boxer could get. The new engine used a tunnel-type crankcase similar to the one used on the R2 single. After the introduction of the R5, this type of crankcase would be a feature of every air-cooled engine BMW would build. The engine retained pushrod-actuated overhead valves, but the pushrods were lighter and shorter than in the past, allowing the engine to rev higher before the onset of valve float. To further increase

ABOVE: The main event in the Kompressor show rests behind the canister at the front of the engine: the supercharger.

RIGHT: The pad was for the rider to rest his chest on when riding the Kompressor in anger. Even BMW's baddest racing motorcycle had to have some civility.

FAR RIGHT: The R6, built for just one year in 1937, reintroduced the tubular frame to the side-valve lineup.

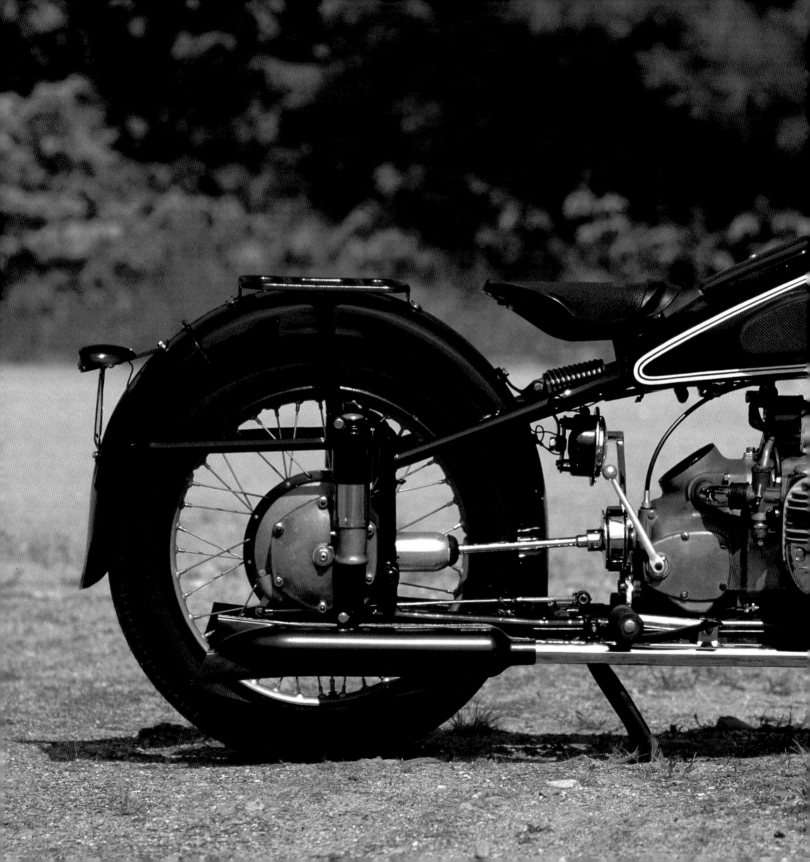

The R61 replaced the R6 in 1938. The main difference was that a plunger-type damper now suspended the rear wheel.

1939 R61

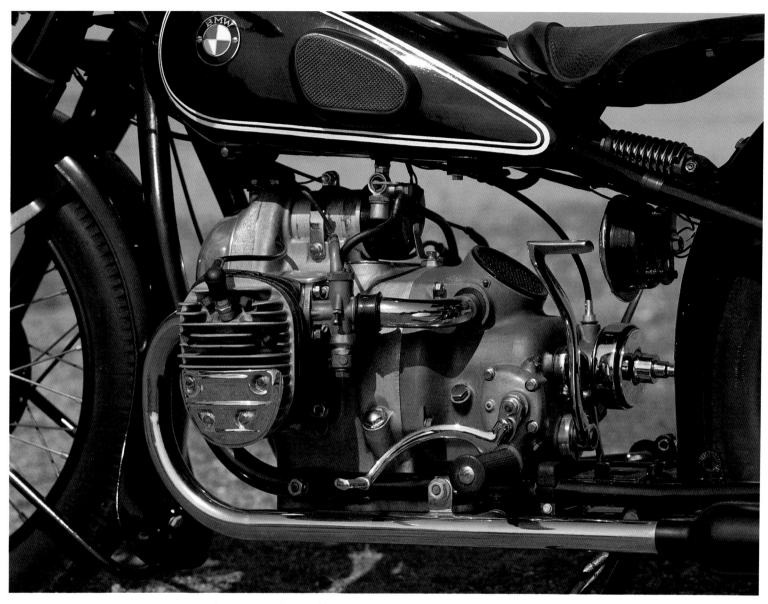

ABOVE: The 597cc R61 and 745cc R71 were the last BMW's to feature side-valve engine. A 1939 R61 is shown here.

FAR RIGHT: Although the R71 pumped out prodigious torque and a respectable 22 horsepower, the age of the side-valve engine was over.

engine revs, the R5 powerplant used hairpin valve springs from BMW's race bikes rather than traditional coil-type valve springs. While not adopting the advanced in-head cam design from the racing *Kompressors* (see below), the new engine did use an advanced twin-cam design that allowed for straighter pushrods and more advantageous valve angles.

With the R5 BMW began the process of ditching the heavy pressed-steel Star frame design. Instead, it used a strengthened version of the tubular frames used on BMW racers. Unlike the troublesome frames of earlier street-going

BMWs, which had been brazed, the joints on the R5 frame were welded.

The sophisticated hydraulic fork again appeared, now featuring a control for adjusting damping characteristics. The rear suspension remained the same as on all previous BMWs, which is to say it was still nonexistent, though the R5 did feature the sprung saddle from the R7 concept bike.

While the R5 lacked rear suspension, it finally featured a sophisticated foot-operated shift lever with positive stops for the gears, a change appreciated by just about everyone. As a bone to

the Luddites among BMW's customer base, the new bike retained a vestigial hand-shift lever sprouting from the transmission case. Though this lever was essentially useless for anything other than finding neutral when coasting to a stop, it survived until 1955. Though this was by far the most advanced motorcycle BMW had ever built and is considered by many to be the finest road-going motorcycle made during the 1930s, the R5 actually cost less than the last overhead-valve 500-cc BMW had built, the R57, which went out of production in 1929.

THE NEW KOMPRESSORS

The National Socialist Party's rise to power precipitated a return to racing for BMW. While Adolf Hitler wasn't a personal fan of motor sports, the Nazis understood the propaganda value of racing. They understood that success in motor sports increased German prestige on the world stage, so Hitler encouraged manufacturers to go racing. BMW needed little arm twisting to comply, and soon a new Kompressor race bike was developed.

The new 500-cc road racer used BMW's basic boxer architecture, and like all other opposed twins built by the company, transmitted its power to the rear wheel via a drive shaft. The road racers retained a tubular frame design rather than adapting the pressed-steel Star frames from BMW's production bikes of the period. The new Kompressor was the first BMW to use the foot-shifted four-speed transmission and hydraulically damped telescopic fork that would later appear on the R5 street bike. Like the R5, it also retained a rigid rear frame.

The 492-cc engine, designated Model 255, featured an undersquare 66-x72-millimeter bore and stroke ratio and was designed to be supercharged from the beginning. The supercharger was moved from its earlier location above the transmission to the front of the engine, where it could be driven directly from the end of the crankshaft.

By this time the benefits of overhead cams were well known. Compared to pushrod-operated valvetrains, overhead cams allowed higher revs before the onset of valve float. Unfortunately, the basic boxer architecture doesn't lend itself to overhead cams. Opposed-twin engines are wide engines; the addition of overhead cams outboard the cylinder heads would make the engines too cumbersome for even street use. On road-racing circuits this width would make them completely uncompetitive.

To obtain most of the benefits of overhead cams while keeping the engine width manageable, BMW turned to a system that proved so advanced, the company would resurrect it 60 years later on the R1100RS Oilhead boxer. This system used two cams mounted in the heads, operating short pushrods that opened and closed the valves via rocker arms. Unlike the later Oilhead system, the original cam-in-head design used shafts with bevel gears to

operate the cams. While the system didn't allow the engine to rev as highly as a true overhead-cam system, it did allow the engine to rev much higher before valve float set in.

Wiggerl "Ludwig" Kraus piloted the new machine during its maiden race at the Avusring near Berlin in June 1935. A Husqvarna-mounted Swede named Ragnar Sunnqvist won that race, but at that year's ISDT the BMW-mounted team of George Meier, Josef Forstner, and Fritz Lindhardt won the gold medal.

BMW kicked its road-racing efforts up a notch in 1936. The Kompressor proved to be the fastest motorcycle on any given track, but handling difficulties kept the factory team from the top of the podium at most races. Otto Ley took second at the Swiss Gran Prix, but it wasn't until late August that BMW scored its first win. Ley finally beat the dominant Nortons at the Saxtorp circuit, a track that favored top speed over handling, allowing Ley to fully exploit the superior power of the Kompressor.

BMW's luck improved in 1937. Englishman Jock West rode a Kompressor to a sixth-place finish at the Isle of Man TT, and Karl Gall won the German and Hungarian Grans Prix as well as the Dutch TT. West went on to win that year's Ulster Gran Prix.

In 1938, BMW returned to the Isle of Man with a new frame for its race bikes, one featuring a sprung rear suspension. Jock West still rode a 1937 Kompressor with a rigid frame, while Gall and George Meier rode the new sprung-frame bikes. The Germans fared poorly. Gall crashed and Meier broke down early in the race, but West finished in fifth place. Meier went on to win the Belgian, German, and European Grans Prix, as well as the Dutch TT, and West again won the Ulster Gran Prix.

Even though war seemed imminent in the spring of 1939, BMW once again fielded a factory team at the Isle of Man TT races. Once again Gall crashed, this time so severely that he died from his injuries four days after the crash. Given what the future held for Germany, it was probably a good time to die. Norton didn't enter a factory race team that year because it was too busy preparing for war. Without the dominant Nortons, Meier cruised to an easy victory.

Meier again won the Dutch TT and Belgian GP, but the certainty of war cast a pallor over the 1939 racing season, a pallor that would have been even greater had anyone suspected that the season would prove to be the end of the line for the mighty Kompressors. World War II put an end to motor sports in Europe for the better part of a decade, and when racing resumed after the war, sanctioning bodies prohibited motorcycles with supercharged engines from competing, ending road racing's supercharged era. Few people alive today have actually seen these bikes turn a wheel in anger, but in their day, the fabled Kompressors gave race fans quite a show, their superchargers shrieking as they ripped past crowds at speeds approaching 140 miles per hour, a spectacle that may never be seen or heard again.

By 1938, BMW's telescopic fork was universally accepted as the industry standard for front suspension.

THE R6

In 1937, BMW entered the 600-cc class, a displacement category that would prove extremely important for the company in the coming decades. The company's first 600-cc-class motorcycle, the R6, featured most of the cutting-edge technology from the R5, like the foot-shifted four-speed transmission and the telescopic fork, but since the engine was a side-valve design, BMW wasn't able to use the twin-cam arrangement from the more sporting 500. The R6 did use BMW's advance tunnel-design crankcase, but the side-valve arrangement forced BMW engineers to use the older single-cam setup. In its single year of production, 1,850 R6s rolled off BMW's assembly line.

A NEW SINGLE

BMW introduced its final 200-cc-class motorcycle, the 192-cc R20, in 1937. The R20 shed the pressed-steel frame of the R2, replacing it with a tubular frame similar to the one used on the company's twin-cylinder motorcycles. The new thumper still featured a rigid rear frame, but now used a telescopic fork, though of a much simpler design than the hydraulically damped fork used on the more expensive models. The new fork simply relied on springs for shock absorption. The R20 did feature the new foot-shifted transmission from the twins, but with only three cogs in the gearbox instead of four. It also lacked the positive stop mechanism used on the other foot-shifted models. Perhaps the R20's most identifiable feature was its tank top–mounted steel tool kit. BMW sold more than 2,000 R20s in the two years the model was produced.

BMW also replaced its R3 single with the R35 in 1937. The only changes in the conversion from R3 to R35 involved boring the engine to 340 cc and mounting the nonhydraulically damped telescopic fork from the R20. Unlike the R20, the R35 continued to use the pressed-steel frame, marking BMW's final use of the Star frame concept. This was also the last civilian motorcycle to feature a hand-shifted transmission. While the R3 had been a marketing failure, the R35 proved to be the exact opposite, selling 15,000 copies over a three-year period. The year 1937 found Germany's Wehrmacht on a buying spree, and the vast majority of R35s ended up going to the German military.

REAR SUSPENSION

In 1938, BMW replaced the R6 with the R61. The R61 was an R6 with a plunger-type rear suspension similar to the one used on BMW's Kompressor road racers. This crude system simply mounted shock absorbers in the rear frame, providing the rear hub with a couple of inches of travel. The system required universal joints on the drive shaft to compensate for hub movement. The sprung rear axle was far from ideal and likely would

1938   R 66

have been relegated to the status of failed experiment in short order if World War II hadn't effectively halted all streetbike development at BMW for more than a decade.

In all, BMW introduced five new models for 1938. In addition to the R61, BMW produced a 745-cc version of the side-valve twin, the R71. This replacement for the pressed steel framed R12 was primarily intended for sidecar use.

The company fitted the R5 with the sprung rear axle used on the R61 to create the R51 and introduced an overhead-valve motorcycle for the 600-cc class, the R66. Rather than an overbored R51, the R66 had a new engine, which featured a single camshaft, like the side-valve R61 instead of the twin-cam system used on the R51. It did retain the hairpin valve springs used on the R51. For the first time BMW offered optional Bing carburetors on the R66, helping this 597-cc machine become BMW's first production model capable of topping 90 miles per hour.

BMW's other new machine for 1938 was the R23, which was an R20 bored out to 247 cc. BMW built this motorcycle in response to a change in German law. Beginning in June 1938, motorcycles under 200 cc were no longer exempt from licensing requirements, but bikes under 250 cc could be operated with a special restricted license. Other than a slight overbore, the only other noticeable change was that the toolkit that had been mounted atop the fuel tank of the R20 was now recessed into the tank. BMW sold more than 6,000 R23s in 1938 and likely would have sold many more in the years to come, had World War II not interrupted production.

BOXER MOTORCYCLES AND JET AIRPLANES

Max Friz earned a place in motorcycle history when he designed BMW's first motorcycle, the R32, a bike that would influence BMW motorcycle design into the next millennium, but he also earned a spot in the history books for a nonmotorcycle-related design. As noted in chapter 1, Friz' passion was aircraft, not ground transport. Friz returned to the pursuit of that passion soon after designing the original R32 and during World War II developed one of the world's first operational gas turbine jet aircraft engines, the BMW 003. The German Luftwaffe used the BMW engine in a number of planes like the wood-and-cloth Heinkel HE 162, but by the time the engine had been sufficiently developed and tested, Germany had already nearly lost the war. Friz' design did see use in Russia. After the war, the Russians began producing jet engines based on the 003.

WAR

The big model roll out of 1938 marked a high point for BMW. The company's motorcycles set the industry standard, both on the road and on the track, and its other products prospered too. By 1939 the company employed 27,000 people, but with war once again on the horizon, it was clear that BMW could not continue doing business as it had for the past couple of decades. After war broke out on September 3 of that year, production of civilian transportation declined at a dramatic rate. BMW tried to continue supplying its customers, even defying Nazi orders by releasing cars to dealers, but in the chaos of war, few resources were available for building civilian transportation. Soon all of the company's production would focus on supplying the Wehrmacht's war effort. The Nazi Party allowed an occasional small production run of vehicles to reach the public, but in 1941 BMW produced its last war-time motorcycle for civilian use. This final run of R71s marked the last side-valve motorcycles ever produced by BMW.

Not that war was bad for BMW's bottom line. By 1941 the company's workforce had risen to 35,000 people, though most were engaged in building aircraft engines. By May of that year, BMW ceased building all vehicles except the R75 military motorcycle.

THE R75

The R75 was a classic war baby, a machine created solely for military use and never intended for civilian riders. Introduced in 1941, the bike was designed specifically for the Wehrmacht to use in the deserts of North Africa and on the Russian Front. Because the R75 was manufactured at BMW's automotive plant in Eisenach, which became part of the Soviet-controlled German Democratic Republic after the war, all production records related to the R75 have been destroyed. The actual number of R75s produced remains unknown, but has been estimated to be between 10,000 and 20,000 units. BMW's U.S. website puts the number at 18,000.

Designed to be a sidecar rig from the outset, it is not possible to separate the R75 motorcycle from its chair. When the Wehrmacht needed a solo motorcycle, it used the R35. The chair came with a machine gun as standard equipment, one of the more unusual features ever to be included in a motorcycle's purchase price.

The R75 used American-style 16-inch wheels at all three corners, lowering the bike's center of gravity as well as lowering the overall gearing. To compensate for the reduced final drive ratio, the R75 featured what was then considered a massive 5.25-gallon fuel tank. The motorcycles used in Europe and on the

HARD LESSONS

Besides its machine gun, the R75 featured one other unique feature: a driven sidecar wheel. This was not the first use of a powered wheel. Ernst Henne had used a powered wheel on his record-breaking sidecar runs in the 1930s, although his rig consisted of little more than some lightweight tubing connecting the wheel to the motorcycle. While not the first, the R75 does hold the honor of being the most sophisticated driven-wheel sidecar rig of the era, and perhaps of all time.

The sophistication of the design came about in an attempt to prevent casualties among the Wehrmacht soldiers. Operating a sidecar rig with a driven wheel on the chair presents some formidable challenges. While the system provides tremendous traction in mud or sand, on dry roads the driven wheel can pitch the chair into the ground on right-hand turns. On a sidecar rig without a driven wheel, the chair will rise into the air on right-hand turns. This is known as "flying the chair" and is harmless fun. Getting pitched into the pavement, however, is not much fun at all. In fact, it's about the most dangerous type of single-vehicle accident you can have on a sidecar rig.

To minimize the potential for augering the chair machine-gun first into the ground, the R75 featured an advanced automotive type differential mounted outboard of the driveshaft pinion gears on the rear axle. The differential could be locked out in low-traction conditions, effectively creating a solid axle between the driven wheels on the chair and the bike. Many operators undoubtedly forgot to unlock the differential when they were back on dry roads, though most likely they made this mistake just once. It's amazing how fast the human animal can learn something when the curriculum includes a high-speed face plant into the road.

Russian front used dual-purpose tires, but the bikes destined for Northern Africa featured full-blown off-road knobbies. A dual-range transmission further enhanced the bike's off-road capabilities. A hand-operated lever selected either high or low range, and a second lever engaged reverse gear, a handy feature on a bike that weighed 925 pounds with machine gun in place. Reverse could be used in either high or low range.

Although it used an overhead-valve design, the 745-cc engine had more in common with the side-valve 750s than with the other overhead-valve engines from the period. It used the same perfectly square 78-by-78-millimeter bore and stroke as all the side-valve 750s. In fact, the R75 was based on the side-valve R71. The R75 used an overhead-valve design because side-valve engines tend to run hotter than overhead-valve engines, an important consideration for an ultra-heavyweight machine intended for low-speed work in difficult conditions. The tuned-for-torque engine cranked out 26 horsepower, enough to propel the massive machine to just a tick under 60 miles per hour.

A single high-level exhaust pipe enabled the R75 to pass through deeper water than would be possible with traditional low-level pipes, and a monstrous auxiliary air cleaner could be mounted atop the fuel tank for desert duty. The rigid rear frame was probably a good idea, considering the heft of the bike. The company's sprung axle design could be overwhelmed even on the lightweight street machines of the era. The suspension would have come completely unhinged if it had to cope with the R75's mass. The beefy steel frame featured massive bracing to cope with the unprecedented weight of the motorcycle. To adequately stop the beast, both the rear wheel and the chair featured hydraulically operated expanding drum brakes.

Unlike motorcycles used in World War I, this sophisticated new machine was not intended for dispatch duty. The Wehrmacht intended to use the R75 as a replacement for the horse in a motorized cavalry. The R75 was an attack vehicle. As such, it almost succeeded. Almost, but not quite. While the R75 was a competent sidecar rig, the four-wheel-drive Jeeps used by the Allies were clearly superior. The Jeeps were much easier to drive and didn't require specially trained operators. They were more versatile and had far greater towing capacity. Ultimately the Wehrmacht replaced the R75 with the Kubelvagon, a Jeep-like vehicle based on the Volkswagen.

A COMPANY IN RUINS

While the military buildup instigated by the Third Reich initially was profitable for BMW, the Nazi regime ultimately proved ruinous for the company. Karl Popp, BMW's managing director since 1917, retired in 1943 and Max Friz left the company soon after the war, leaving something of a void in company leadership. Not that there was much of a company to lead. The Allies began bombing BMW's Allach plant, located just outside Munich, on June 13, 1941, and by the time Germany surrendered on May 8, 1945, the Allach plant was in ruins. The situations at the company's plants in Eisenach and Berlin were even worse. Before things got better, they would get worse still. BMW was about to enter the darkest period of its entire history.

CHAPTER 3

AFTER THE
WAR

Even as Hitler hunkered down in his Berlin bunker, waiting for Germany's final defeat at the hands of the Allies, he continued to attempt to inflict his will on the German people. On April 11, 1945, just days prior to committing suicide, Hitler ordered BMW's Allach factory destroyed to prevent the Allies from using anything that remained. Surviving members of BMW's board of directors ignored Hitler's final ravings from his bunker.

Not that there was much left of the Allach plant for BMW's directors to save. Allied bombing had reduced the factory to rubble, and it would deteriorate even further in the days immediately following the war. Just as Hitler had feared, what little remained of the factory was soon liberated from the premises in a frenzy of looting. While American forces have been accused of carting off the contents of the Allach factory as war booty, the arrival of the American forces actually put an end to the pilfering taking place at the time, at least in the initial stages of occupation. The Allied occupational forces ordered the remains of the Allach plant confiscated along with all BMW's other facilities, but the Americans had that order nullified

ABOVE: One of the few differences between the R51/2 and the original R51 was the use of the split-valve cover on the /2 version. This style of valve cover was first used on the Wehrmacht R75 sidecar rig.

LEFT: Even the most minor details of BMW motorcycles exude an air of elegance, like these combination spotlights-rear view mirrors.

RIGHT: When BMW returned to the business of building motorcycles, their first postwar boxer twin was the 1950 R51/2, which was basically a copy of the prewar R51.

FAR RIGHT: Although the R51/3 introduced in 1951 looked almost identical to the /2 version, its engine was completely new, and formed the basis of all future BWM boxer twins until the introduction of the /5 series in 1969.

URAL MOTORCYCLES

After World War II, the Soviets occupied the city of Eisenach, Germany, the wartime home of BMW's motorcycle manufacturing plant. After Germany surrendered, the Soviets dismantled an entire motorcycle assembly line and carted it home as war booty. They reassembled the equipment in Irbit, Russia, where the BMW-based Ural has been assembled ever since. The Ural currently sold in the United States is somewhat of a mongrel, displaying lineage from several prewar and wartime models, most notably the R75 and R66. Except for the addition of a twin-shock swinging-arm rear suspension, not much has changed in the intervening decades.

The Ural is a bit crude by today's standards, but possesses an earthy, proletarian charm, like Russian Vodka or a fresh potato. Most Urals come with an attached sidecar as standard equipment. Solo bikes have to be special ordered. The bike itself could be worse. While it's more crude than the antique BMWs upon which it's based, it's more sophisticated than, say, an Ironhead Harley-Davidson Sportster from the 1970s. Ural motorcycles may be a bit crude, but the chairs are sturdy and well finished and constitute one of the best sidecar values available today.

Once Ural motorcycles reach U.S. shores, their engines are completely disassembled and reassembled using quality aftermarket components. As delivered from the Irbit factory, Ural quality is notoriously lacking. Tales of Russian laborers pounding ill-fitting bearings into the crankcases with wooden mallets abound.

Today's Ural motorcycle is still built on the assembly line that the Soviets carted home after World War II as war-booty.

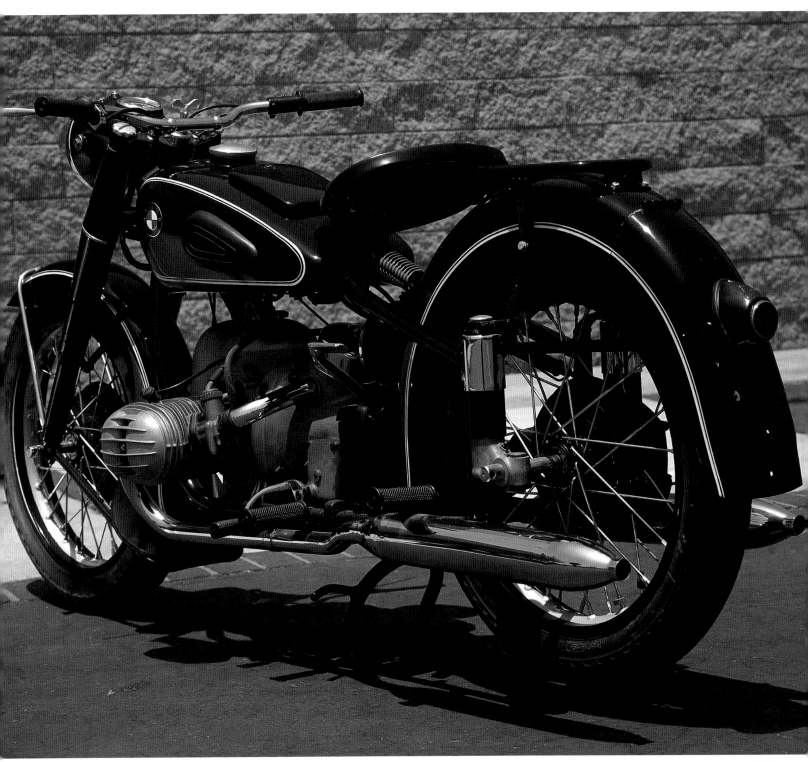

Introduced in 1952, the R68 marked BMW's return to the sporting market.

to save the Allach factory, which they hoped to use as a repair facility. Eventually the Allies took much of the equipment at the Allach plant as part of war reparations, but early American intervention prevented a complete dismantling of the factory.

BMW's Eisenach factory wasn't as lucky. The Soviets took over that facility. They moved an entire assembly line back to Russia, where it was used to build Ural motorcycles.

The Eisenach factory remained in use after the war, producing the pressed-steel-framed R35 single under East German management. The bikes produced at Eisenach bore the EMW (*Eisenach Moteren Werke*) banner. In addition to pilfering BMW's equipment, EMW even copied BMW's spinning-propeller badge, though the sky blue of the BMW badge was changed to blood red on the EMW motorcycles.

Motorcycle production at Eisenach began in 1946, two years before motorcycle production was restarted in West Germany. EMW motorcycle quality was much higher than the quality of the BMW knock-offs being built in Russia, partly

because EMW was staffed by experienced factory employees who had once built motorcycles to BMW's high standards. To be fair, material availability also played a role in quality, since the materials available in East Germany were of higher quality than the materials available in Russia.

STARTING FROM SCRATCH

While the Eisenach facility was a total loss for BMW, the Allach factory had narrowly avoided complete dismemberment. Thanks to financial intervention by the Deutsche Bank and some clever maneuvering by BMW personnel, the company retained some potential capacity to begin manufacturing motorcycles in the future. Unfortunately, it was forbidden to do so. The terms of Germany's surrender prohibited BMW from manufacturing motorcycles.

Even if the company had been allowed to build motorcycles, it had lost many of its top engineers. BMW had produced sophisticated jet engines during the war. After the war, the Soviet and

With its simple, angular lines, the R68 ranks as one of the most elegant BMW motorcycles.

American governments brought the engineers who designed those jet engines to their respective countries to continue jet technology development, leaving BMW without its brightest technical minds.

Another obstacle to getting back in the motorcycle-manufacturing business was BMW management, which wasn't certain that resuming motorcycle production would be in BMW's best interest. Thankfully Georg Meier, a prewar racing hero and winner of the 1939 Isle of Man TT, convinced BMW management that resuming motorcycle production was indeed the company's best course of action. Meier sold BMW executives on the idea that Europe would need inexpensive transportation in the coming years, and that they could make money by building motorcycles to meet that need.

When the Allies finally lifted the ban on motorcycle production in Germany, the company had to start entirely from scratch because its blueprints and schematic drawings had been either confiscated or destroyed by the Russians. Company engineers were forced to tear down surviving prewar motorcycles and create new plans by measuring each part individually.

THE R24

BMW introduced its first postwar motorcycle at the 1948 Geneva Motor Show. Essentially a prewar R23, the new R24 incorporated some details from the Wehrmacht R75 model. The rockers worked in bolted-on pillars rather than pillars cast into the heads, and the valve covers consisted of two separate pieces held in place by a clamp with a single central bolt. This valve-cover design would be used on every future BMW single until the advent of the Rotax-engined F650 in the mid-1990s.

Engine horsepower increased to 12, up 2 from the R23, thanks to an increased compression ratio, an improved valve angle, and a new 22-millimeter Bing carburetor. The new bike also featured a modern four-speed transmission, but it still made do with no rear suspension.

Production began in December 1948, and in 1949 BMW produced more than 9,200 units. By 1950 production surpassed 17,000 motorcycles. The new BMW motorcycle

The plunger-type rear suspension had never been the most effective design. With swinging arm rear suspensions becoming popular in the 1950s, the design became downright archaic.

was a hit, providing German citizens with much-needed transportation, just as Georg Meier had promised BMW's board of directors.

RETURN OF THE BOXER

The success of the R24 brought much-needed funds into BMW's coffers, money the company put back into product research and development. In 1950, BMW updated the R24, giving the little single a beefed-up crankshaft, larger intake valves, and most important, a plunger-type rear suspension. These improvements earned the upgraded bike an upgraded title. The R24 became the R25.

But improvements to the single-cylinder bike were hardly noteworthy compared to BMW's big news for 1950: the return of the Boxer twin.

Like the R24 single, BMW's first postwar boxer twin was basically a modified version of one of the company's prewar bikes. In the case of the R51/2, as the new boxer would be called, the donor bike was the prewar R51. And like the R24, the R51/2 featured the split-valve covers from the wartime R75. One noticeable change was that the control levers of the R51/2 pivoted from the inside end of the lever, like nearly every other motorcycle in the world, instead of from the outside end, as had every BMW motorcycle since Max Friz' R32.

BMW might have been banking some money from the success of its single-cylinder motorcycle, but the company was hardly rolling in money, and the R51/2 exhibited some evidence of cost-cutting measures. The rear main bearing was pressed directly into the crankcase instead of being mounted in its own housing, which meant that if an owner spun the bearing, he would have had to replace the entire crankcase. To further cut costs, the needle roller bearings were replaced with plain bearings, and traditional coil valve springs replaced the exotic hairpin valve springs used on the original R51.

The polished lever beside the footpeg is a handy neutral finder.

ABOVE: While never a huge success on the world's racetracks in solo form, the RS54 Rennsport was certainly an aesthetic success.

FAR RIGHT: The Earles-type fork used on the Rennsport was one factor that limited its success on the racetrack.

The R51/2 appeared on the cover of the magazine *Das Motorrad* during Christmas 1949, and the first 1,000 units built were sold to the French police force. The model became available to the general public later in 1950. In a road test from its November 1950 issue, the magazine *Motor Cycle* marveled at the engine's "turbine-like" power delivery, but noted that clumsy gear changes hampered overall performance. Of the lack of suspension travel, the magazine noted that "suspension was largely provided by the tyres." The writer of the test did note that the stiff suspension contributed to remarkably stable handling and described the steering as "pluperfect."

The R51/2 became the R51/3 in 1951. The /3 looked like the /2 version, but it featured a completely different engine with an improved valvetrain. A single camshaft replaced the dual-camshaft

design of the original R51, and the valvetrain now resided under redesigned rocker covers. The new engine was now narrower overall, and the magneto and generator were tucked away under covers in front of the engine. The new engine looked much cleaner and more modern and would set the pattern for every BMW twin to be manufactured for the next two decades. A larger fuel tank (4.5 gallons, up 1 gallon from the R51/2) further distinguished the /3 version visually.

THE R67

Later in 1950 BMW produced its first completely new motorcycle since the Wehrmacht R75, the R67. Many fans hoped for a flat-out sporting successor to the prewar R66, but such fans were disappointed. Rather than being a fiery sporting mount, the R67 was designed for pedestrian sidecar duty. BMW designed the new bike to fill a hole in the company's line-up left by the demise of the prewar side-valve models like the R61 and R71. Based on the new single-cam 494-cc engine introduced in the R51/3, the 594-cc engine featured a slightly undersquare 72-by-73-millimeter bore and stroke ratio, and pumped out a less-than-heart-stopping 26 horsepower. The frame used the already antiquated plunger-type sprung rear axle. The new bike did, however, feature a double leading shoe front brake, which represented state-of-the-art equipment in 1950.

It's new models were well received and sold in respectable numbers, but BMW knew it would take more than aging prewar designs if the company wanted to remain competitive in the motorcycle market. The company wanted to regain its position as one of the world's premier motorcycle companies, but money was still in short supply in the early 1950s, so company engineers were forced to settle for incremental improvements to BMW's line-up rather than making huge technological leaps. Such leaps would have to wait for a few more years.

The R25 became the R25/2 in 1951, thanks to a few minor engine modifications, a sportier looking fender, and a new sprung saddle. In 1953, it became the R25/3, when the bike finally received a telescopic fork with hydraulic damping instead of the crude spring damping it had inherited from the R23.

In another example of incremental improvements, the R67 became the R67/2 in 1952, thanks to a few engine tweaks that raised power from 26 horsepower to 28 horsepower. Sales continued to increase, but BMW knew it had to bring more exciting motorcycles to the market if it hoped to build on that success.

THE R68

At the 1951 Frankfurt Motorcycle Show BMW introduced its first postwar sporting motorcycle, the R68. The R68 featured a hot-rodded version of the new 594-cc single-cam engine from the R67. Compression was bumped from 5.6:1 to 7.5:1 and the venturi throat sizes of the Bing carburetors were increased from 22 to 26-millimeter. Intake valves increased from 34 to 38-millimeter in diameter, and exhaust valves increased from 32- to 34-millimeter. The new valves operated under covers that featured just two ribs. This served no functional purpose but became a stylistic hallmark of sporting BMW motorcycles that would last until the demise of the unpainted valve covers in 1977. The show bike featured a high-mounted two-into-one exhaust pipe similar to the pipe used on ISDT bikes, in part to distinguish the sporty new bike from the utilitarian R67 upon which it was based. When the bike was finally available to the general public in the summer of 1952, it wore normal street-going exhaust pipes, though a competition

RIGHT: With the RS54
Rennsport, BMW adopted
its trademark shaft drive to
a modern swinging arm
rear suspension.

version of the bike with the high-mounted exhaust system could be specially ordered.

The changes to the engine helped extract 35 horsepower from the 594-cc engine when the rider spun the boxer twin to its 7,000-rpm redline, enough to make the R68 BMW's first genuine 100-mile per hour production motorcycle. BMW capitalized on this ability, advertising the R68 as "The 100 mph motorcycle!"

Undoubtedly the R68 was the most potent street-going motorcycle BMW had ever built, but by 1952 just being The 100 mph motorcycle! was no longer enough. There were other motorcycles available that would also go 100 miles per hour. None could do it with the big BMW's unruffled style, but many could achieve 100 miles per hour a lot more cheaply than the R68. BMWs were expensive bikes, and the R68 was the most expensive machine in the company's line-up. BMW sold less than 1,500 total units before the R68 was replaced by the R69 in 1955.

POSTWAR RACING

Although Allied bombers virtually destroyed BMW's production capacity and the company's brain power had been drained through attrition and postwar pilfering of top engineers by the war's victors, a surprising number of competition machines survived the war. Quite a few top German racers also survived, and legend has it that these racers played a significant role in saving BMW's racing motorcycles. Stories abound of BMW racers hidden in pigpens around the German countryside during the war. Prewar racer Georg Meier was said to have hidden a Kompressor race bike in a haystack. Whether or not that was the case, Meier did indeed have a Kompressor to campaign once racing resumed in Germany, which occurred almost immediately following Germany's surrender.

Meier and his Kompressor dominated German racing after the war, but he was unable to repeat his prewar success on the world stage for political reasons. While racing in Germany resumed at the national level after the war, the Federation Internationale Motocycliste (FIM), the sanctioning body that initiated the World Championship Series in 1949, excluded Germany from competing in its events.

In 1951, the FIM relented and allowed Germany to rejoin the World Championship series, but with a caveat that ensured BMW motorcycles would not dominate the competition: a total ban on supercharging. This effectively eliminated BMW from serious contention, because while the company had been able to pattern its initial postwar motorcycles on its prewar machines, the ban on supercharging meant the company would have to create an all-new design if it had any intention of being competitive in international racing.

BMW could not afford to develop an entirely new racing engine when it was still struggling to resume motorcycle production, so the first BMWs entered in the World Championship series were simply old Kompressors castrated of their superchargers. These neutered engines were much more compact than the old Kompressors, but in normally aspirated form, they were 30 horsepower down on their prewar ancestors. BMW needed an all-new engine if it had any hope of being competitive.

THE RENNSPORT

In 1953, BMW introduced its much-needed all-new racer, the Rennsport. A pair of overhead camshafts outboard each cylinder distinguished the Rennsports from any other motorcycle BMW had ever before produced. Driven by a pair of bevel shafts, these heavily finned double-overhead-cam cylinder heads looked like they meant business. The original versions of the engine displaced 492-cc through an undersquare bore-and-stroke ratio of 66-millimeter by 72-millimeter. This long stroke combined with the tall DOHC cylinder heads led to a wide engine. The engine produced 55 horsepower at 8,000 rpm.

That power passed through a four-speed transmission and was directed to the rear wheel by a driveshaft, just as on every other motorcycle the German firm had ever built. BMW experimented with both carburetors and fuel injection on its factory racers, but when it built a production batch of 25 RS54 Rennsports to be campaigned by carefully selected privateers during the 1954 racing season, two 30-millimeter Fischer-Amal carburetors pumped fuel into the combustion chambers. Unlike prewar 500-cc-class motorcycles BMW sold to privateer racers, which were essentially modified street machines, the 25 RS54 Rennsports were almost identical replicas to the factory works racing motorcycles.

While the Rennsport engine represented a dramatic break from BMW tradition, its chassis represented a break from just about every chassis tradition to date. The RS54 featured a frame with swinging-arm suspension front and rear. While a swinging arm rear suspension was an established design in 1953, the swinging-arm front suspension was not. BMW described this suspension design as "a pivot fork with spring struts." This was, of course, a variation of the Earles fork that would shortly appear on BMW production road motorcycles.

The Rennsport was a technological tour de force, but that didn't make the bike a successful racer. It may have used

Another limiting factor in the Rennsport's racing success was the width of its bevel-drive, overhead-cam engine. It was pretty, though.

While the Earles fork lent heavy steering characteristics to a solo motorcycle, it helped to stabilize the bike with a sidecar mounted. Since the width of the cylinders don't matter on a sidecar rig because the machine doesn't lean, the RS54 Rennsport proved perfect for sidecar racing, and dominated the sport well into the 1970s.

ground-breaking technology, but using radically different technology forced engineers to seek out design solutions that compromised the bike's racing abilities. The bike's primary problem was one of balance. To gain adequate ground clearance with such a wide engine, engineers were forced to mount the powerplant high in the frame, raising the motorcycle's center of gravity and making it feel awkward and top-heavy in corners. But the Rennsport also suffered for its swinging-arm suspension, which was heavy and contributed to ponderous steering.

BMW engineers modified the Rennsport engine, experimenting with different bores and strokes until finally arriving at an undersquare bore and stroke ratio of 70- by 64-millimeters. This helped raise overall power output to 65 horsepower at 10,000 rpm. Many racers also improved the transmission, converting it into a five-speed instead of a four-speed.

The Rennsport had some success. Walter Zeller won the 1953 German Grand Prix aboard a Rennsport. Dickey Dale won the Czechoslovakian Gran Prix and Ernst Hiller won the Austrian Gran Prix, both in 1958. By the end of the decade, however, with corporate funds running low, BMW abandoned solo Gran Prix racing.

AND NOW FOR SOMETHING COMPLETELY DIFFERENT

The R68 may not have been a sales success for BMW, but it injected a spark of life into a postwar line-up that was conservative to the point of being stodgy. But the powerful engine of the R68 highlighted the deficiencies of the sprung-axle frame inherited from the company's prewar motorcycles. Clearly a modern sporting

THE THREE-WHEELED RENNSPORTS

While technologically magnificent, BMW's RS54 Rennsport achieved very little success in international motorcycle racing, at least of the two-wheeled variety. BMW made a host of improvements to the machine during its international Gran Prix career, but the design had a fundamental flaw: a high center of gravity necessitated by the need to attain sufficient ground clearance when using such a wide engine. This flaw doomed the Rennsport to footnote status in the world of two-wheeled racing.

But take away the need for cornering clearance, and suddenly the basic Rennsport engine design, which has an inherently low center of gravity, changes from hindrance to help. When used in sidecar racing, where the machines steer like cars rather than lean into corners like motorcycles, the Rennsport powerplant is just about ideal. Rennsport-powered sidecar outfits dominated international sidecar racing well into the 1970s, winning 18 World Championships and 20 constructor titles between 1953 and 1974.

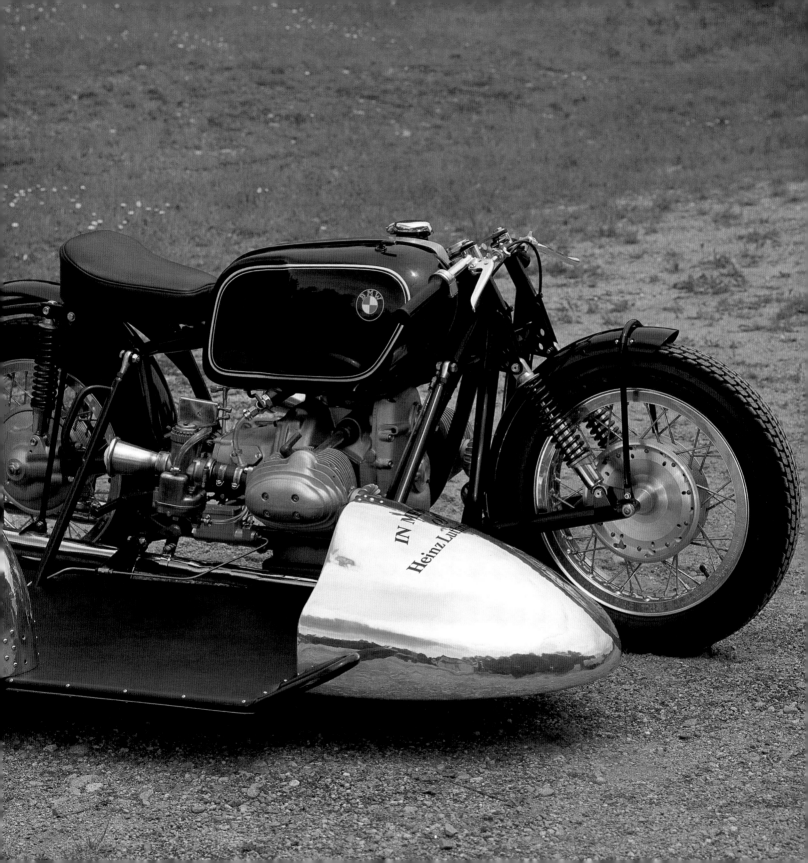

In 1955 BMW brought the Earles fork concept to the street, and introduced a line of boxer twins that featured swinging-arm suspensions front and rear.

motorcycle required a swinging-arm rear suspension to be competitive. But BMW engineers decided that a modern bike needed even more innovation than a swinging-arm rear suspension. What was good for the rear suspension must be good for the front suspension too.

THE EARLES FORK

For its next big thing, BMW turned to the work of Englishman Ernie Earles, who had developed a leading-link swinging-arm front suspension for motorcycle use. BMW used a version of Mr. Earles' design on its Rennsport racers beginning in 1953, and the RS54 Rennsport production racers built in 1954 continued with the design.

At the Brussels Motor Show held in January 1955, BMW introduced two new road bikes with a version of the company's exotic front racing suspension: the R50 and R69. The version of the Earles fork concept that appeared on these new models used a rigid fork that angled back from the centerline of the axles. The bottom of the rigid fork connected to short links that ran forward to the axles, effectively acting as swinging arms. A pair of shocks connected to the swinging arms just aft of the axles, though this location could be adjusted for sidecar use. The tops of the shocks connected to the rigid fork at the bend where it angled back to meet the links. Basically the new streetbike suspension mimicked the design of the racers, except that it used much stouter (and heavier) components to withstand the rigors of sidecar duty. This design had the advantage of preventing the fork from diving under braking. Its major disadvantage was tremendous unsprung weight, a major factor in the Rennsport's difficult handling.

The rear suspension design of the new machines was not quite as unique as the front suspension, but neither was it a typical design. The rear frame looped around much as it has done on the old rigid-framed bikes from the 1930s, but steel cups jutted out behind the rear of the top loops. These cups held the tops of shock absorbers that were attached to the rear swinging arm, just ahead of the axle. These shocks featured levers at the bottoms of their bodies that allowed the rider to adjust spring preload, making this one of the world's first adjustable suspensions. The swinging arm ran from the rear axle to a pair of cross braces inside loops behind the transmission. The driveshaft ran through the right side of the swingarm. To compensate for excessive driveshaft movement generated by the long-travel rear suspension, the U-joint was moved from the axle to the transmission end of the driveshaft.

A few other details differentiated the new models, as if they weren't different enough. The tool kit was moved from a recessed compartment in the top of the fuel tank to a recessed compartment in the side of the tank. Otherwise not much changed. The R50 used the same 494-cc engine used in the R51/3, and the R69 used the high-performance 594-cc engine from the R68. While the engines were relatively unchanged, the transmissions were greatly improved, as were the clutches.

Road tests from the period universally commented on the cleanliness of BMW motorcycles, and a road test of the new R50 published in the July 7, 1955, issue of *Motor Cycle* was no exception. According to the magazine, "The machine could be ridden in ordinary walking clothes without any fear of their becoming soiled."

The bike's performance, while respectable, certainly wouldn't contribute to the rider soiling his ordinary walking clothes.

The magazine recorded a quarter-mile time of 16.8 seconds at 76 miles per hour and a top speed of 94 miles per hour.

As for handling, the magazine noted that the bike was "slightly heavy at ultra-low speeds" but was "otherwise superb." The combination of swinging arm suspension front and rear provided "leech-like road holding at all speeds." Although the magazine noted that the tendency for the fork to rise instead of dive when the brakes were applied was initially unsettling, it raved about the brakes' performance. In past tests, braking had been a weak area for BMW motorcycles.

The plunger-framed R67, now designated the R67/3, remained in production strictly for sidecar use, though the Earles-forked models proved superior for sidecar duty. The telescopic fork flexed more under the high side loads generated by a sidecar rig than the swinging arm Earles design. Perhaps the greatest benefit of the Earles fork in sidecar use was its adjustability for rake and trail. The swinging arm pivot had two positions. Moving it to the forward position reduced trail, allowing the bike to turn with less effort when a sidecar was attached. Because of this most BMW buyers looking for a motorcycle for sidecar use opted for the newer models, and the R67/3 sold primarily to fleet buyers such as police forces, where a low purchase price was a primary consideration.

EARLES FORKS FOR EVERYONE

In 1956, BMW introduced two more models with the new swinging arm front and rear suspensions: the R60 and the R26. The R60 replaced the R67/3 for sidecar duty, using that bike's 28-horsepower 594-cc engine. The R26 brought the Earles fork design to BMW's single-cylinder line-up.

The 245-cc single-cylinder engine developed a claimed 15 horsepower, enough to propel the 350-pound machine to 80 miles per hour, according to factory data. In its February 16, 1956, issue, England's *Motor Cycle* magazine could only wring 73 miles per hour out of the little beast. A parenthetical note to the top-speed entry read: "conditions: moderate side wind; rider wearing two-piece plastic suit and overboots." Perhaps the aerodynamic drag created by the rider's two-piece plastic suit and overboots contributed to the discrepancy between the magazine's test speed and official factory claims. The magazine managed to get the little thumper through the quarter mile in 20.5 seconds, clocking in at 62 miles per hour.

The less expensive R25/3 still sold well enough, and for a short time it was sold alongside the new R26, but by 1956 the market had changed. Mopeds and small automobiles had taken over the small-displacement motorcycle's role as cheap transportation.

JOHN PENTON'S RECORD COAST-TO-COAST RUN

At 5:59 A.M. on June 8, 1959, John Penton went for a ride on his BMW R69, a ride that ended 52 hours and 11 minutes later, on the opposite side of the North American continent. Penton left New York on Monday morning and arrived in Los Angeles Wednesday morning, the new holder of the transcontinental motorcycle record. Since 1935 Earl Robinson, who rode his 45-cubic inch Harley-Davidson coast to coast in 77 hours and 53 minutes, had held that record.

On his trip, Penton slept 45 minutes, ate two ham sandwiches and a bowl of soup, and drank two cups of milk. "I didn't have any dope, either, like they have today," Penton said when asked about the trip forty-three years later. "I wouldn't say I wasn't tired. Of course I was a hell of a lot younger than I am now."

Penton's motorcycle held up as well as he did. He didn't experience a single mechanical problem with his R69. "I was lucky, and the reason I was lucky is because I chose the right machine. I rode for 52 hours steady, and I never touched my machine except to put in a quart of oil, one pint at a time."

FINANCIAL PROBLEMS

BMW entered the 1950s with an outlook that could be best described with the cliché "cautiously optimistic." Sales of single-cylinder motorcycles were strong, and production of the boxer twins was resuming. The car division was doing well, German aircraft manufacturing was booming, and the FIM was about to lift its ban against German competition in motorcycle racing at the international level.

As the decade progressed, motorcycle sales in most of the world's major markets plummeted. Partly this was because the world was experiencing an economic recession; but like all recessions, that was cyclical. The availability of large numbers of inexpensive automobiles for the first time since before the war proved to have a more far-reaching impact on motorcycle sales than any economic downturn could ever have.

In 1957, three of BMW's major German competitors—DKW, Horex, and Adler—went out of business, and BMW seemed likely to follow suit. In 1954, BMW produced almost 30,000 motorcycles, a new record for the company. By 1957 that number had fallen to less than 5,500. Exports were one of the few bright spots. Demand was increasing in some major markets, most notably the U.S. market, where riders were becoming interested in the sporting bikes like the R69. By the late 1950s, BMW exported more than 85 percent of its boxer twin production to the United States. At the time, BMW credited much of its U.S. success to Butler & Smith, Inc., the sole U.S. importer of BMW motorcycles from 1954 onward.

Strong U.S. motorcycle sales helped, but not enough to offset the soft domestic market, where BMW's automotive division was also in financial trouble. By 1959 it looked like BMW was about to be taken over by Mercedes Benz, but many Germans did not want to see BMW disappear. Banker Herbert Quandt was one such German. Quandt secured financing to restore the financially strapped firm to solvency by selling off the aircraft engine business, and in so doing thwarted Mercedes Benz' attempted takeover.

Quandt was in the right place at the right time. Just as the company's cash hemorrhaging was stopped, the company introduced a small automobile called the 700. This rear-engined car, introduced in August 1959, received its motivation from a 697-cc fan-cooled version of BMW's boxer motorcycle engine. This successful car helped return BMW to profitability, and its success marked a change in company philosophy. From that point on, the company management would shift its focus from motorcycles to automobiles.

NEW MODELS

Business took a sharp turn for the better under Quandt's leadership, and by 1960 BMW was ready to introduce its first new motorcycle models since 1956. That August the company rolled out four new motorcycles at the Nurburgring: the R50/2, the R60/2, the R50S, and the R69S.

Money was still tight, so these new models were developments of existing machines rather than all-new motorcycles. Most changes involved tweaking engines to increase power output. The engines received strengthened crankshafts, camshafts, clutch assemblies, and crankcase bearing housings. The piston rings were made of hardened chrome, and the crankcase and transmission were redesigned for better breathing. All this beefing up allowed engineers to increase power, presumably without compromising reliability.

The second generation (or /2) versions of the R50 and R60 models didn't look much different than the originals, but their engines featured much stronger internals, improving reliability and performance. The new R60/2 now produced 30 horsepower. The S version of the R69 now extracted 42 horsepower from its 594-cc powerplant, and the new R50S massaged 35 ponies from its 494-cc mill. BMW fitted both S models with hydraulic steering dampers to tame the Earles forks' high-speed behavior, and both models used close-ratio four-speed transmissions to make the most of their high-revving engines. The R50S in particular was a screamer, revving to 7,650 rpm before hitting its redline.

Like every other magazine, *Cycle World* complained about the slow-shifting transmission of the R69S but went on to list

LEFT: A close-up view of the cup holding the rear suspension damper on the Earles forked BMWs.

FAR LEFT: The R69, with BMW's new front and rear suspension systems, replaced the R68 as BMW's top-of-the-line sporting model.

the bike's many virtues. The road test concluded by saying that the R69S was "a near perfect choice in a machine for serious travel." With its new models, particularly the high-performance R69S, BMW had created the definitive touring bikes for the 1960s.

In 1960, BMW also introduced the final version of its long-running shaft-drive single-cylinder motorcycle, the R27. By 1960 power output of the 245-cc R26 was up to 18 horsepower, which put a lot of stress on the little engine. Vibration had become a problem. The R27 used a system of rubber mounts to isolate engine vibration from the frame.

Though the editors of *Cycle World* appreciated the rubber mounts, the R27 confused them when they tested it for their May 1964 issue. "There is nothing very exciting about the engine," the magazine wrote. "Most motorcyclists' interests are centered on the sporting aspects of the game. They like to indulge in a bit of high-speed riding." The magazine did acknowledge the existence of a small group of riders who "ask nothing more than to ride gently along and enjoy the fresh air and the scenery." The article concluded that the R27 was comfortable and reliable, but it was also complex, heavy, expensive, and slow. It was a bike for "natural-born BMW riders," but would be of little interest to average motorcyclists.

In 1960 the R69S took over the R69's spot as BMW's top dog. It's 594cc engine pumped out 42 horsepower.

In the early years, buyers of BMW's new top-of-the-line sporting bikes received a feature they never expected from a BMW motorcycle: mechanical problems. Both the S models proved problematic in the first years of production. The R50S model in particular suffered from reliability problems. High-rpm operation led to engine failures, mostly because of over-stressed crankshafts. Building a strong-enough crankshaft for the boxer engine had always been a major challenge for BMW engineers. The problem was that putting a bearing between the two piston-rod journals meant offsetting the cylinders to the point where the boxer engine's famous perfect primary balance would be compromised. The solution was to build

stronger crankshafts, and the addition of ever-stronger crank-shafts was a BMW tradition throughout the entire 73-year production life of its air-cooled boxer engine.

While the new motorcycles proved adept at hauling side-cars, they proved to be less well-suited for riding of a more sporting nature. The swinging-arm front suspension offered benefits such as extreme stability and zero dive under braking, but steering was heavy and slow. Nimble British motorcycles would run circles around the ponderous German machines. The early engine failures were easily addressed, at least on the more sedate R69S, and reliability issues soon disappeared, but the handling problems weren't as easily solved.

LEFT: As BMW's 247cc single-cylinder engine became more highly stressed in an attempt to attain more power, vibration levels increased. To solve this, the company used rubber motor mounts on the R27, which was introduced in 1960.

BELOW: BMW's Earles forked machines excelled for sidecar duty, but by the 1960s, sidecar suitability was not an issue. People wanted the sportiness offered by the lightweight bikes from Japan.

The R50S sold poorly, and BMW dropped the model from its line-up in April 1962, after having built a bit more than 1,600 copies of the bike. The R27 was dropped after 1966. Originally conceived to be the volume leader in BMW's line-up, bad timing prohibited the little single from achieving that lofty goal. The R27 was a rugged but unexciting and terribly expensive motorcycle that happened to hit the market just as Germany's wartime Axis partner, Japan, began to hit its stride in the small-displacement motorcycle market. Buyers could get reliable 250-cc motorcycles from Japan that smoked the stodgy offerings from BMW in any contest of speed and get them at prices that were far lower than the German machines.

THE U.S. MARKET

While the German motorcycle market remained flat, the export market was growing, especially in the United States, where there was a strong demand for the large twins. Even though BMWs sold relatively well in the United States, they were still novelties and not selling in huge numbers. The problem was that BMW sold a motorcycle designed primarily for sidecar duty long after sidecars had ceased to be an important consideration for the vast majority of riders. *Cycle World* reminded readers of this in its September 1966 road test of an

Although the return of the telescopic forks made the US models much more nimble and better suited for solo riding, these bikes were just stopgap measures, something to sell while the new /5 series was being prepared.

R69S: "Just because the R69S has an 'S' in its name doesn't mean that one is buying into a fireball solo machine. It must be remembered that BMW does yeoman service pulling a sidecar." In the swinging 1960s, this couldn't have made a great pull quote for BMW's marketing types to use when trying to generate exciting ad copy.

GIVING ERNIE EARLES HIS WALKING PAPERS

BMW knew full well that continuing to build motorcycles designed primarily for sidecar use meant almost certain extinction. The 1960s were all about being cool, and riding a motorcycle with a sidecar was about as cool as dating your own grandmother. The company took its first cautious step toward hipdom in 1967, when it introduced versions of its standard twins with optional telescopic forks, primarily to help sales in the important U.S. market. BMW called these new models, appropriately enough for their intended mission, the R50US, R60US, and R69US.

BMW adopted the telescopic front forks used on these new models from machines it had designed to compete in the International Six Days Trials earlier in the decade. That ISDT attempt was unsuccessful in that the BMW machines had had their collective clocks cleaned by the lightweight two-stroke competition, but it was successful in that it led to the development of BMW's modern telescopic front forks.

The fork itself was fairly advanced for the time. It featured 8.4 inches of travel and used a tapered rod to achieve progressive damping characteristics. In its June 1968 test of the R69US, *Cycle* magazine wrote, "At high speeds the forks provide positively superb handling. BMW, for years the last-surviving champions of Earles-type leading-link forks, has moved in the direction of the rest of the world's manufacturers."

Other than new forks, the US versions were almost identical with the Earles-forked versions, although the US models didn't include standard sidecar mounting lugs. "From the steering head back, our BMW was mainly old news," *Cycle* wrote. As usual, the magazine commented on the BMW's reliability, but it observed that this reliability might be at least in part attributed to the motorcycle's sheer bulk. The frame, as the test noted, "is sturdily made to resist the rigors of sidecar attachment."

The US models cost $12 more than the Earles-forked models, and all things considered, it seemed like $12 well spent. Performance was up, mostly because of the reduced weight of the new front suspension. *Cycle* magazine achieved a 15.3-second quarter mile and a top speed of 103 miles per hour with its R69US test bike. The R69S tested by *Cycle World* earlier passed through the quarter mile almost 1 second slower, at 16.2 seconds and 101 miles per hour.

STOPGAP MEASURE

New fork or not, BMW's new US models still presented an old-fashioned, stodgy image. In its July 1968 road test of an R60US, *Cycle World* wrote, "[The R60US] stands high and proud, and offers few concessions to modern styling." The test also noted that the combination of low power output, high weight, and clumsy transmission meant that the R60US was slower than most inexpensive 250s from Japan, at least around town.

BMW knew that introducing the US models would just be a stopgap measure. The company knew it would need a modern design to compete in the important U.S. market. The company was busily preparing such a motorcycle even as it introduced the US models.

During the 1960s BMW's most successful motorcycle was also its most expensive; the R69S sold more than 11,000 copies during its nine-year production run. The significance of that bike's success was not lost on BMW. It showed company management that the road to future success was paved with high-end luxurious sporting motorcycles, and not utilitarian transportation devices. This realization would forever change the way BMW built motorcycles.

CHAPTER 4

LIVING IN THE
MODERN WORLD

BMW's motorcycle operations ended the 1960s with a shift in both production location and marketing philosophy. These two elemental changes manifested in the form of an entirely new motorcycle.

The company could likely have ended the 1960s with the decision to get out of the motorcycle market entirely. Something had to give. BMW's motorcycle sales continued to drop throughout the decade. Automobile sales shot up 33 percent during that same period. The obvious solution would have been to quit building motorcycles and devote all the company's production capacity to building the more profitable automobiles. But BMW had never been noted for seeking obvious solutions. Instead of throwing in the towel, BMW introduced the most radically different motorcycle series in the company's history.

BMW introduced the /5 series late in 1969, offering it in 496-cc (R50/5), 599-cc (R60/5), and 745-cc (R75/5) capacities. The /5s retained Max Friz' original boxer layout, but just about every other aspect of the series was new. For starters, the engines were much taller than the old mills. The crankcase tunnel had grown to encompass the air cleaner housing as well as the new electric starter motor, and now filled the entire space between the engine and fuel tank.

ABOVE: Although the R75/5 featured full instrumentation, the gauges were still housed in an old-fashioned headlight nacelle.

LEFT: The original BMW Superbike: the R90S.

With the /5 series that was introduced in 1969, BMW entered the modern motorcycling world. The R75/5 shown here was the firm's top model.

To further differentiate the new powerplant, the entire engine was flopped. The camshaft, which had always resided above the crankshaft, now rotated below it. In turn, the pushrods migrated from their historic position above the cylinders to the bottom of the jugs. In practical terms, this allowed BMW engineers to maintain a fairly low center of gravity while raising the cylinder heads to improve ground clearance, avoiding the handling problems of the old Rennsport racer. A consideration that likely meant more in marketing terms was that flipping the engine upside down hid the pushrod tubes from sight, giving the engine a more-modern overhead-cam look.

REAL IMPROVEMENTS

While flopping the engine may have achieved as much of an aesthetic advantage as a technical one, most changes to the new engine marked definite mechanical upgrades, like the switch from cast-iron to aluminum alloy cylinder barrels. The new barrels featured cast-iron liners that were molecularly bonded to the aluminum alloy. The improved heat dissipating capability of the new cylinder design combined with a 10 percent increase in cooling fin area led to a 40-degree reduction in the engine oil's operating temperature.

The switch from a low-pressure oil system to a high-pressure system allowed the use of plain bearings instead of roller

bearings. Plain bearings distort less than roller bearings under the heavy side loads generated by a boxer engine, and allowed engineers to extract more horsepower from the motor. Plain bearings also made the engine more suitable for use with modern multigrade oils. All these changes combined to make the new engine, in the words of *Cycle* magazine, "A remarkable piece of work."

The two smaller bikes used traditional needle-jet carburetors, but the new 750 used constant vacuum carburetors with butterfly throttle valves. Automobiles had used such instruments for mixing fuel for years, but the idea of CV carburetors on a motorcycle still bordered on radical in 1969 and generated

much controversy. Honda had used the system on its CB450 vertical twin, with mixed success, and one of the few complaints testers had about the new R75/5 was that the carburetors didn't work well at lower engine speeds.

BMW's switch to a 12-volt electrical system proved less controversial. BMW had introduced its modern 12-volt system on the final R69US models, but the system used on the new /5 series represented a significant upgrade from the one used on the older bike. The major difference was the use of an automotive-type 200-watt alternator, the most powerful such device ever mounted on a motorcycle up until that time.

The red frame is non-standard, and probably a bit of overkill since the chrome-bedecked R75/5 was flashy enough as it came from the factory.

THE TOASTER TANK

The optional tank BMW offered for the R75/5 in 1972 featured chrome side covers, and became known as the "toaster tank" in the United States. At the time this was considered a derogatory description of the unit, which proved unpopular in many parts of the world. Some markets found the chrome gaudy and the tank boxy, but the look caught on in the United States. The chrome side covers were dropped after one year in most markets, but became standard issue on U.S. models. Today toaster tank bikes are highly prized by collectors and BMW enthusiasts, especially in the United States, and a nice, clean toaster-tank model commands a better price than a standard version.

The infamous "toaster" tank.

BMW received some criticism for retaining a four-speed transmission in the new series, but the handling prowess of the /5s overshadowed the complaints. The front suspension consisted of the telescopic forks from the US models, no bad thing since it was a fairly advanced design for its day. The chassis was most notable for being remarkably normal, an unusual characteristic in a BMW motorcycle. For the first time, BMW followed standard industry practice rather than shuffling off to the distinct beat of its own peculiar drummer. The frame was a standard twin-cradle design, with a conventional swinging-arm suspension in the rear. The whole setup was not all that different from the featherbed frame Norton had developed a couple of decades earlier. In a decided break from the past, BMW engineers did not include sidecar-mounting lugs on the new frame. In fact, the company

forbade sidecar usage. Mounting sidecars to the new models voided the factory warranty.

In spite of having additional features like an electric starter, turn signals, and a 19-inch front wheel, the new /5 machines gained little weight compared to their /2 predecessors. A 10-pound reduction in the weight of the /5 frames when compared to the /2 frames deserves much of the credit for the relative svelteness of the new machines. *Cycle World* measured the weight of the new 745-cc R75/5 at 457 pounds with half a tank of fuel, just 5 pounds more than the 594-cc R69S it had tested in 1966. *Cycle's* R75/5 test bike weighed in at 3 pounds less than the R69US it had tested the previous year, though presumably both measurements were taken with an empty fuel tank. Standard fuel capacity was up 2.2 gallons on the U.S. market models, eliminating the need for the larger

Even with a two-inch longer wheelbase, thanks to a stretched swingarm, a casual observer would be hard-pressed to tell the difference between the /6 and /5 series.

ANY COLOR YOU LIKE, AS LONG AS ITS'S NOT BLACK

In another radical departure from hidebound tradition, the /5 series was available in an ever-widening variety of colors. Previous models were mostly black, with the rare off-white version finding its way off the old Munich assembly line. Other colors could be specially ordered, but to do something as blasphemous as ordering a red or green R69S was to admit you were a dope fiend, a fornicator, or were in some other way deviant and living outside of societal norms.

BMW offered colors besides black and cream, but people who ordered flamboyant colors were shunned in polite society.

tanks that had been popular options on previous BMW models. In fact, when BMW did make an optional tank available in 1972, it was smaller, not larger.

AN AESTHETIC TRIUMPH

BMW had grown used to receiving praise for the quality and engineering of its motorcycles, but the new series earned BMW praise for its style. Since BMW restarted motorcycle production after World War II, the styling of its bikes had mostly garnered criticism. *Cycle* wrote, "For BMW the new models, and particularly the R75, signify a great leap forward into the present." For all the technological advancements in the new series, this great leap *Cycle* referred to was as much an aesthetic leap as it was a technological leap. For the first time since before World War II, BMW had produced a motorcycle with cutting-edge styling.

"The R75 truly is a fine looking machine," *Cycle World* wrote, listing a myriad of reasons why the new bikes looked better than the motorcycles they replaced. "Previous BMWs, including the R69US, featured a frame which was a hand-me-down from the rigid frame era."

The magazine was only stating what everyone, including BMW management, already knew. The motorcycles BMW had produced during the postwar years had looked like refugees from some long-forgotten past; the new /5 series looked right for its time. *Cycle World's* sole aesthetic criticism involved the exposed battery, which the magazine called "the only ugly spot on an otherwise pleasant design."

"SHOCKINGLY FAST"

An increase of 15 horsepower meant that the new R75/5 had much more sporting potential than any previous "sports" model. Top speed showed no improvement—*Cycle* attained the same 103 miles per hour top speed with its 1969 R75/5 as it had with its 1968 R69US. But quarter-mile times improved dramatically. *Cycle World* rode its R75/5 through the quarter mile in 13.89 seconds, while it took 16.2 seconds to complete the same task aboard the magazine's last R69S test bike. "You move out fast, really fast. Shockingly fast," *Cycle* wrote. "It may be disappointing at the top end, but the BMW has splendid midrange acceleration and an operating smoothness that's yet unequalled by any of the multis."

This paint scheme was called "smoke," and remains one of the most handsome liveries ever to grace a motorcycle.

All the magazines shared *Cycle's* enthusiasm for the new /5 series, especially the R75/5 version. "That redesigned flat-twin delivers 57 bhp at 6200 rpm, which puts it squarely among the new superbikes," *Cycle* wrote in its first full road test of the R75/5.

Cycle World criticized the action of the fork springs. "The rebound stroke is, in our estimation, mostly wasted," the magazine wrote in its road test of the R75/5. "Under normal conditions, the forks would not bottom, but under heavy braking they did with a resounding thump." The magazine suggested potential buyers mount heavier fork springs immediately.

Still, most reports on the handling of the new bikes were extremely positive. "It's got all the touring stuff: electric start, turn signals," *Cycle* wrote in its November 1969 road test. "But you can corner it honked way over, stand it on end with a throttle twist, and cruise full-song all day. The R75 corners superbly—very steady, very firm, very controllable. The whole machine has been set up for hard cornering."

Cycle Guide magazine concurred. Putting the new BMW's prowess into the more colorful lexicon of the day, the magazine

A pair of 38mm Dell'Orto slide carburetors put the S in the R90S.

While modest by modern standards, the bikini fairing on the R90S caused quite a stir when the bike appeared in 1973.

The motorcycle market had undergone a fundamental change since BMW had last introduced major new models nearly a decade earlier. The introduction of inexpensive, lightweight, reliable motorcycles from Japan that were easy to ride and maintain had opened up the sport to tens of thousands of new riders. As the motorcycling population grew, so too grew the motorcycling press. When Joe Parkhurst created *Cycle World* in 1964, he single-handedly killed the old, drab newsletter-style motorcycle publications that were little more than shills for corporate sponsors. Motorcycle magazines thrived during the 1960s, and as their popularity grew, the content of the magazines matured and became more sophisticated.

Gone were the days when a handful of hard-core, socially challenged enthusiasts learned of new models only by stumbling over them in the poorly lit showrooms of greasy motorcycle shops. By the late 1960s, new model introductions were widely heralded in the enthusiast press. And few new models were more widely heralded than BMW's /5 series. In fact, the amount of press the new BMWs received might seem surprising when one considers the other new motorcycles being introduced at the time: Honda's world-changing CB750, Triumph's three-cylinder 750 Trident, Kawasaki's explosive Mach III two-stroke triple. But fans of the fabled German boxer twins comprised an important part of the motorcycle magazine audience. In its preview of the upcoming /5 series, *Cycle World* wrote that BMW devotees had "developed into the most rigid, adamant bunch of 'individuals' in motorcycling." The article discusses the enormous amount of money these "individuals" spend on accessorizing their expensive mounts, and continues, "He also reads every word published anywhere in the world for and against his brand." Like the other magazines of the period, *Cycle World* did its best to provide those rigid individuals with plenty of words to read. And most of these words were for, rather than against, BMW's new motorcycles.

described the R75/5's handling as "out of sight, a real mind bender." Thankfully the editors showed enough restraint to refrain from describing the handling as "groovy."

Although in all fairness, the new BMWs were pretty groovy. At the conclusion of its first R75/5 road test, *Cycle* summed up the significance that this new machine held for BMW's future: "Cornering and acceleration—two new trump cards for BMW and two good ones."

SHOCKINGLY EXPENSIVE

All the improvements to the new /5 series came at a cost, especially on the West Coast of the United States, which had by 1969 become BMW's single most-important market for both motorcycles and automobiles. In July 1968 *Cycle World* listed the price of an R60US as $1,376. When it tested an R75/5 two years later, the magazine quoted a list price of $1,848. The situation appeared a bit different on the U.S. East Coast, where the $1,696 R75/5 *Cycle* tested in 1969 cost $16 less than the R69US it had tested the year before. Still, BMW motorcycles cost more than any of the motorcycles produced by the company's direct competitors.

A CHANGE OF SCENERY

The introduction of the /5 series marked another monumental change for BMW. Unlike past changes, which were often designed to help BMW survive in the face of market or political shifts, success drove this particular change.

While motorcycle sales remained stagnant throughout the 1960s, automobile sales boomed, and the company desperately needed to increase production capacity. The easiest solution was to convert the motorcycle factory, located next to BMW's automobile plant in Munich, to automobile production. But once corporate management committed to producing a new generation of BMW motorcycles, the company needed to retain the capacity to produce those motorcycles.

BMW's answer to this conundrum was to convert an aircraft-engine manufacturing plant in Spandau, a suburb of West Berlin, into a motorcycle manufacturing facility. The sprawling complex had originally been built by the Prussian government to house a weapons manufacturing factory. Siemens bought the property in 1928 and converted it into an aircraft-engine manufacturing operation. In a prescient move, Siemens called its aircraft motor works "BMW," though in this case the "B" stood for *Brandenburgische* instead of *Bayerisch*. This just saved the genuine BMW from having to put up new signage and buy new letterhead, because in 1939 the BMW that is the subject of this book bought out Siemens, acquiring the ersatz BMW in the process.

Just because the plant itself dated back to Germany's prehistory didn't mean the facilities were antiquated. In fact, BMW's Berlin plant was at least as modern as any of the motorcycle manufacturing facilities used by its Japanese rivals. It was a fully automated factory with state-of-the-art robotics. BMW opened this futuristic plant in September 1969 and has been building motorcycles there ever since.

A CHANGE OF IMAGE

The new /5 models embodied the lessons learned from the success of the R69S as well as the failure of the R27: sexy, sporty bikes sell better than sensible utilitarian machines. The new models presented an image that appealed to the young enthusiasts who were buying Japanese motorcycles by the shipload, and the /5 series was a commercial success. In four years BMW produced 68,956 /5 models. Further proving that fast, expensive machines outsold less-expensive utilitarian models, well over half of all /5 production (38,370 units) consisted of the top-of-the-line R75/5, while the least expensive model, the R50/5, sold a mere 7,865 units during that same period.

KRAMM

The success of the new models represented a major reversal of fortunes for BMW's motorcycle operations. Wilfried Kramm, who was promoted to works director of the motorcycle operation in 1968, deserves much of the credit for that reversal. Kramm, who had a solid background in both business and engineering, earned a reputation as a top turn-around executive within the Quandt financial group prior to his appointment as motorcycle works director. Within three years of his assuming control of motorcycle operations, motorcycle sales topped 18,000 units per year, pretty remarkable, considering BMW sold a mere 5,074 motorcycles the year Kramm took the helm. This accomplishment was all the more amazing considering the difficult labor situation in West Berlin, at the time one of the world's political powder kegs.

"Having a works in a political hot-spot brings its problems," Kramm told a *Motorcyclist* reporter in 1972. "Quite often much-needed parts are held up at frontier posts for all sorts of peculiar reasons. So that production isn't disrupted we have to have duplicates flown in at great cost."

In addition to looking cool, the fairing on the R90S provided a place to house an ammeter and an electric clock.

IMPROVEMENTS

As good as the new bikes were, they weren't perfect, and BMW made consistent improvements to the /5 series throughout its production run. Solving the low-speed carburetion problems mentioned in early tests was easy enough. Although BMW continued to hamper the /5 models with a four-speed transmission, company engineers reshuffled the gear ratios in 1971, improving acceleration.

A more serious problem proved more difficult to solve. In spite of the initial glowing reports of the exemplary handling of the new /5 machines, further testing revealed a few snags. Both *Cycle Guide* and *Motorcyclist* complained of high-speed instability. In 1971, BMW altered the steering geometry, raising the front end a bit. *Cycle* attributed the high-speed head shake to the fork itself, and BMW massaged the fork for 1971. While all this helped, a more comprehensive solution was needed. In mid-1973 BMW cured the handling foibles once and for all when it braced

This is the bike Motorcyclist magazine called "The Fastest OHV Twin Road Racer in AMA Annals."

The sparse cockpit of Pridmore's 750 racer was all business.

"'An odd paradox,' some call it. And the skeptics—plus some realists—continue, 'This sort of race effort can't be serious. BMW racing engines belong in sidecars where they can't lean over.'"

So began an article published in the February 1975 issue of *Motorcyclist* magazine. The subject of the article? Reg Pridmore and his remarkable 745-cc BMW GP road racer. "It is in some ways a technological brontosaur," author Mike Griffin wrote of Pridmore's mount, but Pridmore and his Butler & Smith (U.S. importers of BMW motorcycles) crew refused to let such realities dampen their enthusiasm. These men were on a quest, the goal of which was nothing short of saving four-stroke racing against the onslaught of two-stroke monsters swarming from Japan, as Griffin put it, "like vengeful wasps." It was a bad time for four-stroke fans. Though Phil Read had won the FIM 500-cc GP title in 1974 aboard a four-stroke MV Agusta, his victory would mark the last time a four-stroke would ever win a 500-cc GP title. Winning that title represented the pinnacle of motorcycling achievement from 1948 until 2001.

In AMA racing in the United States, two-strokes had all but taken over road racing. Harley-Davidson, which had dominated AMA racing for nearly a quarter of a century with its antiquated side-valve machines, had finally thrown in the four-stroke towel and withdrawn its XR750s from road racing competition. While Norton still achieved some success on the world's road courses, in the world's showrooms the once mighty twins were for all practical purposes extinct, the victims of corporate mismanagement and labor disputes, and in hindsight it seems a too-small gene pool among England's ruling class.

None of which deterred Pridmore and his optimistic crew. These folks liked a good challenge, and they met that challenge with very little factory support. The number 63 bike Reg campaigned was nothing terribly exotic. "Rather, it appears more the result of sweaty-browed tenacity and deliberation," Griffin wrote. The chrome-molybdenum tube frame was fashioned by Rob North, who had earned his reputation by crafting frames for such racing legends as Dick Mann, Dave Aldana, and Gene Romero. North's frame utilized a traditional double-cradle design. Though Griffin describes the swingarm as "positively gargantuan," it looks rather spindly next to the massive aluminum swingarms found on many modern street bikes.

The engine retained the stock displacement of 745-cc but featured a wider bore and shorter stroke. This improved reliability by lowering piston speeds and improved handling by making the boxer engine narrower. Most of the engine's grunt came from straightforward

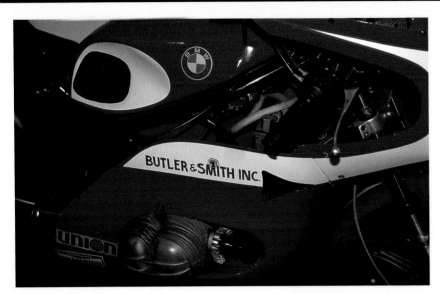

Butler & Smith, BMW's U.S. importer at the time, built this radical machine in an attempt to compete against the Japanese two-strokes that dominated AMA racing.

hot-rodding techniques. Butler & Smith's technicians installed a specially ground camshaft, larger oil sump and oil cooler, high-compression pistons, and 2-millimeter-larger intake valves. They also reshaped the intake ports, which originally angled up on the stock bike, creating an intake tract that was as straight as possible. A pair of 36-millimeter Mikuni racing carburetors filled these straightened tracts.

Next everything that could be eliminated was, including the starter, alternator, and all associated hardware. Pridmore's team modified the engine's cases and covers to eliminate the housings for these components, giving the engine an almost R69S look in the process. Pridmore's team eliminated weight from inside the engine as well as from outside it. They machined 4.5 pounds of metal off the 8-pound flywheel, then gave the stock two-main bearing crankshaft a "gnat's whisker balancing job." This kept the crankshaft from grenading inside the 90-horsepower engine when it spun up to its 9,500-rpm redline. (Pridmore admits to spinning the engine past 10,000 rpm.)

The team achieved additional weight savings by removing excess metal wherever possible. For example, the driveshaft housing was shaved to remove unsprung weight. Since a disc brake was used in the rear, the drum brake housing was machined off the hub, and cast-magnesium wheels were used front and rear. All this weight-saving effort resulted in a 310-pound machine, heavier than Kawasaki's potent H2R triples, but lighter than the liquid-cooled Suzukis and, more important, the Yamaha TZs that dominated road racing at the time.

All this work resulted in a motorcycle capable of out accelerating the dominant Yamahas on the uphill section of Road Atlanta. The Butler & Smith 750 was capable of pulling a genuine 165 miles per hour, which placed it solidly midpack compared to the competition, so Pridmore needed to make up time in the corners if he planned to beat the two-strokes. A good suspension helped his effort. The combination of Ceriani fork and Betor triple clamps mimicked the setup used on MV Agusta's successful road racers, creating a motorcycle that "handled like a wizard's wish," according to Griffin.

"Against the arrogant, incredibly powerful two-strokes, this machine, to be frank, poses at best a modest threat," Griffin continues, but outright domination was not the point. Griffin said the goal of the Butler & Smith effort was simply "to keep the four-stroke in the fray."

That was a tall order. "Competing against the TZ Yamahas was pretty difficult," Pridmore says today. While not particularly successful in outright wins, the pioneers of modern production four-stroke racing were extremely successful in that their efforts led to the creation of four-stroke classes like the AMA's Superbike Production class, saving four-stroke racing from extinction.

"Rego" would refer to Reg Pridmore, winner of the first-ever AMA Superbike racing series.

the swingarm and lengthened it by 2 inches. The later 1973 /5 bikes with the longer swingarms are easily identifiable because the swingarms were lengthened by welding in sections, and the welds are easily visible. From 1974 on the welds disappeared.

"The difference is night and day," *Motorcyclist* wrote in its July 1973 issue, stating that in addition to improving high-speed stability the new swingarm improved overall handling by moving the weight bias forward, giving the front tire better traction. The longer wheelbase provided other more subtle benefits too, like a longer seat area, which allowed the rider's footpegs to be placed farther back, providing more space between the rider's shins and the carburetors. It also allowed engineers to mount a larger battery for more reliable starting.

By 1973 the /5 series needed freshening. Sales remained strong and magazines still marveled at the bikes' overall competence, but some aspects, like the four-speed transmission and

the drum brakes, along with a plug-type ignition that allowed anyone with a BMW "key" to start any other BMW motorcycle ever built, had reached their expiration date.

LIVING LARGER

The announcement of a bigger, better version of BMW's /5 series came as a surprise to no one. In its September 1969 preview of the new models, *Cycle World* wrote that a 900-cc version was imminent. BMW as much as said such a motorcycle was under development. The fact that the /5 series had been so heavily over-engineered backed this up. Of the R75/5, *Cycle* magazine wrote, "Everything seems set up for 80 bhp."

BMW motorcycle director Wilfried Kramm denied the existence of a future 900-cc machine in a 1972 *Motorcyclist* magazine interview, but he obviously lied to the reporter, because a little more than a year after the interview was published just such a machine appeared on showroom floors. Of course Kramm had to fib a bit in such a situation, since letting the 900-cc cat out of the bag might have had a negative impact on 750 sales. Kramm was not one to kill sales. Kramm's coyness aside, BMW's upcoming big bike was one of motorcycling's worst kept secrets. Even before the public introduction of the /5 series in 1969 BMW motorcycles with suspicious engine capacities had been appearing at such high-profile events as the Isle of Man TT races.

BMW released updated versions of its existing bikes in October 1973. Or rather, most of its existing bikes: the slow-selling R50/5 disappeared from the line-up. Though smaller displacement bikes like the R45 would be produced to meet licensing requirements in various markets over the coming years, this deletion effectively marked the end of the 500-cc-class twin as a major part of BMW's motorcycle line-up.

The surviving R60/5 and R75/5 became /6 models. To earn their sixth-generation designation, the bikes gained an extra cog in their transmissions, as well as a stronger 280-watt alternator for more reliable starting. The R75/6 also received a much-needed disc brake up front.

When it introduced the /6 models, BMW finally released its long awaited big bike, the 898-cc R90/6. For all practical purposes, BMW created the R90/6 simply by boring out the cylinders of the R75/6. Though both machines shared the same 70.6-millimeter stroke, the R90/6 cylinders were bored out 8 millimeters to 90 millimeters. The two machines even shared the same Bing CV carburetors and single-disc front brake. The only way to identify the larger machine from the visually identical 750 version was by the identifying badge on the crankcase tunnel.

Cycle World's R90/6 test bike weighed 460 pounds with its 4.75-gallon gas tank half filled. Magazine test riders ran the bike through the quarter mile in 13.45 seconds and measured a top speed of 115 miles per hour, though the 898-cc machine likely would have performed better in both tests if it had used the lower final drive ratio from the R75/6.

PUTTING THE "SPORT" BACK IN THE "S"

Frankly, there was nothing terribly surprising or exciting about the R90/6, but that bike didn't need to be exciting because BMW had another bike up its sleeve for the 1974 model year, one that surprised just about everyone in the motorcycling community: the R90S. While BMW's high-quality touring bikes had always had a sporting bent when compared to other touring bikes on the market, like Harley-Davidson's Electra Glide, the R90S marks the one time in BMW history that the company produced a truly cutting edge sports bike for its time.

The major mechanical components separating the new S model from its pedestrian counterparts were a pair of 38-millimeter Dell'Orto slide carburetors in place of the 32-millimeter Bing CV carburetors used on the R90/6 and R75/6. With a higher compression ratio—9.5: versus 9.0:1—and a hotter camshaft, the S model cranked out 67 horsepower, up 7 over the R90/6. Twin disc brakes up front slowed this biggest-yet BMW (*Cycle World*'s S model test bike weighed 26 pounds more than the R90/6 it had tested seven months earlier).

Raw power was not the reason the R90S earned its status as BMW's first genuine superbike. Its 67 horsepower only equaled the Honda CB750's power output. The 82 horsepower of Kawasaki's new 903-cc Z-1 eclipsed both motorcycles. *Cycle World* ran its R90S through the quarter mile in 13.05 seconds, a respectable time, but hardly earth shattering. The new BMW was about much more than drag racing anyway. Americans, as *Cycle World* noted, "think in terms of the quarter mile, and BMW has never been a threat here. But the European regards performance as getting from point A to point B in the shortest time possible." At this task, BMW's new sport bike had few peers.

BMW's new superbike was about poise. Poise and style. The R90S became the first BMW that contributed as much to the aesthetic evolution of the motorcycle as it contributed to the technological evolution of the species. Sporting details abounded on the bike. Longtime BMW enthusiasts recognized the sporting mission of the S by the two fins on its valve covers; if that hadn't given away the plot, the plastic hump encapsulating the taillight would have. But the new S needed no such subtle sporting signifiers. The bike's handlebar-mounted bikini fairing screamed "Café racer!" at the volume of a Who concert. It's tough to imagine today, when even lowly commuter bikes sport racy fairings, but in the fall of 1973 a production motorcycle with a fairing as standard equipment broke virgin ground. The fairing was a nice piece of plastic, too, well finished inside and out. It even incorporated a clock and ammeter just above the speedometer and tachometer.

As if all this racy bodywork wasn't enough to make the R90S a standout, the paint was unlike anything ever seen on a production motorcycle. A comma-shaped silver panel on the sides of the fuel tank gradually shifted to black, earning the color scheme the name "Smoke." It was hard to get one's mind around the fact that this flashy superbike was the product of a company that just a few years earlier had lived up to its reputation for building archaic black machines best suited for powering the sidecar rigs favored by arthritis-riddled geriatrics. According to *Cycle World*, the R90S "tells you that the BMW image of yesterday (stodgy, conservative, unexciting) has at last departed the scene."

With an out-the-door price of $3,800, the R90S cost more than just about every motorcycle sold in the United States at the time, but enough people were willing to pay that high price to make the bike a sales success. Butler & Smith sold every S model it imported into the country. When speculating why such an expensive motorcycle sold so well, *Cycle World* asked, "Just what is it that makes the Sport so special, exceptional and remarkable?" The magazine answered its own question: "A combination of everything, actually." BMW had produced a motorcycle that met just about everyone's needs. It was reliable, fast, comfortable, stylish, and it handled very well. The R90S undoubtedly qualifies as the classic BMW of the 20th century. "More cubic inches," *Cycle World* wrote in its December 1973 issue. "More class. Fantastic."

REFINING A REFINED MACHINE

BMW began improving its new /6 line-up almost immediately, just like it always did when introducing new models. As *Motorcyclist* magazine wrote, the "dogmatic Teutonic quest for perfection never ends." The company paid special attention to its R90S flagship model. Early versions of the big Dell'Orto carburetors used on the S lacked chokes. To start the bike when cold, a rider had to rely on messy, old-fashioned ticklers. By the summer of 1974 these had been replaced by modern chokes.

Everyone appreciated the extra gear in the /6 transmission, but the shifting action of the five-speed unit fell short of the standards set by the inexpensive competition from Japan. All five-speed transmissions in BMW's 1974 model line suffered from difficult shifting, but the problem was most pronounced on the 898-cc models. The higher final gearing on the S model exacerbated the transmission's shortcomings even more. "As a result," *Cycle World* wrote, "in-town riding is more pleasant on the roadster version of the 900." BMW corrected the problem for the 1975 model year and made available a kit to modify the shift forks on 1974 models. While still not bringing shifting action up to Rising Sun standards, the new shift forks were a tremendous improvement.

BMW made a host of improvements to its flagship S model for 1976. The company now drilled holes in the brake discs, just as Butler & Smith had done on Reg Pridmore's race bikes. This helped prevent water from building up between the discs and pads, an even more important consideration than the removal of a few grams of unsprung weight. A reshaped oil pan improved lubrication and lowered the oil's operating temperature. Internal changes included new rocker-arm bearings and cylinder base gaskets. In 1976, BMW began its long-standing tradition of offering Krauser saddlebags as optional equipment for all its models.

"Embarrassingly little constructive criticism can be leveled at the BMW Sport," Bob Greene wrote in the February 1976 issue of *Motorcyclist*. BMW had even improved the bike's aesthetic quality. The pinstriping, which had been taped on the original 1974 models, was now hand-painted. For 1976 that striping was available in red, applied over a striking orange-and-silver livery that came to be known as Daytona Orange.

In its three-year production run, BMW sold nearly 1,000 more examples of the /6 series than it had sold of the highly successful /5 series during its four-year production run. The expensive 898-cc /6 models outsold its 745-cc /5 predecessors 38,525 units to 38,370 units, further driving home the point that people weren't afraid to spend large amounts of money on a motorcycle if it was the right motorcycle.

WE WERE SPEECHLESS

Because of strong sales of the /6 series, BMW had little incentive to make wholesale changes to the line-up. When the company released the 1977 model year bikes in the fall of 1976, all models featured minor across-the-board changes, like stiffer, more heavily braced frames that significantly improved handling. The most obvious changes to the two smaller models were a switch to the sleek S model gas tanks and new, more modern looking valve covers. A slight overbore on the R75 engine created a new model, the R80/7. This soon replaced the R75/5 model.

The real news for the new /7 series involved the big bikes. BMW gave the 898-cc engine a 4-millimeter overbore to bring capacity up to 980-cc, resulting in a liter-class motorcycle dubbed the R100/7. Power output actually fell on the R100S when compared to the R90S (65 horsepower versus 67 horsepower), thanks to a switch from the 38-millimeter Dell'Orto carburetors to a pair of Bing CV carburetors, the same units used on the pedestrian R100/7.

That move would seem a step backward for BMW's range-topping model, except the S was no longer the range-topping model. The new R100RS now occupied that role. Mechanically the new model stuck pretty close to the formula set by its /7 siblings, though a pair of 40-millimeter Bing CV carburetors brought horsepower up to an even 70. The new RS model's real claim to fame was that it was the first motorcycle with a full fairing to be mass-produced in the modern era.

If the plastic bubble fairing on the R90S had stirred up the motorcycle press, the wind tunnel-developed bodywork on the R100RS sent motorcycle journalists into apoplectic spasms of superlatives. When BMW first showed the futuristic motorcycle to members of the U.S. press, according to *Motorcyclist's* Bob Greene, "We were speechless. We weren't ready for the dynamic years-ahead machine pedestalled before us, a high-speed touring bullet in shimmering German silver."

The entire /7 series received the sleek tank from the R90S. Shown here is a 1977 R75/7.

DAYTONA ORANGE

In spite of the work of dedicated four-stroke racers like Reg Pridmore and his Butler & Smith team, the two-strokes continued their inexorable ascension and would continue to dominate the top levels of international road racing until the demise of the FIM's 500-cc GP class in 2002. But in a way the efforts of Pridmore and his contemporary four-stroke aficionados were successful beyond their wildest hopes.

The year after *Motorcyclist* published its article on Pridmore's 745-cc GP racer, the AMA inaugurated a production-based four-stroke series. Production four-stroke racing had been taking place sporadically since 1974, but in 1976 the AMA made it an official part of its national series.

On March 5, 1976, the AMA held its first official Superbike Production race at Daytona as a support race for the 200-mile main event. The race proved a real battle, with Pridmore leading on the final lap aboard his Butler & Smith–prepared R90S. Just as he was about to cross the finish line, Steve McLaughlin, riding another Butler & Smith R90S, passed to take first place. Third-place Cook Neilson almost drafted McLaughlin on his Ducati 750 Super Sport to take second, but Pridmore held him off, making it a one-two BMW win. Pridmore went on to finish first in the rest of the season's events, earning the distinction of being the first national champion in the history of AMA Superbike racing.

The Butler & Smith Superbikes featured many of the same performance modifications as Pridmore's earlier 745-cc GP bike, as well as benefiting from two years of research and development. "The Daytona[s] were quite a bit more highly developed than the '74 bike," Pridmore says today.

Pridmore thought the monoshock rear suspension was a step backward. "I couldn't get on with the monoshock. I went back to the dual Konis. The monoshock system used a Koni car shock. It was too hard for me. McLaughlin was getting kind of fat, so maybe it worked for him."

Initially a support class for the two-strokes, the AMA's new Superbike series proved so popular that it eventually became the AMA's premiere class. American-style Superbike racing's popularity caught on at the international level too. In 1987, Steve McLaughlin formed the World Superbike series (WSB). WSB became so popular that by the 1990s it rivaled 500-cc Gran Prix racing for fans' affections. In fact, the popularity of WSB was one of the factors contributing to the demise of the 500-cc GP class. The MotoGP class that replaced the 500-cc GP class in 2002 pits 990-cc four-strokes against 500-cc two-strokes, and it is in many ways a direct result of the dedication of four-stroke diehards like Pridmore and his Butler & Smith team.

Unfortunately BMW wouldn't be a significant part of the four-stroke racing revival it helped spawn. The 1976 AMA Superbike season would prove to be BMW's road racing swan song. BMW motorcycles would never again win a major racing series, adding to the mystique of the bikes Pridmore and McLaughlin rode to victory at the first-ever Daytona Superbike Production race. The distinctive orange-and-silver paint of those machines, a new offering for BMW's 1976 production R90S models, became so associated with the racing achievements of the Butler & Smith bikes that the color has become known as Daytona Orange.

Reg Pridmore at speed aboard his R90S Superbike racer. Tom Riles

A SPORT-TOURER IS BORN

In addition to its stunning appearance, the new RS fairing offered several functional benefits, the most obvious being protection from the elements. "It is virtually impossible for the rider to determine speed without consulting the meter," Greene wrote. Unlike previous chunks of plastic used in the past, the fairing did much more than just block the wind. Rather, it cut the wind, reducing air resistance by 5.4 percent and front wheel lift by 17.4 percent, according to BMW's wind-tunnel research.

These were all important benefits, no doubt, but what really took journalists' collective breathe away was the bike's wicked-cool looks. "Appearance is shocking," Greene wrote in his trademark telegraphic style. Greene compared the RS to a Porsche Carrera, writing, "In one bold move the German's have advanced motorcycle styling several years."

Cycle World was a bit confused about the bike's intended mission. "Just whose bike is it, anyway?" the magazine asked in its May 1977 road test. "The tourers won't like the 1 1/2 person seat and lack of space for storage; the sporting group will probably find the fairing a bit too large." What *Cycle World* could not have known at the time was that it had just witnessed the birth of an entirely new class of motorcycle: the sport-tourer. Buyers suffered no such confusion about the identity of the new R100RS. Even though its $4,595 purchase price set a new record, the RS went on to become BMW's single best-selling model until the advent of the four-cylinder K100RS almost a decade later.

In summing up his original article on the RS, *Motorcyclist*'s Bob Greene captured the appeal of Germany's expensive new R100RS: "Most impressive is the air of pure excitement that accompanies the ride, as if you were climbing

The R90S had been a shocker, but nothing had prepared the motorcycling world for the space-age R100RS.

91

In a famous magazine advertisement for BMW's 1968 US models, the company's marketing folks ask, "Why does a BMW cost more than an ordinary motorcycle?" The ad offers "craftsmanship" as the reason for the high cost. Years later in an article entitled "Why do BMWs Cost So Much," *Motorcyclist* magazine took BMW to task for this explanation. While not questioning the quality of the motorcycles themselves, the article outlined a variety of reasons that had more economic validity than craftsmanship.

At the time the *Motorcyclist* article appeared in 1978, BMW's top-of-the-line motorcycle, the R100RS, cost $5,750. For that much coin a rider could purchase two Yamaha XS750 triples and pocket $1,149 in change. He or she could buy three Kawasaki KZ650 four-cylinder bikes or, as the article pointed out, nine Hodaka Road Toads.

According to the article, a primary reason for the high price of BMWs was the exchange rate between the German mark and the U.S. dollar. Other factors included the high wages paid to German workers and the costs of Germany's social system, which the article described as "staggering."

Yet another set of expenses arose because of BMW's relatively low volume and market position. "Cost of materials is more for a 5,000 unit production run than a 50,000 unit run," the article stated. "A prestige product such as a BMW must be advertised heavily to maintain a visible and confident profile." Certification by various environmental and transportation departments around the world represented another enormous expense. All these costs have to be spread out over a company's production run. Because of high volume, Japanese makers were able to spread those costs over many more motorcycles. With small production runs, these costs proved much more significant for a company like BMW and contributed more to each unit's overall cost.

But even taking into account all these factors, the article estimates that there is still a certain percentage of the price difference between a BMW and a Japanese motorcycle that was due to BMW's exploitation of its reputation for quality. "It is clear that BMW is pricing for prestige," the article stated. But it goes on to say that BMW was in no way "ripping off" American consumers. "[BMW motorcycles] pretty much have to cost as much as they do," the article concluded.

FAR RIGHT: The wind tunnel-designed fairing on the R100RS was unlike any bodywork any manufacturer had ever offered to the general public.

into the cockpit of a jet fighter plane. BMW has gone far beyond building a fine motorcycle; they've captured a thrill you know will never go away."

HANS MUTH REDEFINES THE MOTORCYCLE

In 1978, BMW created two new smaller bikes by taking the basic /7 platform and shortening the engine's stroke from 70.6 millimeters to 61.5 millimeters. A 70-millimeter bore used in the R45, the smaller of the two machines, gave the engine a capacity of 473 cc, while the new R65 featured an 82-millimeter bore, leading to a total capacity of 649 cc. Even though both bikes were nearly as large as their big-bore brethren, shortening the stroke helped BMW engineers trim 2.2 inches from the width of the boxer powerplant.

The R45 was primarily a home-market model, designed to comply with Germany's strict licensing laws. The R65 replaced the slow-selling R60/7 in the U.S. market, becoming BMW's smallest U.S. model. The new bike benefited from the work of BMW's in-house designer, Hans Muth. Muth's attention to detail resulted in a design that forever changed the look of the motorcycle. Muth blended the various pieces of bodywork on the new model into an integrated whole, sculpting the seat, fenders, side covers, and tank to bring the same sort of integration of design that Harley Earl had brought to automobiles half a century earlier. Some of the styling, like the automotive-type dashboard that also covered

the top triple clamp, bordered on gimmicky, at least on an unfaired bike, but like the rest of the machine, it foretold the direction in which motorcycle styling would soon take. No longer could bikes look like haphazard collections of cycle parts. When *Cycle World* tested the bike, the magazine's editors seemed to understand the importance of Muth's styling: "BMW's new R65 may be the company's most significant new model since the original four-stroke, horizontally opposed, shaft-driven Twin of 1923."

The R65 sold relatively well in Europe, where smaller displacement machines received heavy discounts in tax, licensing, and insurance costs, and even sold in respectable numbers in the displacement-hungry United States.

THE RUBBER COW

In 1978, BMW introduced a motorcycle for riders who were more interested in the "tourer" part of the equation than the "sport" part. The new R100RT featured an enlarged version of the R100RS fairing that offered the most complete weather protection ever available on a stock motorcycle, though some critics felt the bike looked like an RS model with a case of the mumps. In addition to isolating the rider from the elements, the new RT model isolated him or her from as much mechanical commotion as possible on an air-cooled motorcycle with rubber handlebar mounts.

Even though the R100RT was the heaviest bike BMW had ever built—*Cycle World*'s June 1979 test bike weighed

550 pounds with half a tank of fuel—it was the lightest full-dress touring bike on the market. Suzuki's GS850 weighed 649 pounds, Honda's GL1100 Gold Wing weighed 737 pounds, and Harley's monstrous FLT weighed 781 pounds. "The big BMWs haven't gotten any lighter," the magazine wrote, "but have gained less weight than the other bikes and in the process have gone from being considered heavy bikes to being considered light bikes."

With its wind-tunnel–developed touring fairing and standard Krauser saddlebags, the R100RT certainly looked the part of a high-buck touring rig. "The Beemer is not just attractive," *Cycle World* wrote, "it's striking; it doesn't look like any other motorcycle on the highway."

The price of the new machine was even more striking than its appearance. *Cycle World*'s 1979 test bike cost a record setting $6,345. Critics expected a lot more than simply good looks from the most expensive mass-produced motorcycle ever unleashed upon the public. "Does the striking look lend itself to superior function?" *Cycle World* asked. "The answer, generally, is no." The article aired a long list of reasons why the RT failed to live up to its astronomical purchase price: "The seat that will make a man confess sins he hasn't yet committed, handlebars that managed to alienate all our riders, hand grips which compound the problems." The magazine's most grievous complaints centered around the fairing, which produced an "abnormally high amount of buffeting around the head. … All the wind-tunnel testing apparently was done to reduce aerodynamic drag, not to improve protection from the wind." The heel-and-toe shifter also drew complaints.

Considering the RT was designed specifically for the lucrative U.S. touring market, its negative reception among stateside journalists bode poorly for the bike's reception elsewhere. The first-generation R100RT was, in fact, one of the most poorly received models BMW had produced in recent memory. The compromised handling even earned the bike a derogatory moniker that has stuck to this day. The rubber handlebar mounts that kept pesky vibration away from the rider's sensitive mitts also gave the RT vague steering, earning the motorcycle the nickname *Gummikuh* ("Rubber Cow" in German) among fans of BMW's more sporting mounts.

The sales figures of the /7 generation R100RT tell the story of BMW's overall situation in the late 1970s. In seven years of producing the bike, BMW sold just 13,516 of these exorbitantly expensive motorcycles. BMW sold 8,400 more examples of the unfaired (and far less expensive) R100T model during that same period and sold almost as many of the more popular RS sport-touring model than it sold of the T and RT models combined. With the pricey RT, BMW had

When originally
introduced, the R100RS
came with a racy solo seat.
Because so many riders
chose the more traditional
dual saddle, the solo seat
soon disappeared. Today
the original solo saddles
are almost as rare as
R100RS sidecar rigs.

at last reached the breaking point, discovering just how much the public was willing to pay for a certain level of performance. This did not mean the company had discovered the absolute limit it could charge for a motorcycle. The success of the expensive RS model indicated fans were willing to shell out amazing amounts of cash for a BMW motorcycle. That motorcycle simply had to offer fans something they couldn't get elsewhere.

CHANGING TIMES

BMW made more improvements to its line of motorcycles during the 1970s than it had in any previous decade in the company's long history. If it had been building motorcycles in a vacuum BMW would have dominated the industry. But the motorcycle industry did not exist in a vacuum. Japanese motorcycles wrought hurricane-force havoc on the industry during the 1970s. When BMW introduced its /5 series for the 1970 model year the bikes had been, if not state-of-the-art, at least up to speed with current technology. For a time BMW had even been ahead of the curve, producing such ground-breaking models as the R90S and R100RS. But in a few short years the competition had advanced at such a rapid pace that by the time the new RT model came out for the 1979 model year, BMW's model line-up had become almost irrelevant.

No longer could the company trade on reliability and exclusive features. If anything, the motorcycles coming from the Far East were even more reliable than the vaunted German bikes, and by the end of the 1970s, each of the Japanese manufacturers produced bikes with shaft drive. Honda even produced a motorcycle with a boxer engine: the Gold Wing. Most Japanese motorcycles featured technology that BMW owners could only dream of, like overhead cams. Exotic technology like four-valve cylinder heads and liquid cooling were becoming commonplace on Japanese motorcycles. BMW found itself in a very difficult market position as the Reagan era dawned.

FLYING BRICKS AND
THE REVENGE OF
THE AIRHEADS

"**D**oes BMW have a future in motorcycling?" C. D. Bohon asked in an article published in the February 1981 issue of *Motorcyclist*. "And does anyone care?"

The early 1980s found the motorcycling world turned on its head. Tradition and history were marketing liabilities instead of marketing assets. BSA had shuffled off to the great showroom in the sky, and Norton was for all practical purposes dead and gone, though the tortured company would continue to crank out an occasional rotary-engined motorcycle over the next decade or so. The Italians continued to produce bikes, though the Italian propensity for designing exquisite machinery and then failing to actually produce or market these machines meant few Italian motorcycles escaped Italy's borders. Then as now, the Italian motorcycle manufacturers existed in a perpetual state of near financial insolvency.

ABOVE: The 1984 R100 models were the last of the Airheads to feature the original high-performance version of the 980cc boxer engine. BMW discontinued production of the biggest boxers after introducing the K series for the 1984 model year.

LEFT: The longitudinal multi-cylinder engine flopped on its side, nicknamed the "Flying Brick," was BMW's first new engine design in 60 years. The K75RT, shown here, was the most popular of the 740cc three-cylinder models.

By the time BMW introduced the Flying Bricks in 1983, the old air-cooled lineup had begun to show its age. The R100RS was still a visual stunner, though.

The three remaining longtime major manufacturers—Harley-Davidson, Triumph, and BMW—also teetered on the brink of bankruptcy. Gambling types were giving odds on which company would be the first to crumble, and as the 1970s drew to a close, it looked like BMW was the odds-on favorite. In 1979, even lowly Triumph, at the time still producing virtual replicas of Ed Turner's ancient Speed Twin, outsold BMW in the critical U.S. market. Considering the fact that new Triumph's almost universally elicited the response, "They still make those things?" BMW was not in a happy place.

How could a company that experienced record sales in the mid-1970s fall on such hard luck in such a short period of time? Much of BMW's financial hardship came about as a result of its Japanese competition. Compared to the technological marvels emanating from Japan, BMW's air-cooled, pushrod twins lacked the sex appeal needed to woo the Baby Boomers fueling Japanese motorcycle sales. At the time many enthusiasts considered BMWs to be overpriced, over-rated, and outdated.

Period magazine tests reinforced this mindset. In a six-bike comparison test published in the June 1979 issue of *Motorcyclist*, the BMW R100RT, at the time the most expensive motorcycle sold in North America, cost almost twice as much as the test-winning motorcycle, Suzuki's GS850. In addition to being the most expensive bike tested, the $6,345 BMW was also the slowest and had the worst brakes. The magazine's editors picked the BMW as one of the test's losers, writing, "Every time we got on the bike, there was another annoyance." The list of the editors' complaints took up several column inches of text. "BMW has had 56 years to refine the flat twin," the article concluded, "but somehow they still haven't done it, at least not with this machine."

The test riders' individual comments stung even more than losing the test. Or rather, it was their lack of comments that worried BMW. The sole statement directed at the BMW was Maurice Brouha's: "The BMW is an expensive exercise in sticking with tradition." The lack of interest shown in the BMW by the six other test riders provided a microcosmic view of BMW's problems in the broader motorcycle world. The brand had fallen off the radar of the average motorcyclist.

Building an uncompetitive product was only part of the reason for BMW's economic woes. BMW suffered at the hands of Japanese business practices almost as much as it suffered from Japanese engineering genius, specifically the Japanese manufacturers' practice of adjusting their prices for different markets. BMW sold its motorcycles at the same price in each different country. For example, Honda's 1981 CB750K sold for about $4,400 U.S. in Germany, while BMW's R65 sold for about $4,000 U.S. In the United States, BMW's R65 sold for $4,250, reflecting the shipping and distribution costs associated with transporting the motorcycles, while the Honda sold for a mere $2,975.

BMW's manufacturing situation hadn't improved by 1981 either. Berlin was still an island surrounded by the Soviet Union, and the Cold War still raged on. In spite of paying extremely high wages, BMW had difficulty retaining skilled workers. "Young people don't want to live here," a BMW employee told Bohon. But BMW remained committed to manufacturing motorcycles in Berlin, and when Bohon visited the plant in 1981, the company was in the process of investing $80 million in a complete refurbishment of the facilities.

Still another factor contributing to BMW's precipitous decline involved problems with BMW's U.S. distributor Butler & Smith. Where BMW had credited the firm with its U.S. market success in the 1960s, company insiders now attributed the lion's share of its problems to Butler & Smith, according to the *Motorcyclist* article. "Many people we talked to alleged Butler was not interested in stocking parts for and servicing the machines it sold, and raised retail prices higher than they reasonably should have been," Bohon reported.

By 1981 BMW had started to turn its motorcycle division around. The first step was to install new management. On January 1, 1979, BMW hired a new team to oversee its motorcycle operations, a team that included Dr. Eberhardt C. Sarfert, Dr. Wolfgang Aurich, and Karl Gerlinger. In October 1980 that new management gave Butler & Smith the boot and took U.S. distribution in-house. At that time, BMW North America (BMWNA), which had been distributing automobiles in the United States since 1975, became the sole U.S. distributors of BMW motorcycles. "That means from now on Munich will have its fingers directly on the pulse of the U.S. market," Bohon wrote, "and should be able to offer far better service than BMW owners have been used to."

By 1981 BMW no longer appeared on the verge of joining BSA on the list of extinct motorcycle manufacturers. Things were looking up for the German manufacturer in spite of the fact that the other remaining traditional manufacturers—Triumph and Harley-Davidson—were both in such financial straights that they operated at the day-to-day discretion of their creditors. In all fairness, BMW produced an unquestionably superior motorcycle to the offerings from Triumph and Harley-Davidson, even if the company was using a design created 58 years earlier. In some ways, such as cooling and vibration control, even Max Friz' original M2B32 boxer engine from 1923 was superior to the V- and parallel-twin 1981 offerings from Harley-Davidson and Triumph.

Although the fairing design was nine years old when this 1984 R100RS hit the streets, the cockpit was still one of the most pleasant places to spend time while crossing multiple state lines.

The fact that BMW was part of a larger company, one with a thriving automotive division, provided BMW's motorcycle operation with another advantage over its competition in the traditional motorcycle market. Harley-Davidson had been a division of AMF, a large U.S. conglomerate best know for manufacturing railroad cars and bowling balls, but by the time Bohon's article appeared in *Motorcyclist*, AMF was in the final stages of selling its financially troubled motorcycle division to a group of private investors. No one could quite figure out who owned Triumph. "Don't forget, we are associated with a company that produces the finest motorcars in the world," an anonymous BMW executive told Bohon. "We can call on our parent company's expertise in design, engineering, wind-tunnel testing, automated manufacturing, whatever we need. We are definitely not a Harley-Davidson, definitely not a Triumph."

Still, to survive the final decades of the 20th century, BMW needed a motorcycle that had more going for it than just being a better relic than the relics produced by Harley-Davidson and Triumph at the time. "BMW recognizes the limits of the flat-twin design and has plans for an entirely new motorcycle, which should debut around 1984," Bohon wrote in his 1981 article.

BMW was typically cagey about its future plans. While the company's work on developing a new engine was commonly acknowledged, BMW refused to publicly commit to the form that engine would take. Rumors abounded. The new engine would be a liquid-cooled in-line four. It would be a V-four. It would be a boxer-style flat-four, like the powerplant used in Honda's Gold Wing. It wouldn't be a four at all; rather, it would be a twin or a triple. Or there would be no new engine but just a refined version of the existing boxer twin.

BMW's continual process of improving the boxer lent credence to that final rumor. BMW may have been developing an entirely new line of motorcycles deep in the bowels of its research and development facilities, but in the meantime it kept its boxer line-up fresh. The company introduced several radical (for BMW) new boxer-powered models in the years leading up to the unveiling of its all-new machines.

GELÄNDSTRASSE

Even though the company's wide, heavy boxer twins were poorly suited to off-road riding, BMW continued to dabble in off-road competition and competed in the International Six

The idea for a GS80-based production bike sprang from the mind of a single man: ISDT veteran and BMW engineer Rudiger Gutsche. His idea was to build a huge 800-cc boxer trail bike based on his own personal /5 off-road prototype, only with off-the-shelf production parts in place of the one-off exotica on his own machine. The point of this machine was simply to get BMW back on the motorcycling world's radar. This was a stop-gap machine designed to get people talking about BMW; actual sales would be secondary. No one involved with the GS project would have guessed that the strange machine Gutsche designed primarily for shock value would go on to create an entirely new market, becoming BMW's best-selling bike and likely saving the motorcycle division from oblivion in the process.

Like the ISDT-winning bike, the new model BMW introduced late in 1980 featured a single-shock rear suspension. Unlike the works racer, which used a centrally mounted cantilevered shock located beneath the rider's seat, a layout which represented state-of-the-art motocross technology at the time, the production motorcycle's single rear shock attached to the right member of the swingarm in a more-or-less conventional fashion. The fact that this section of the swingarm also housed the driveshaft left little for the opposite member to do, so BMW eliminated it entirely. The asymmetrical appearance of BMW's new "Monolever" rear suspension took some getting used to, but it worked. The right swingarm member was already hellaciously strong in order to house the driveshaft, and getting rid of the left member helped alleviate the unsprung weight penalty imposed by the shaft-drive system. A high-mounted two-into-one exhaust pipe on the left helped balance the machine both mechanically and aesthetically. It also left a clear view of the rear wheel.

ABOVE: The R80G/S might have been a bit cumbersome for serious off-road use, but it was a svelte, nimble streetbike.

ABOVE RIGHT: Simplicity and light weight define the original G/S. Nothing as extraneous as a tachometer was included in the bike's specifications.

Days Trials event throughout the 1970s. The company's efforts paid off at the 1979 ISDT, which was held in Poland. That year rider Fritz Witzel won the 750-cc-and-over class. BMW spent a fortune developing the winning motorcycle, the 872-cc GS80. At the time the expenditure seemed to make little sense. Creating a production bike based on that over-weight, overpowered monoshocked behemoth seemed unlikely at best, insane at worst. Yet that is exactly what BMW did, introducing a GS80-based production machine a year after Witzel won the ISDT.

Oddball rear suspension aside, the new model was mechanically similar to the R80/7. It featured a high-mounted front fender, a 21-inch front wheel, and Metzler dual-purpose tires developed especially for the bike. Otherwise it featured the same across-the-board changes as did other 1981 BMW models. An improved clutch helped eliminate BMW's trademark clunky shifting, and an 8-pound lighter flywheel let the engines rev more freely than had any previous BMW powerplant. Like the other bikes in BMW's line-up, the new model used an electronic capacitor-discharge ignition system in place of the traditional breaker-points-and-coil system. The most significant change to the powerplant involved the cylinder liners, or rather, the lack of cylinder liners. In a move that would soon be adopted across the entire production range, BMW eliminated the steel liners inside the aluminum cylinder barrels. Instead, engineers coated the cylinder walls with a material called "Scanimet," a nickel and silicon-carbide plating. This allowed the metals in the engine to expand at a uniform rate, lowering oil consumption but prohibited overboring of the cylinders.

BMW called its new model the R80G/S. The G/S stood for *Geländstrasse*, which, depending on whose translation you choose, means "forest/pavement," "cross-country/highway," or "dirty little road burner." BMW intended to define the bike as a trail/street machine, but riders soon discovered the G/S excelled as a dirty little road burner.

The new machine absolutely befuddled many members of the motorcycle press. Most journalists focused on the obvious differences between the G/S and pretty much every other motorcycle ever built. The swingarm represented the bike's most apparent break with tradition, but its benefits were clear to even the casual observer. "Tire repair or replacement is a breeze," *Cycle World* wrote, noting that in addition to easy, automotive-type wheel removal, the tires could be repaired or replaced without removing the wheel. The bike included a high-quality flat-tire repair kit to further alleviate any flat-tire fears a rider might harbor.

Like other magazines, *Cycle World* picked up on the bike's other most-obvious feature: It was big. At least it was big for a dirt bike; as a street bike, it weighed less than most bikes in its class. As the magazine noted, "A 400-pound 800-cc street machine is a lightweight."

While not really an off-road machine, the G/S worked remarkably well on dirt roads and well-groomed trails, considering it weighed 437 pounds with its 5.1-gallon gas tank half full and that its cylinders stuck out nearly a foot in either direction. "Dirt suits the G/S right down to the semi-knobbies," *Cycle World* wrote after riding the new BMW down to the southern tip of the Baja Peninsula and back. "Assuming the rider remembers it isn't a YZ465 or an XR750, that is. Assuming speeds are held down and a hazard around the next curve is expected, the G/S works quite well."

The brilliant Monolever rear suspension debuted in 1980 on the R80G/S.

THE BIRTH OF THE ADVENTURE-TOURER

Cycle World may not have grasped the sport-touring concept when it first tested the R100RS, but the fact that editors put the new G/S through such an ambitious test meant the magazine understood the significance of this ground-breaking motorcycle. BMW wasn't just trying to compete in the then-crowded dual-purpose niche; BMW had created an entirely new type of motorcycle: the adventure-tourer. This was a motorcycle for riders who wanted "to cross Tunisia or go from Alaska to the tip of South America," the magazine wrote.

At first BMW offered electric starting as an option, reasoning that the weight saved by deleting the starter would help the bike perform better off-road. Most buyers knew they would be doing little if any off-road riding on a machine that weighed as much as two normal dirt bikes, and they were almost universally willing to accept a small weight penalty for the convenience of electric starting. BMW soon got the message and made the electric starter a standard feature.

MADMAN MUTH

The R80G/S had been the first bike in BMW's renewed assault on the motorcycle market. The odd adventure-tourer turned out to be a surprising success, and the company quickly followed up with the R65LS. BMW based the new model on the Hans Muth–designed R65. With the LS version of the bike, BMW gave the mad-scientist designer free reign.

The resulting motorcycle, introduced for the 1982 model year, was a visual stunner. "What makes the attention-demanding motorcycle look different from previous Bavarian boxers is the small cockpit spoiler/fairing," *Motorcyclist* magazine wrote in its June 1982 issue. More a spoiler than a fairing, the little hunk of plastic provided more down force on the front wheel than wind protection. BMW claimed the spoiler reduced front-wheel lift by one-third at highway speeds.

Stylistically, the rest of the bike took Muth's integrated look to a new level. "The 5.8-gallon gas tank looks smaller than it is and blends gracefully into the mildly stepped seat," *Motorcyclist*

wrote. "The seat ends in a stylish fiberglass housing with integral passenger grab rails." The bike looked like no other middleweight on the market.

In addition to beating its 650-cc-class competition on the styling front, the R65LS beat them on weight, undercutting Yamaha's XJ650 Seca, a bike that blatantly aped Muth's earlier R65 styling, by 22 pounds. It weighed 27 pounds less than Suzuki's GS650G and 39 pounds less than Honda's CB650 Nighthawk. "That light weight, combined with the bike's low center of gravity, neutral steering, and overall excellent handling, make the motorcycle a delight to slip through the mountains on," *Motorcyclist* wrote.

The R80ST cloaked the basic R80G/S platform with the ground-breaking Hans Muth bodywork from the R65.

The R65 may have had it going on in the style department and in lack of flab, but when it came to acceleration, the competition absolutely stomped the flashy new BMW. *Motorcyclist* recorded a quarter-mile time of 14.23 seconds. *Cycle World* bested this, but not by a large margin. That magazine coaxed its LS through the quarter-mile traps in 13.99 seconds. Unfortunately for BMW, U.S. customers still measured performance in quarter-mile increments. The underachieving LS confused both journalists and the public alike. While *Cycle World* called it "BMW's most charming bike," the magazine admitted most people didn't know what to make of the unusual-looking motorcycle. It looked like a high-tech, high-performance superbike. Yet underneath its stylish duds, it was a typical middisplacement motorcycle, and a slow one at that. The LS proved a slow-selling model. During its four-year production run, BMW cranked out fewer than 6400 LS versions of the R65.

OTHER BOXERS

BMW introduced a couple of other new boxer-powered models while biding the time until the introduction of its first all-new engine in six decades: the R80RT and the R80ST. The R80RT, which was based on the existing R80/7 model, represented a fairly straightforward reusing of existing parts. BMW simply mounted the fairing from the R100RT to the basic R80 chassis. The result of adding 53 pounds of fiberglass to a machine that put out 55 horsepower in the wildest dreams of BMW's most hyperbolic advertising copywriters (more like 40 horsepower at the rear wheel) was a predictably slow motorcycle. *Motorcyclist* tried to put a brave face on the powerplant's lack of motivating force, opening its July 1983 road test of the R80RT: "BMW will make you a mellow man. To ride one is to take a sublime holiday from the frenetic pace of today's wonder bikes. It is a sort of hypokinetic, relaxing experience in modern leisure augmented by the certain mystique that has always surrounded the machines from München." All of which was an eloquent way of saying the bike was slower than a box of rocks, a fact the test later confirmed. "The R80's best quarter-mile run was a 14.57 at 85.57, which is substantially slower than the Honda VT500 tested last month."

The R80RT formula may have resulted in a slow motorcycle, but it also resulted in a relatively cheap one, at least when compared to other BMWs. The $5,490 machine brought the virtues of BMW's luxury-tourer to a wider audience. The 797-cc interpretation of BMW's RT concept wasn't a huge success, but it sold better than its more expensive big brother, the R100RT.

The R80ST, the other new 797-cc model BMW introduced for the 1983 model year, claimed the innovative and popular R80G/S as the source of its corporate DNA. The new ST model retained the high-mounted exhaust pipe of the G/S along with its Monolever rear suspension, but traded the big adventure-tourer's 21-inch front wheel for a 19-inch wheel, which was a common size for street bikes of the era. The rest of the bike looked familiar to BMW fans because it borrowed its Hans Muth bodywork from the R65.

The lightweight R80ST (452 pounds with its 5.1-gallon gas tank filled) performed better than the heavy R80RT, but it was still no fireball. As *Motorcyclist* noted in its October 1983 road test of the bike, outright performance was beside the point: "No one, not even a demented Yankee, buys a BMW to exercise his or her speed demons. It's like asking Pavarotti to do the splits—an interesting exercise, perhaps, but more revealing of the underlying motivations of the viewer than any real deficiency in the subject himself."

Motorcyclist concluded the test by speculating that the new model would "capture a lot of hearts just by being what it is— a lightweight, torquey sport/tourer that wears the magic blue-and-white BMW crest." Unfortunately for BMW, the bike only managed to capture 5,963 such hearts and was dropped after two years of production.

The R80ST was the first street-only BMW to feature the Monolever rear suspension from the R80G/S adventure-tourer.

105

THE STATE OF THE MOTOREN WERKE

Of the new models introduced since the ground-breaking R100RS, only one could be considered an unqualified success. Even though the strange R80G/S stumped journalists and defied conventional categorization, a lot of people seemed to have been waiting for just such a machine. Adventure touring proved to be popular enough to make the odd-duck R80G/S one of BMW's most popular models. With the G/S, BMW had created more than just a new marketing niche; it had created a profitable new marketing niche, one that it owned, at least for the time being.

Several other factors contributed to the overall improvement in BMW's bottom line in the years leading up to the middecade introduction of the company's new generation of motorcycles. Moving distribution from Butler & Smith to BMWNA helped the company improve customer relations in the critical U.S. market. BMWs had also become more competitive on the retail-price front. A combination of more efficient

When BMW introduced the four-cylinder K100 series, the Flying Brick came in three distinct flavors: the naked K100, the sport-touring K100RS, and the luxury-touring version shown here, the K100RT.

manufacturing techniques and better control of distribution helped BMW bring the prices of its motorcycles more in line with the Asian competition. BMW kept the prices of some models the same throughout the early years of the decade and managed to cut prices on other models. The R100S, which sold for $6,600 in 1981, listed for just $5,190 in 1983 despite several mechanical upgrades. By 1983 BMW no longer had the distinction of selling the most expensive mass-produced motorcycles on the U.S. market. Harley-Davidson now held that honor.

The price difference between German and Japanese motorcycles was about to get even more narrow, thanks to a U.S. tariff on imported motorcycles over 700-cc. The Reagan administration instituted this tariff at the urging of Harley-Davidson. It was designed to punish Japanese manufacturers for dumping motorcycles into the U.S. market below their production costs, an allegation BMW had long made about the Japanese companies. The tariff also benefited European manufacturers because it allowed companies to import a specific number of motorcycles each year, depending on the country of origin. This benefited the Europeans because all the European manufacturers fell well within the specified limits set by the tariff.

As a result of all these factors, BMW motorcycles slowly backed away from the edge of extinction. Sales in the benchmark U.S. market had fallen to less than 2,000 units in 1980. By 1982 U.S. sales had risen to more than 4,800.

THE FLYING BRICK

The only forward motion the outside world saw at BMW were refinements of the company's venerable boxer twins, but behind the scenes huge changes were taking place. A small team headed by Josef Fritzenwenger had been working on a new engine design since 1977, when Fritzenwenger laid out what would become the basic design for BMW's next generation of powerplants, internally known as the K589 project. This early proto-team laid out the basic architecture for an engine family that would redefine BMW motorcycles.

BMW was rumored to have had an opposed flat-four ready to go in the early 1970s, but the use of that configuration in Honda's Gold Wing, introduced in the fall of 1974, precluded that option. Something as momentous as BMW's first new motorcycle engine in 60 years couldn't be perceived as being a mere copy of a Japanese design. This would be especially devastating if the Honda was perceived as being of higher quality than the BMW. Given the phenomenal quality of the Gold Wing, such a prospect was not beyond the realm of the possible.

The engine design Fritzenwenger settled on would not be mistaken for a copy of any motorcycle engine ever built. The basic configuration—in-line four-cylinder—wasn't terribly unusual,

THE HARLEY-DAVIDSON TARIFF AND BMW

In the early 1980s it wasn't just BMW and the other traditional manufacturers that were on the verge of extinction; the entire motorcycle industry was in trouble. The motorcycle industry had generally been on an upward trend since the end of World War II, and that upward trend increased exponentially as the American baby boom generation became old enough to ride motorcycles. Between 1965 and 1981 the number of American motorcycle registrations grew from 1.4 million to 6 million. The vast majority of those extra 4.6 million motorcycles came from Japan. After nearly three decades of record growth, the Japanese motorcycle industry had no reason to believe the situation would ever change.

Apparently they hadn't given much thought to their market demographics. As the 1980s dawned, the American baby boom generation that had fueled the motorcycle boom of the previous decades was growing up. They were getting married, raising families, and increasingly trading in their motorcycles for child transportation units. Goodbye motorcycle boom, hello minivan craze. Between the years of 1981 and 1984, the motorcycle market severely contracted. From 1981 until 1982 total inventory of unsold heavyweight motorcycles (700 cc and above) rose from 108,000 units to 200,000 units. But even in the face of a changing marketplace, the Japanese manufacturers kept proceeding as if plummeting sales were just an aberration instead of the new reality. In 1982, the Japanese imported 160,000 heavyweight motorcycles into the United States. The four major Japanese manufacturers introduced a combined total of 117 new motorcycle models in 1982 and another 119 new models for 1983. This led to a glut of unsold machines and drastically reduced prices of all motorcycles.

While the Japanese could afford to ride out the economic depression that hit the motorcycle industry in the early 1980s, the situation was much more dire for the struggling traditional companies. Harley-Davidson lost money in 1981 and 1982. Harley's share of the heavyweight motorcycle market had fallen from nearly 100 percent in 1972 to less than 14 percent a decade later. Bankruptcy loomed large for Harley, which had been bought out from parent company AMF in 1981 by a consortium of investors headed by Vaughn Beals. In September 1982 Harley-Davidson petitioned the U.S. International Trade Commission (ITC) for relief from the importation of heavyweight motorcycles. The ITC investigated and found that imports of heavyweight motorcycles did indeed pose a threat to the American motorcycle industry and instituted a five-year tariff plan. The tariff, which at the time was set at 4.4 percent, was raised to 49.4 percent in 1984, then lowered to 39.4 percent for 1985, 24.4 percent in 1986, 19.4 percent in 1987, and 14.4 percent in 1988. It was to go back to the original 4.4 percent in 1989.

Prior to adopting the ITC recommendations, the Reagan administration instituted some changes that proved particularly advantageous for the small European manufacturers. The administration appended provisions that allowed West German motorcycle companies to import 5,000 heavyweight motorcycles in 1984, 6,000 in 1985, 7,000 in 1986, 8,500 in 1987, and 10,000 in 1988. The British, Italians, and even Japanese received similar exemptions, though they weren't quite as generous as Germany's exemptions. This came too late to save Triumph, which rolled out the last of its original Speed Twin-derived models in 1983, but it occurred just as BMW was about to introduce its first completely new motorcycle in 60 years, which was a most opportune time for the struggling German company.

nor did the use of liquid cooling differentiate the new BMW from its Japanese competition. Likewise the engine's longitudinal orientation, while different from the hordes of transverse four-cylinders emanating from Japan, had been a common design on early four-cylinder motorcycles. What really set the engine apart was that the entire unit was flopped over on its side, so that the cylinder head stuck out by the rider's left foot, and the crankcase hung out by the rider's right foot. Laying the engine on its side helped BMW maintain the low center of gravity for which it was famous while

A KIDNEY ON THE NEW MOTORCYCLE

To drive home the relationship between the new engine and BMW's successful automotive division, the new line of bikes sported split grilles over their radiators that resembled the famous kidney-shaped grilles used on BMW cars. David Robb, BMW's head of motorcycle design, explains the symbolism of this relationship: "We are the only company in the world with its motorcycle and car design under one roof. It creates a synergy of technology, resources, designers, sculptors, and creativity. We get the chance to inspire each other. It ties together our passion for ideology, personality, and character."

With the K100 four-cylinder series, BMW tried to stress the relationship between BMW motorcycles and the popular cars the company produces by incorporating its famous kidney-shaped grille into the front of the bike. Today BMW continues to incorporate the design on its latest offerings, such as the popular K1200LT.

avoiding the excessive width of the traditional boxer design. The new powerplant measured 19 inches across, making it 8 inches narrower than Honda's Gold Wing flat four and a full 10 inches narrower than the 797-cc and 980-cc boxer twins.

To test this novel layout, Fritzenwenger's crew shoehorned the aluminum engine from a Peugot 104 automobile into a test-mule motorcycle chassis. The result of this experiment proved the longitudinal flopped four had a great deal of promise.

The downside of the chosen configuration was that when coupled to BMW's automotive-type transmission, the entire package was a bit long. BMW could have followed Honda's lead with the Gold Wing and mounted the transmission under the engine, but this would have raised the center of gravity and compromised handling. Besides, BMW was not too keen on following Honda's lead. BMW minimized the length of the bike with a clever, compact frame design. This resulted in such an innovative layout that BMW patented it as the Compact Drive System (CDS). The engine acted as the central stressed member in this design, with a minimalistic tubular frame surrounding the engine, tying the various other cycle parts together.

Even with the CDS frame, the drivetrain was still long. BMW engineers used an extremely short swingarm to keep the wheelbase to a reasonable length, but the K bikes, as BMW labeled the new models, still measured 59.7 inches from axle to axle. One unfortunate side effect of the vestigial swingarm was that its short length meant it lacked the leverage to control the up and down jacking inherent in a shaft-driven motorcycle. This had been a BMW quirk since the company started using rear suspension systems, but as power outputs rose, the unsettling effects the driveshafts had on the chassis went from endearing quirk to annoying deficiency.

The new engine design quickly became a top priority when new management took over BMW's motorcycle operations. One of the first acts of the new regime was to increase Fritzenwenger's team to 240 members. From that point on, the pace of development increased dramatically. Martin Probst, an engineer with experience designing motors for BMW's auto racing program, was placed in charge of the team designing the new engine. The powerplant, which was primarily designed by Stefan Pachernegg, a young Austrian engineer BMW had

The sport-touring K100RS proved to be the most popular version of the Flying Brick.

109

poached from scooter maker Puch, displayed its racing heritage in its technological wizardry. Computer-controlled electronic fuel injection took the place of carburetors, and the engine incorporated a sophisticated electronic rev limiter.

Other than its sophisticated electronics, its fuel injection, and of course its unusual layout, the engine broke little new technological ground. The unfashionably undersquare powerplant did use double overhead cams, but DOHC systems were used in all but a handful of Japanese motorcycles. In its first K100RS road test, *Cycle World* wrote, "Poking around in the RS's twin-cam, 987-cc engine reveals anything *but* cutting edge hardware." If anything, the engine's two-valve-per-cylinder design was a bit old-fashioned by the fall of 1983, a time when most Japanese motorcycles featured at least three valves per cylinder, and more often four. Yamaha was on the verge of releasing the world's first five-valve cylinder head.

BMW took the opportunity to address one of the traditional weak areas with BMW motorcycle engines. Since Max Friz had first condescended to designing his "stupid conveyance," BMW crankshafts had been a source of problems. The basic design of the boxer engine was the culprit. To keep the pistons close

together on the boxer, an important design criteria for maintaining the near perfect primary balance of the boxer design, Friz and every BMW engineer who followed in his shoes was forced to use just two main bearings on the crankshaft. Putting a bearing between the piston-rod journals would have offset the pistons enough to upset the primary balance. Probst and company were under no such constraints when designing an in-line four, so they made the bottom end of the new K motor as stout as possible, spinning a forged steel crankshaft inside five main bearings.

While BMW chose not to mimic the basic architecture of Honda's flat-four Gold Wing mill, it did borrow at least one clever design from its Japanese competitor. Longitudinally mounted engines have a tendency to rotate in the same direction that the crankshaft spins when the throttle opens. This is described as the engine "torquing," and on BMW boxers, it makes the bike feel as if the engine is twisting down and to the right when the throttle is blipped. This isn't too noticeable at speed, but at a stop it can be disconcerting. All motorcycles with longitudinally mounted cranks experience this, but Honda solved this dilemma on its Gold Wing by spinning the alternator in the opposite

direction of the crankshaft, effectively canceling out the torque reaction of the engine. BMW took this idea one step further with the new K bikes, rotating both the generator and oil pump in the opposite direction of the crankshaft.

The new motorcycle that would house all this high-technology featured the company's most up-to-date suspension system, a beefed-up version of the Monolever introduced on the R80G/S. BMW initially offered the new K bikes in three versions. The standard K100 was an unfaired roadster. Like the R100 boxer series, there was also a sport-touring version of the new machine, the K100RS, and a full-boat touring version, the K100RT. There was no S version of the new four. BMW unveiled the new models in September 1983, at a press launch in the south of France. By this time everyone who might possibly care about the new bikes had already seen spy photographs of BMW's latest creations. The company made such a half-hearted effort to keep the bikes secret that it almost certainly intended to let the world know it was producing a radically different motorcycle. By the time of the official unveiling the engine had already earned the nickname "The Flying Brick."

FLYING IN THE FACE OF "MONKEY-SEE, MONKEY-DO"

Even though they knew the details, the new BMW captivated the assembled press. At a time when 24-valve six-cylinders and liquid-cooled V-fours were old news, the unusual new K bikes stood out from the crowd. "BMW has flown in the face of monkey-see, monkey-do design trends and produced a machine that is utterly unorthodox and positively oozes stately and sporting character," *Motorcyclist* wrote after getting a chance to ride the new German bike for the first time. "It is an assemblage of high-quality components waltzing in harmony with no invisible barbs or treacheries."

BMW may have avoided what *Motorcyclist* called "monkey-see, monkey-do design trends," but functionally the new K bikes were remarkably mainstream, which surprised many observers. People did not expect riding a BMW to be a normal experience. After the French press introduction, *Motorcyclist* wrote, "While many expected the K to produce a feel and sound as unique as the boxer's distinctive rumble and pop, the flat four feels much like any well-designed four-banger. It makes no great impression

on the ears, only a competent, chuffing whirr inaudible at highway speed, and the engine's battle cry sounds like nothing so much as a nameless UJM out on Sunday maneuvers."

The styling of the new BMW was as mainstream as its performance. While it was contemporary and tasteful, other than its oddball engine orientation and Monolever rear suspension, the Muth-styled bike did not stretch the boundaries of design. In the years since the introduction of the R65, Muth's integrated look had become the industry standard, and by the time the K bikes appeared on showroom floors in late 1983, most manufacturers offered sleek sporting bikes with Muth-inspired bodywork. Or at least, in the case of BMW's competition from the Land of the Rising Sun, they attempted to offer Muth-esque styling. For some reason Japanese designers seem incapable of letting a motorcycle

out of their design studios without tacking on at least one incongruent design element. The new K bike might not have stretched any stylistic boundaries, but it did set a new standard for elegance. Every surface was exquisitely finished and no element on any version of the new BMWs appeared extraneous. "There isn't a rough edge or thoughtlessly executed part on the K100," wrote *Cycle World*'s Steve Anderson. "It looks functional and expensive, just as its designers intended."

Motorcyclist's Dexter Ford shared Anderson's judgment on the overall unity of design: "As a piece of sculpture, the K100 is unrivaled; the design of the bodywork, the glorious aluminum castings and perfect candy-apple red finish make the K bike worthy of inclusion in any museum's industrial design section. It's the first motorcycle I've seen in the past 10 years I would not hesitate to call beautiful."

BMW THROUGH AND THROUGH

The K bikes went on sale in most markets late in 1983, but the new machines wouldn't arrive in the U.S. market until late in 1984, as 1985 models. The U.S. press didn't receive official test bikes until the summer of 1984. When they finally got their mitts on the new K bike's optional heated grips, members of motorcycling's fourth estate were suitably impressed. "It is a BMW through and through," *Motorcyclist* wrote in its first road test of the naked K100, "supple, stark, dignified, comfortable, maneuverable, light and uncharacteristically fast."

The new K bikes were fast, and not just for BMWs. Outright performance numbers like quarter-mile times and top speed were just average, which in itself represented a tremendous improvement for the German company. In its February 1984 road test of a German-specification K100, *Motorcyclist* managed a quarter-mile time of 12.4 seconds, and the bike topped out at an indicated 120 miles per hour. BMW still wasn't building American-style drag bikes, but they were no longer building slugs, either. In midrange roll-on tests, which better measure real-world capabilities, the new BMW fours excelled, beating such shaft-driven rivals as Yamaha's XJ900 Seca and Suzuki's GS850.

Even though the K bikes were the first BMWs that could legitimately be described as fast, like every motorcycle BMW had ever built, the new bikes offered a lot more than just sheer velocity. Again from the pages of *Motorcyclist*: "BMW has chosen, as always, to coddle the rider. ... This is a machine of quality and strength, with broad-range muscle that purrs and devours miles with seven-league strides."

When the new BMWs finally reached U.S. showrooms, BMWNA set prices at $5,990 for the naked K100, $7,200 for the K100RS sport-tourer, and $7,500 for the K100RT touring bike. By this time, magazine editors had had ample opportunity to test the new machines, both in Europe and in the United States, and in addition to their virtues, the press had discovered a few vices in the K formula.

The virtues continued to impress most riders. The new K bikes took BMW's tradition for building fine high-speed touring bikes to a new level. "The K100 has the kind of powerband, the kind of suspension, the kind of overall handling that simply make the fine art of riding quickly a whole lot easier," *Cycle World* wrote in its September 1984 road test of a K100RS. The other magazines concurred, attributing the balance of the new K bikes to the low center of gravity created by the basic design.

In hindsight, it seems that the centralization of mass also contributed to the balance, helping to mask the weight, which ranged from 540 pounds for the naked K100 to 595 pounds for the K100RT tourer. While a wet weight of nearly 600 pounds was shocking for a BMW, its K100RT undercut its Japanese luxury-touring competition—Honda's Gold Wing, Yamaha's Venture, and Suzuki's short-lived Cavalcade—by 200 pounds. It undercut Kawasaki's massive six-cylinder Voyager by 300 pounds. BMW's engineers openly disdained the gigantic tourers coming from Japan, calling them "battleships." They had no intention of saddling their new flagship with such excessive poundage.

As good as the new K series was, it was far from perfect. The two main criticisms centered on engine vibration and the driveshaft's torque reaction. Thanks to a great deal of engineering trickery the antics of the abnormally short driveshaft upset the chassis less than the wild gyrations of the old boxer driveshaft. But even though it was better than the boxer, the up and down jacking of the shaft when the throttle was opened and closed proved problematic. When *Motorcyclist* tested a K100RT for its September 1984 issue, the magazine reported, "The RT must be handled carefully during fast cornering because of the relatively short swingarm. ... Any sharp throttle input will put the chassis through some long-excursion gyrations that will keep the rider from making any aggressive action until the movement dies out."

What U.S. journalists didn't know was that even before the K series made its way stateside, BMW was in the process of developing an ingenious and effective solution that would tame the driveshaft for all time.

The problem with engine vibration proved more severe, and ultimately took far longer to resolve. "Despite being rubber-mounted in the front, the engine buzzes noticeably more than a Japanese inline-Four of comparable size, and certainly more than any Boxer Twin ever managed on its worst day," *Cycle World* wrote of its K100RS test bike. "It's a fairly high-frequency vibration, too, that is strongest right at about 55 miles per hour in top gear, and it's most often felt through the footpegs. And the vibes didn't go unnoticed by the heat shield on the muffler, which self-destructed its front mounting tab after only a few hundred miles of testing."

MOTORCYCLE OF THE YEAR

Vibration aside, the overall competence of the K bikes, their ability to cover vast expanses of highways at highly illegal speeds (illegal in 55-mile per hour America, anyway), and their exquisite attention to detail made the new K series a success. The K bikes won just about every international Motorcycle of the Year award given out in 1984 and won a couple more the following year, when the bikes hit the U.S. market. In the first year of production, BMW motorcycle sales were up 120 percent, and that was before BMW began exporting the new series to the United States. In 1985, when the big K bikes were

finally spinning their tires on U.S. tarmac, BMW's total motor-cycle sales topped 37,000 units, an all-time record for the German firm. By the time the next generation of K bikes replaced the original eight-valve models in the early 1990s, BMW had sold 85,510 copies of the various models.

IF FOUR ARE GOOD, COULD THREE BE BETTER?

If BMW had done a poor job at keeping the development of the four-cylinder K bikes secret they fared even worse at keeping the upcoming 740-cc three-cylinder K bike series under wraps. When the new K75 was unveiled in late 1985, even the technical details were common knowledge. The new triple was essentially a K100 with one cylinder lopped off. The crankpins were staggered 120 degrees apart, and adding a couple of weights to the water-pump driveshaft made the shaft act as a counterbalancer to control vibration. The press knew all these details well in advance of the bike's release. What they didn't know was just how good the little K bikes would be.

Power output proved one area where the K75 exceeded expectations. Working with a 25 percent reduction in engine displacement, the smaller K bikes only gave up 15 horsepower to their 987-cc siblings. To squeeze out the extra ponies from each cubic centimeter, BMW engineers resorted to typical hot-rodding techniques: higher compression (11:1, up from 10.2:1 on the K100), redesigned combustion chambers, and massaged intake and exhaust systems.

The new three-cylinder K bike was initially available as the K75C, with a small handlebar-mounted cockpit fairing, and later available in a naked version—the K75T—as well as a sport version with upgraded suspension and a small frame-mounted fairing—the K75S. The smooth, torquey three-cylinder engine made the most of the new machines' lighter weight. The sporting K75S model weighed 32 pounds less than the K100RS sport-touring model. "The power range is so broad that it's hard to know what rpm the engine is turning without looking at the tach," *Cycle World* wrote after testing the K75C for its April 1986 issue. "But it doesn't matter; the engine always seems to pull, regardless. When going through a turn, you can shift now, you can shift later, or you don't have to shift at all. The K75 has a torque curve that is as broad as most liter bikes."

The smaller K bikes were not the stoplight-to-stoplight rockets that still made the collective American motorcycling public go slack-jawed with desire. "But," *Cycle World* wrote, "it's BMW's philosophy that a motorcycle doesn't *have* to produce enough power to spin the earth on its axis."

Most measurements between the K100 and K75 series were almost identical. In addition to sharing the same bore and

stroke, both the three-cylinder and four-cylinder versions featured the same frames, and thus the same wheelbase length, the same steering geometry, and the same seat height. But the two series could not have felt more different on the road. "If you're still not sure which is the 1000 and which is the 750," *Cycle World* wrote, "any twisty road can show you the light. The triple feels much smaller and lighter."

The use of a balance shaft created the greatest difference between the road manners of the two series'. The system virtually eliminated the annoying vibration of the four-cylinder models. "Unlike K100s we have tested," *Cycle World*'s Steve Anderson wrote after his first ride aboard the new triple, "the K75 doesn't buzz its footpegs at these speeds. Above 6,500 rpm in top gear there is some vibration, but it's not intrusive. Ten-hour days on this motorcycle are completely reasonable."

When *Cycle World* first put a K75C through a full road test, the magazine's staff was even more impressed with the smoothness of the new powertrain: "Unlike the K100, the K75 is dead smooth. … There's no hint of the left footpeg vibration that loosened the toenails of most early K100 riders. In fact, the K75 will hold its own against any bike when it comes to engine smoothness."

Like its bigger brothers, the new K75 series wasn't perfect either. While the balanced engine eliminated the bothersome vibration of the 987-cc K bikes, the new K75 models were still hobbled by the shaft drive antics and overly soft suspension common to all BMWs. Or at least the initial versions of the new triple suffered from these traditional BMW foibles. When BMW introduced the sporting S version of the bike, these problems were largely absent. Besides the sleek sport fairing, the most significant change to the new S model was its upgraded suspension. BMW used stiffer springs in the fork and on the rear shock, and also increased rebound damping at both ends. This helped lessen the traditional BMW tendency for the fork to bottom under heavy braking, and also helped settle the driveshaft-induced jacking of the rear end.

Journalists raved about the new S model like they had never before raved about a BMW motorcycle. The increased back-road velocities allowed by the better-controlled suspension did highlight some other shortcomings inherent in the K series, like the need for better brakes, but for the most part the new triples sent journalists on a quest for new superlatives. *Motorcyclist* concluded its November 1986 road test of the new S model: "The K75S is a versatile machine, fully capable of being flailed on the back roads and still taking you and a partner cross country in comfort. The S's suspension improvements are terrific, and they give the bike the sporting competency to back up its radical look and S designation. The S is, by far, the finest-handling BMW we have ever ridden."

THE REVENGE OF THE AIRHEADS

The K100 series had been intended from the start as a replacement for the aging R100 series. When the new model was released for 1984, BMW announced its intention to quit producing the 980-cc versions of the boxer twin.

Before BMW released its new K bikes, it surveyed various BMW owners' clubs about possible engine configurations for future models, including flopped fours and boxer twins. More than 90 percent of respondents selected the boxer twin as the configuration BMW should pursue. A survey conducted after the release of the new K models showed an apparent change of heart, because 90 percent of respondents now said they approved of the company's new engine configuration. It seems BMW had made the correct decision by choosing to ignore boxer aficionados' wishes and abandon the boxer, at least in 980-cc form.

With the introduction of the three-cylinder K75 series, the next logical step would seem to be dropping the 797-cc boxers from the line-up. After all, the old boxers' main competition would be the new K bikes. After that, BMW would likely replace the R65 with a 493-cc flopped, longitudinal, liquid-cooled twin in the K formula.

But an odd thing happened on the way to the elimination of the old air-cooled boxers, or "Airheads," as fans call them. It turned out that when BMW asked people if they approved of the K bike, they obviously weren't the same people who said the company should pursue the boxer twin formula. The 90 percent of owners who felt the company should stick with the boxer contained some stubborn individuals, enough of them, in fact, to be a problem for BMW. It seemed a certain percentage of Beemerphiles would never buy a K bike no matter how much the company improved the basic design. As the initial excitement about the new K bikes faded, it became apparent that that group was too important to ignore. Instead of killing the remaining boxer-powered models, in 1986 BMW resurrected the R100 series in both RS and RT trim.

Actually they didn't resurrect the bikes, exactly. During the 980-cc engine's hiatus, BMW had introduced an updated version of the R80RT, as well as a new standard version of the bike, the R80. The most significant improvement to the new machines was the inclusion of the Monolever rear suspension from the popular R80G/S adventure-tourer. Rather than dusting off the old tooling for the original R100RS and R100RT, BMW created new 980-cc bikes by boring out the cylinders of the R80 series. Max Friz' old boxer design proved difficult to kill, as if it had a touch of *Nosferatu* in its blood.

NOT REALLY THE LAST EDITION

While the rest of the world received the new K models in 1984, the brave new Beemers didn't arrive stateside until late in the year, as 1985 models. In the meantime BMW marketing folks tried to score a few extra boxer sales in the U.S. market.

The company had already announced it was discontinuing production of the 980-cc versions of the boxer bikes after the 1984 model year. The decision made sense. BMW dealers in the United States had plenty of unsold 1983 and older machines on showroom floors, bikes available at heavily discounted prices. Without the new K bikes to sell in 1984, U.S. BMW dealers needed some reason to entice buyers into purchasing brand-new 1984 model year boxers instead of discounted carryover models. So BMW capitalized on the big boxer's demise and marketed special Last Editions of the old beasts.

A couple of years later, when it turned out that rumors of the big boxers' demise were greatly exaggerated, some of the people who shelled out big bucks to get their special Last Edition found that by not really being last, the Last Editions were somewhat less special. This created some hard feelings among BMW fans that persist to this day.

MARKETING HERITAGE

BMW's motorcycle division had entered the 1980s as one of the weakest motorcycle manufacturers in the world, selling even fewer bikes than ailing Harley-Davidson and terminally ill Triumph. During the course of the decade the company had turned itself around, managing to log record sales in the process. And it accomplished all this at a time when the motorcycle industry was in an overall decline. The original Triumph went out of business, and a number of other European brands floundered or quit building motorcycles all together. Even powerful Japanese companies like Yamaha found themselves struggling to remain in the motorcycle business.

BMW accomplished this amazing comeback partly by introducing innovative new motorcycles that genuinely offered buyers something they couldn't get elsewhere. But part of BMW's financial turnaround involved the savvy marketing of a more intangible commodity: heritage. A retrograde move like bringing back the ancient 980-cc boxer twins must have stung an engineering-driven company like BMW, but it indicates company management had at last embraced the company's legacy, realizing it was something they could capitalize on rather than something from which they had to run away.

LEFT: While the old Airhead boxer might have been dated, it still had enough to offer for fans to demand it be brought back into production.

CHAPTER 6

FROM MONOLEVERS
TO PARALEVERS

After releasing its first new motorcycle engine design in well over half a century, most observers expected BMW to return to something resembling a semi-dormant state for at least a decade or three. For a short time, that appeared to be the case. After introducing the K75S for the 1987 model year, not much happened on the K front for a couple of seasons. BMW swapped the handlebar-mounted fairing on the K75C model for a stylish plexiglass windshield for 1987 and dropped the slow-selling C version of the triple altogether after 1988. The company had introduced a decked-out version of the K100RT tourer, the K100LT, a bike designed to compete head to head with the ultra-luxurious Japanese "battleships." The LT took the RT formula to new extremes, featuring color matched luggage, complete with passenger backrest, touring saddle, cassette radio, and just about every other amenity the touring hedonist could imagine. The American tourists that BMW hoped to lure would still have to bungee their own Teddy bears to the luggage rack, however; the Teutonic mindset of BMW's engineers still demanded some owner involvement. To a degree the LT succeeded, at least more so than the RT, and in 1990 the LT supplanted the RT all together.

ABOVE: The R100GS, introduced in 1987, took the Monolever concept one step further with its brilliant Paralever system. Through clever geometry, the Paralever tamed the up-and-down antics of a shaft-driven motorcycle.

LEFT: The Paris-Dakar version of the R100GS proved to be BMW's most popular model prior to the introduction of the Oilhead series.

While it had the trappings of an off-road racer, the R100GS was simply an excellent streetbike with the capacity to keep going when the pavement ended.

A large percentage of BMW aficionados still bought boxers no matter how much BMW improved the bricks. This group made the R80RT a surprising success in BMW's post-K-bike line-up. The original R80RT introduced in 1982 had not been well received, and BMW sold just 7,315 examples during the three years it produced the bike. BMW introduced a new motorcycle bearing the R80RT designation for the 1985 model year. The new RT was based on the technologically innovative R80G/S. Like the G/S, the R80RT used BMW's monolever suspension, although in RT application the Boge rear shock attached to the ring-gear housing instead of the driveshaft tube. This provided a stronger structure for the heavier touring bike. The thicker front fork featured an aluminum fork brace bolted across the top fender. When combined with stronger suspension components sourced from

the then-new K bikes, the R80RT proved to be a competent handler. This was not another rubber cow.

Even though the R80RT brought many of the technical innovations from the K-bike line-up to the boxer family, its most innovative feature was its price. When introduced for the 1985 model year, the improved R80RT cost just $5,700, $240 less than the previous iteration had cost when it was introduced three years earlier. In 1985, the R80RT was the least expensive full-dress touring motorcycle sold in the United States.

Not only was the R80RT less expensive than its predecessor, it was also much more popular with magazine test riders. "It's a pleasant relief from the huge, boring land yachts on one side and the hyper-frenetic sport bikes on the other," *Motorcyclist's* Dexter Ford wrote. "The R80RT is like finding a good jazz station on the radio just when you'd resigned yourself

The Paris-Dakar version of the R100GS was cosmetically altered to resemble BMW's Dakar rally-winning desert racers.

RIGHT: With practical touches, including a 9.25-gallon gas tank, the Paris-Dakar model offered more than just stunning looks.

BELOW: The oil cooler, shown here, was a standard feature on the Paris-Dakar model.

to a choice between an endless opera or a Cindy Lauper retrospective." Apparently many BMW fans found the R80RT's combination of performance and low price made the bike more tempting than the alternative motorcycles the company offered. BMW sold almost 22,000 R80RTs, which meant the 797-cc RT outsold the 980-cc version by a margin of nearly three-to-one.

Like the R80RT, the R80GS (by the time the new K bikes came on line, BMW had abandoned its long practice of using a slash as part of the model designation) also proved a popular and capable model. The popularity of these boxer-powered models likely influenced BMW's decision to use the resurrected 980-cc Airhead platform instead of the new flying bricks to showcase its most innovative technology of the period: the Paralever rear suspension.

PARALEVER

The resurrected R100RS and R100RT seemed at best half-hearted efforts. While they featured BMW's innovative Monolever rear suspension, boxer fans found other features of the new-old twins to be more regressive than progressive. The styling of the R80-based 980-cc machines took a definite turn for the

ABANDONING THE SLASH

The R80G/S was the last 20th-century BMW model to carry a slash in its designation. The tradition began with the company's first postwar boxer twin, the R51/2. The "/2," which indicated that this was the second generation of the R51, was meant to put some distance between the postwar R51 and the prewar R51. In reality, the two models were remarkably similar, the newer model being distinguished by two-piece valve covers, a more deeply valanced fender, and a few mechanical upgrades, as well as a mechanical degradation or two in the name of economy. It was understandable that the two models were so similar, given BMW's precarious financial situation following the end of the war. In some ways, the /2 designation was a marketing ploy to distract buyers from the fact that the struggling company was selling a motorcycle whose design dated back to a previous era.

The company continued using designations with slashes to indicate new generations of a design throughout what was supposed to be the boxer's life span, although the marketing folks strayed from the rigid formula when they wanted to emphasize just how new a product really was. The most obvious example of this slash-hyperbole was when BMW introduced the revolutionary /5 series. Since this was an entirely new design and not a fifth generation of the existing models, BMW's traditional formula would indicate that the new machines should start over with plain R50, R60, and R75 designations. The rhetorical statement behind the use of the /5 designation indicated that these bikes were not just third generations of the existing /2 series. Instead they were at least several steps ahead of the existing models, which was a valid enough sentiment to excuse the labeling hyperbole.

BMW resumed its traditional model designations after the introduction of the /5 series, introducing the /6 series and /7 series in a totally linear fashion. But as the Alpha part of BMW's Alphanumeric model coding system became more prevalent in the codes of popular models like the R90S and R100RS, BMW let the slash designation fade. When company product planners inserted the slash into the R80G/S moniker, it was more due to the force of habit than any logical system of assigning model designations, and it was the last such use of the slash. By the time the R80G/S became the R100GS, the slash had quietly disappeared. In the postmodern world of the 1980s, linearity was no longer cool, and BMW was making a comeback by marketing cool motorcycles.

But don't count the slash out just yet. One of the side effects of the nonlinearity that characterizes the postmodern world is that everything old becomes new again. Harley-Davidson rode this postmodern horse to record profits, recycling its own heritage in the same nostalgic Cuisinart that gave us the black velvet painting of Elvis Presley, James Dean, Humphrey Bogart, and Marilyn Monroe sipping cups of Joe at a diner on the Boulevard of Broken Dreams. The slash is part of BMW heritage, and as long as heritage sells, it may still grace future BMW models.

---

blander, with tail sections that would look more at home on generic Japanese motorcycles than on Germany's distinctive boxer twins. Worse yet, the post–K-bike engines had been trimmed of some horsepower in an effort to meet various pollution- and noise-control regulations. Smaller Bing carburetors (down a whopping 8-millimeter from the Last Edition models of 1984), smaller valves, more restrictive exhaust pipes, and a lower compression ratio brought power back down to R90/6 levels.

The press treated the rereleased boxers as curious artifacts rather than serious motorcycles. They still featured the softly sprung suspensions that had hobbled BMW motorcycles for years, and the driveshaft's antics still tried to buck the ham-fisted operator off the machine when the throttle was opened or closed. And like BMWs of yore, the new boxers tried to flip the rider over the fork if the front brake was applied with anything resembling force. "The R100RS needs a fork that doesn't collapse like a pole-axed mule every time you hit the brakes," journalist Jerry Smith wrote in the May 1988 issue of Motorcyclist.

In that same road test, a comparison between the R100RS, Moto Guzzi's 1000 LeMans, and Ducati's 750 Paso, Bill Stermer compared the new BMW to his own original 980-cc bike, a 1981 R100RS. Stermer's motorcycle, which had more than 74,000 miles at the time of the test, handily outpowered the R80-based mill in the new version. Thanks to a heavily

modified suspension, his bike outran the new machine in the twisties too. When he first climbed aboard the 1988 R100RS, he thought, "Egad, another *Gumikuh* (Rubber Cow)!"

The article was tactful in its assessment of the resurrected RS. "It exists more as a nostalgia piece, a talisman of an era passed," it concluded, which was a nice way of saying the Airhead RS had outlived its usefulness.

The R100GS *Motorcyclist* tested just one month later received no such criticism. In fact, the bike was one of the most highly praised BMWs in the magazine's history. While sharing the same basic frame and engine as the R100RS, right down to its restrictive 32-millimeter Bing carburetors, the new GS was an entirely different animal than any previous BMW, including the well-received K75S. The reason for the bike's warm reception was its revolutionary suspension.

The front fork, a 40-millimeter Marzocchi unit, was fairly conventional, though it could be considered revolutionary for a BMW because it was actually as good as the forks used by other manufacturers. It had the compression damping sorely lacking in any previous Beemers, making the GS the first BMW fitted with a telescopic fork that didn't "collapse like a pole-axed mule" when the brakes were applied.

But the rear suspension was truly revolutionary by any standards. BMW engineers equipped the driveshaft with an extra universal joint between the engine and final-drive housing,

If the standard R100GS was too big for serious off-road work, the Paris-Dakar version was doubly large.

giving the shaft housing an extra pivot point. A horizontal link connected the housing and the frame, creating parallelogram suspension geometry that fed the gyrations of the driveshaft back into the frame in a back-and-forth motion rather than an up-and-down motion. BMW claimed the result was the equivalent of using a 5-foot-long swingarm and the design eliminated 95 percent of shaft-induced chassis movement.

Motorcyclist's testers believed that figure was closer to 100 percent. "In practice the GS feels like a chain-drive bike," the magazine reported. "Not a trace of shaft hop is detectable from the saddle, no matter how hard you hammer the throttle or try to make the motorcycle misbehave."

The new GS featured a host of other nice touches, too, such as spokes that laced to the outer edges of the aluminum Akront

rims, outside the tire bead so tubeless tires could be used. It also had a two-position fender that could be raised from the street position should anyone feel hardy enough to try some serious trail riding with the big BMW, but street riding was the new adventure-tourer's real forte. "Ridden hard, the GS can keep even the fine-handling and fast 600 Katana knocking on its back door by taking advantage of its mondo cornering clearance and superb, confident steering feel," *Motorcyclist* staffer Nick Ienatsch wrote. "The 1,000-cc twin pumps out enough torque to pull hard out of corners, but the truly brilliant piece on the Beemer is the Paralever rear suspension. Don't buy a BMW without it."

Other staffers agreed. Jerry Smith, by his own admission "the guy who sniveled about the limp suspension on the R100RS," wrote, "The difference between the Dakar-look

The K1 was BMW's unique interpretation of a modern sportbike.

ABOVE: The K1 was the first K model to use BMW's innovative Paralever rear suspension.

Approach the K1 from any angle and it remains one of the most unusual-looking motorcycles ever produced.

R100GS and the RS is, as Mr. Twain once said, the difference between lightning and a lightning bug."

Mitch Boehm concurred, calling the Paralever suspension "phenomenal," and the GS "the finest boxer BMW has ever built."

Perhaps Ienatsch best summed up the staff's response to the bike in his one-word sentence:"Perfect."

"The Paralever is one of the rightest things BMW ever put on one of its bikes," the article concluded. BMW had at last engineered the shaft-driven motorcycle into submission.

ANTILOCK BRAKES

To follow up its technological grand slam Paralever rear suspension, BMW borrowed some technology from its thriving automotive division. BMW's automotive engineers had been working on antilock braking systems (ABS) since 1978, pioneering a technology that would become one of the most important automotive safety devices since the advent of the three-point seat belt. While the system BMW developed worked quite well in automotive applications, BMW engineers felt it was too heavy for a motorcycle, and the technology wasn't refined enough for use on a single-tracked vehicle.

In the early 1980s, BMW teamed up with FAG Kugelfischer, another company located in the island that was West Berlin at that time, and began work in earnest on an ABS system for motorcycle applications. The two companies developed a computerized hydraulic ABS system more suitable to use on a motorcycle. This system featured impulse generators bolted to the wheels. These sensors monitored each wheel's rotation speed. If either wheel decelerated too quickly the readings activated a pressure modulator to reduce hydraulic pressure to the caliper or calipers of the offending wheel. It would continue a cycle of pressure reduction to the caliper or calipers up to 25 times per second until road speeds dropped below 2.5 miles per hour. The ABS system added 18 pounds to the already heavy K100RS and K100LT models on which it made its production appearance for the 1988 model year.

The ABS system worked fairly well in its original form, though its application could be a bit disconcerting to uninitiated riders. Over the years BMW has steadily refined the system, making it less obtrusive. Since its inception, rider's have had mixed opinions about ABS in motorcycle applications. Many riders like ABS-equipped motorcycles, while many others feel a skilled rider is better served in most conditions by controlling the brakes him- or herself. Everyone agrees that in certain circumstances, such as panic stops in low-traction conditions, ABS can be a lifesaver. Unlike the automotive industry, which has universally accepted ABS, there has been enough

controversy over the use of ABS on motorcycles to keep it from becoming universally accepted as a positive technology. While most manufacturers have experimented with ABS, by the turn of the century only BMW and Honda continued to offer motorcycles equipped with the system. Honda offers the system on a few select touring or sport-touring models, while BMW makes it available on most models.

PARIS-DAKAR

For the 1990 model year, BMW decided to capitalize on its success in the grueling Paris-Dakar rally and marketed a Paris-Dakar version of its popular R100GS. This was not the first such model offered. BMW built a Paris-Dakar version of the R80G/S in 1984 to commemorate the Dakar victories of BMW riders such as Hubert Auriol and Gaston Rahier. The 797-cc Paris-Dakar version of the R80G/S was a replica in only the most superficial sense. With its massive 8.3-gallon gas tank, solo seat, and luggage rack, the Paris-Dakar model visually resembled the works desert racer, but underneath it was pure R80G/S. The Paris-Dakar edition proved popular in Europe, where the G/S model had become BMW's best-selling motorcycle. Even though it was popular in Europe, BMW never exported the Paris-Dakar version to the United States, where the G/S model took longer to catch on.

Like its R80G/S Paris-Dakar ancestor, the R100GS Paris-Dakar featured visual cues that said "desert racer": solo seat with luggage rack, massive gas tank, and long-travel suspension. It also featured a frame-mounted fairing in place of the handlebar-mounted fly screen from the standard model, along with a thick aluminum skid plate underneath the engine, and tubular steel crash bars around the headlight, fairing, and cylinders. These served more than aesthetic functions should the rider feel like venturing off road aboard a machine weighing 550 pounds with its 9.3-gallon tank filled. Trail riding was within the realm of possibility, provided the trails were extremely well groomed and the rider had the sense not to fill the massive tank more than half full.

The big K1 fairing provided more wind protection than any other sportbike on the market.

SPORT-TOURING COMPETITION

BMW ended the 1980s a fairly prosperous company thanks to its introduction of several innovative new machines in rapid succession. Despite this, corporate management didn't need to consult an infomercial psychic to know it had some potential troubles brewing. One of the most worrisome problems facing the company was the slowing sales of its flagship K100 four-cylinder series.

Company engineers needed to address some basic design flaws in the overall K100 package to keep sales strong after the initial wave of interest in the new Beemers faded. As discussed in chapter 5, most of the problems were directly attributed to the layout of the engine. A combination of factors—high weight, soft suspension, short swingarm, rearward weight bias, and drive-shaft-related misbehavior—combined to make the handling of the bike less than secure when not ridden in a completely smooth fashion. Other problems included engine vibration and heat buildup behind the fairing. And while power output wasn't a problem, more power couldn't hurt, especially in the U.S. market.

As long as BMW was the only manufacturer building motorcycles specifically for the sport-touring market, the company could go its own way, fitting bikes with the suspensions corporate engineers thought the riders should have, and letting owners modify the bikes if they were arrogant enough to disagree with said engineers. The fact that owners almost universally modified their machines, installing stiffer fork springs and aftermarket rear shocks with better rebound and damping control, only meant that most owners didn't get it.

But a funny thing happened the year after BMW brought its first K bikes over to the United States: The company found it had some Asian competition in the sport-touring market. In 1986, Kawasaki introduced the ZG1000 Concours, a shaft-driven, hard-bag-equipped sport-tourer powered by a 997-cc liquid-cooled in-line four-cylinder, although one laid out in conventional upright transverse fashion. The Concours, which cost less than two-thirds of the K100LT, was more than one second quicker in the quarter mile, stomped the BMW in the handling department, and was at least as comfortable on the long haul. When *Motorcyclist* compared the two bikes in its September 1986 issue, the magazine's editors concluded, "The Concours is the new king. The new Kawasaki has the stronger motor, better suspension, sharper handling (up to the 100-mile

THE MOST GRUELING RALLY IN THE WORLD

First run in 1978, the Paris-Dakar rally is one of the most grueling endurance events ever conceived, sending riders through some of the most inhospitable terrain on the planet. Originally run from Paris, France, across the Mediterranean Sea by ferry, then through the African countries of Algeria, Nigeria, Mali, and Senegal, the rally route has shifted over the years to accommodate the unstable political landscape of Africa. Because of changes in the route, it is now known as the Grenada-Dakar rally, but most people just call it "Dakar."

Almost since its inception, BMW motorcycles have been extremely competitive at Dakar, winning in 1981, 1983, 1984, 1985, 1999, and 2000. The highly specialized bikes BMW races in this event bear only the most superficial resemblance to the street-going Paris-Dakar motorcycles the company has sold over the years. While the street versions might lack the alloy frames of the racing versions, as well as their heavily breathed on engines, full knobby tires, and dual fuel tanks, they also lack the six-digit price tags of the works racers. These versatile street-going replicas do offer one of the richest racing heritages in all of motorcycling.

While BMW intended to compete in the sportbike market, in reality, it was more of a sport-tourer.

per hour mark) and better rider accommodations. For about two grand less, that sounds like a good deal to us." Staffer Mitch Boehm called the Concours "the most practical, useful and competent motorcycle made," and editor Art Friedman said it was superior to the BMW in "almost every aspect imaginable."

It would not do for a Japanese upstart to beat BMW's flagship motorcycle like a redheaded stepchild, so BMW engineers turned the full force of their industrious Germanic natures to the problem of improving the firm's four-cylinder K bikes. In addition to the antilock brakes, which finally became available on production machines for the 1989 model year, BMW engineers made numerous improvements to the four-cylinder K bikes. Specifically, they improved the sporting capabilities of the biggest K bikes, drawing on lessons learned from the popular K75S.

When *Motorcyclist* compared the K100RS Special against the Concours, Yamaha's redesigned FJ1200, and Suzuki's GSX1100F Katana in 1989, the K bike was a significantly improved unit from the one the magazine had tested three years earlier. A stiffer yet better-controlled suspension at both ends improved the bike's handling, and lighter pistons helped reduce vibration. Pinned piston rings eased the longstanding problem of smoky start-ups. The rings were combined with a complex labyrinth of air passages designed to keep crankcase oil from being drawn into the combustion chambers by the vacuum created by the cooling engine (a system built under license from Citroën). The most flamboyant technological upgrade to the Special version of the K100RS was the inclusion of BMW's futuristic ABS system.

The Concours had only received minor tweaking to make the riding position more comfortable, but the fact the magazine now had four machines to test in the sport-touring category instead of just two meant the market was becoming more competitive. Performance-wise, the K100RS faired better against the competition than had the earlier K100RT. The one area where the K bike got its pretty pearlescent white-and-blue behind spanked was in value. The ABS-equipped version of the K100RS tipped the financial scales at a breath-taking $11,790, plus another $440 for color-matched luggage, putting the cost of Special ownership to more than $12 grand, almost double the price of any of its competitors.

SPECIAL K

In the summer of 1989, BMW kicked up its K program another notch. While BMW had made a comeback by marketing sport-tourers and adventure-tourers, Japanese sport

bikes and the technology war those bikes instigated defined the 1980s motorcycle market. Beginning with Honda's remarkable 1983 V45 Interceptor, Japanese motorcycles revolutionized the sportbike concept. The 1984 ZX900 Ninja brought to the street the full-coverage bodywork long associated with racing motorcycles. A year later (two years in the U.S. market) Suzuki's GSX-R series one-upped Kawasaki and brought actual racing technology to the street. Honda introduced the aluminum parameter-beam frame with the 1986 VFR750, and Yamaha gave us five-valve cylinder heads with its FZ and FZR models. As the decade ended, BMW decided to take a shot at this hottest of motorcycle markets.

The resulting K1, BMW's interpretation of a sport bike was, to say the least, unique. For starters, it used a driveshaft instead of a chain to transmit power to the rear wheel. By this time the Japanese had completely abandoned all attempts to build shaft-driven sportbikes. Chain technology improved

LEFT: Although BMW updated the overall styling of the K bikes, the 987cc and 1092cc versions lacked the overall integrated styling that would define the company's motorcycles after David Robb took over as chief designer. These were still very much motorcycles with fairings tacked on.

FAR LEFT: This striking two-tone paint job was available on the Special Edition version of the K1100RS, produced for the 1995 model year.

exponentially over the 1980s and the convenience offered by driveshafts no longer outweighed the penalties they imposed in handling and unsprung weight, at least on high-performance motorcycles. While BMW was unable to completely disobey the laws of physics and decrease the unsprung weight of its shaft-drive system, the company's clever Paralever system helped it do a fair job of disobeying those same physical laws when it came to handling.

The K1 used four valves per cylinder rather than two. Since the Japanese competition had been using four-valve systems for the better part of a decade, this was not in any way remarkable. In fact, many observers felt the K series should have had four-valve cylinder heads from the very beginning. The engine also included other detail improvements, like a lighter crankshaft and pistons

and a higher compression ratio. The fuel injection system, the use of which was still fairly unique at the time, also received some attention. The antilock brake system from the K100RS Special, optional in most markets but standard on K1s bound for the United States, added both technology and weight to the new K bike. A new, stronger (and heavier) subframe tied all this future tech together, and when combined with the Paralever rear suspension, added 2.1 inches to the K1's wheelbase.

Technology aside, what was most remarkable about the K1, shocking even, was its outrageous styling. The unusual shapes of the fender, fairing, fuel tank, and tail pod were the results of long hours in BMW's wind tunnel. The goal of the design was to achieve the best possible compromise between aerodynamics and rider protection. For the most part

the design worked as intended, though the heat buildup behind the fairing bordered on unbearable in warm weather. The riding position enforced by the seat also prohibited the kind of hanging off needed to make really quick time down a snaky road when riding such a long, heavy motorcycle. The bodywork was effective in making the bike stand out in a crowd, though. No motorcycle ever built before or since looked anything like the K1.

Style was the main commodity marketed by the new BMW. At 613 pounds with a full tank of gas, the K1, with its claimed 100 crankshaft horsepower, couldn't hope to compete on a pure performance level with the open-class wonderbikes being created in Japan. It couldn't even compete with the 600-cc sportbikes coming from the Far East, bikes that weighed 25 percent less than the behemoth Beemer and cost 60 percent less than the $12,990 big K. But if you wanted a bike that looked like no other, the K1 was your machine. For most people, though, the K1 was a better bike to look at than to ride or to own.

BUILDING A BETTER BRICK

While the K1 was not exactly a failure, BMW's entry into the competitive open-class sport market failed to make much of an impact. BMW planned to produce at least 4,000 K1s per year, but over the machine's three-year production run BMW only built 6,919 examples of its space-cadet sport bike.

Although it wasn't a marketing success, the technology developed for the K1 filtered down and improved BMW's overall four-cylinder line-up. In 1990, the K100RS received the updated four-cylinder engine and Paralever rear suspension from the K1. Because the RS weighed 20 pounds less than the K1 and had a more rational seating position, the four-valve K100RS came closer to the sporting ideal than the K1.

The following year the long-suffering K100LT received the paralever suspension and four-valve engine, though in LT form the cylinders had been bored out to a slightly oversquare 70.5-millimeter, giving a total capacity of 1,085-cc. This necessitated a new name, so the K100LT became the K1100LT. A year later the RS model received the same overbore, resulting in the K1100RS.

By the time BMW introduced the 1,085-cc versions of the four-cylinder K bikes, its flying bricks had established a reputation as competent but not terribly exciting long-distance tools. Meanwhile, the competition continued to improve. In the spring of 1990, Honda released the ST1100, a transverse V-four that was a shot across BMW's sport-touring bow. The big Honda was as good as or better than BMW's bricks by any objective measurement: acceleration, top speed, handling, braking, and even reliability. And the ST1100 was more affordable than the K1100RS, the Honda's closest rival. In 1993, the ABS-equipped K1100RS cost $13,990, while the ST1100, which featured a traction-control system in addition to ABS, listed for $11,399.

The company was in relatively good shape as it entered its seventh decade, but BMW's sales success was not consistent across its entire motorcycle line-up. The GS version of the 980-cc Airhead boxer thrived, but the other big boxers sold poorly. BMW sold just 5,482 resurrected R100RS models in the five years it produced the machine, and just 8,346 R100RT models in eight years of producing that bike. The K models sold in respectable numbers, especially the four-cylinder RS versions, but many people still preferred boxers to flying bricks, no matter how much BMW improved the bricks. As a result, the relatively refined and inexpensive R80RT sold fairly well, providing diehard boxer fans with an unpretentious alternative to the bricks. The success of the R80RT illustrated the challenges BMW faced. When he tested the R80RT for *Motorcyclist* magazine, editor Art Friedman cut to the heart of the problem facing BMW: "At the risk of sounding reactionary, I have to say that I like BMW's twin better than its four."

It seemed BMW could do nothing to woo boxer fans over to the K-side. In a 1988 road test of the flawed R100RS, *Motorcyclist*'s Friedman again echoed the sentiments of many hard-core boxer fanatics: "Given the choice, I choose the twin over the four in a minute. The twin has its foibles, but it has far fewer foibles than the K100s I've ridden." BMW continued to tweak the K bikes, and boxer aficionados continued to prefer boxers. In a June 1990 *Motorcyclist* multibike comparison of luxury-touring motorcycles, the R100RT bested the K100LT in the handling portion of the test.

It was clear that while the flying bricks had a place in BMW's model line-up, they would never replace the boxers. To keep trying to force the issue would lead the company to oblivion. By the time the 1990 comparison test appeared in *Motorcyclist*, BMW was starting to see the results of abandoning boxers for K bikes. In their individual comments, not one test rider mentioned either BMW model. Once again, BMW was falling off the enthusiast's radar.

139

CHAPTER 7

THE OILHEAD

Over the years, the K bikes gained a loyal following, but sales hadn't met company expectations. BMW hoped to sell 10,000 motorcycles a year in the U.S. market. The flying bricks were intended to account for the bulk of those sales, yet the R100GS and R80RT, with their ancient air-cooled, pushrod boxer twin powerplants, proved to be the company's most popular models. It was clear that if BMW hoped to achieve its goals, it would have to do so by offering something other than multicylinder motorcycles that competed head-to-head with the Japanese.

BMW responded by introducing the R100R, a street-only version of its popular GS model stripped of its desert-rally trappings. The bike proved an interesting styling exercise, combining the avant-garde GS mechanicals, including the highly regarded Paralever rear suspension, with retro touches, most notably the unpainted valve covers last seen on the /6 series.

THE THIRD COMING OF THE SINGLE

BMW's next new bike proved even more surprising than any of the K bikes, and even more of a departure from the company established way of creating motorcycles. With the F650, BMW threw out every corporate tradition. For starters, it developed the machine in conjunction with another company. BMW had begun working with Italian manufacturer Aprilia on product distribution and technical development in 1989. In 1990, after seeing Aprilia's Pegaso 650, which was then under development,

ABOVE: The most innovative aspect of the new Oilhead series was its Telelever front suspension.

LEFT: The bike that started the Oilhead revolution: the R1100RS.

The F650 reintroduced many riders to the pleasures of a lightweight single-cylinder motorcycle.

management decided a 650-cc class single cylinder was just the entry-level machine BMW needed.

To minimize development costs, BMW decided to design the new machine in conjunction with Aprilia, basing it on the Pegaso. Because the Berlin plant was operating at full capacity, BMW decided to have Aprilia manufacture the F650 as well. Once such taboos as using outside designers and outside manufacturing facilities had been broken, managers of project E169,

as BMW coded the F650 program, began throwing out BMW traditions willy-nilly. First to go was the driveshaft, making the F650 BMW's first ever chain-driven motorcycle.

The bike that emerged from all this taboo breaking was remarkably mainstream. It shared its liquid-cooled, Rotax-built 652-cc single-cylinder engine with the Pegaso, though in the BMW the engine featured four valves per cylinder while the Aprilia featured five valves. Fed by a pair of 33-millimeter

Mikuni carburetors, the engine pumped out an impressive 42.5 horsepower and 39.2 pounds of torque at the rear wheel, enough to propel the 444-pound thumper through the quarter mile in 13.64 seconds. It managed to do this in spite of being fitted with a catalytic converter, an item that found its way on to all BMW motorcycles in the 1990s. A counterbalancer buried within the engine cases meant that this single-cylinder powerplant was smoother than BMW's four-cylinder K bikes at speed.

BMW produced two versions of the F650, the Funduro (yes, unfortunately that was the actual name of the bike), which had vague pretensions toward being a dual sport, and the Strada, which means "street" in Italian. In reality, both bikes were designed for road use. Besides a few minor alterations in body-work, the only real difference between the two models was the diameter of the front rim. The Funduro featured a 19-inch hoop in front, while the Strada featured an 18-incher.

Though it is the sportiest BMW ever built, the R1100S is still comfortable enough for a transcontinental tour.

Although the F650 was marketed as a dual-sport, it's off-road capabilities were marginal, at best.

BMW introduced the F650 at the September 1993 Frankfurt International Auto Show. Observers were stunned, not so much by the motorcycle they viewed, but by the fact that such a machine had been built by BMW. This was a company that adhered to its traditions with fanatical rigidity, and here it was producing a motorcycle that threw out every one of those sacred traditions. But it worked. All that tradition bending resulted in a competent machine. The little single was nimble, quick, comfortable, and handled well. Being a BMW meant you could even get optional hard luggage. It was inexpensive by BMW standards, though it was still expensive compared to its competition. When BMW finally brought the F650 to the United States three years after showing it in Frankfurt, the bike cost $7,490.

BMW didn't bring the F650 to the U.S. market until late in 1996 because BMWNA wasn't interested in an entry-level model. The best-selling BMWs in the United States remained the most expensive models, as had always been the case with the U.S. market. But European sales of the BMW singles were so strong—BMW sold 30,000 copies in the first three years of production—that BMWNA relented and imported the F650 for the 1997 model year.

Test riders in American magazines, accustomed to every larger and more complex motorcycle, rediscovered the thrill of riding a lightweight single when they finally had the chance to test the F650. As an off-road mount, the new 427-pound motorcycle was a failure, barely better than the 550-pound Paris-Dakar version of the R100GS. But despite

The new Oilhead engine
would power BMW's
boxer motorcycles into
the 21st century.

THE F650 AND THE FALL OF THE BERLIN WALL

Part of the reason BMW was able to cooperate with Aprilia to such an extent on designing and building the F650 was because by the time the F650 project began, Berlin was no longer a capitalistic island in Communist East Germany. In fact, by the time Project E169 began, there no longer was an East Germany. The infamous Berlin Wall that separated West Berlin from the rest of the world no longer existed.

The Berlin Wall came into being at 2 A.M. on August 13, 1961, when a low, barbed-wire barrier was strung between East and West Berlin, dividing the city in half. Within days, East German workers replaced the barbed wire with a concrete structure. Over the years the wall was rebuilt at least three times, each time becoming bigger and stronger, and more of a logistical problem for BMW's motorcycle operations.

On November 9, 1989, the wall came down, torn apart brick by brick by people from both sides of Berlin. In 1990, the German Democratic Republic ceased to exist. East Germany was once again reunited with West Germany. The citizens of the former German Democratic Republic were free from decades of repressive Stalinistic governmental control. And BMW was free to pursue alternative methods of building motorcycles, because it was no longer operating its plant on a free-market island surrounded by a totalitarian state.

the 19-inch front tire of the Funduro version, no one really expected the F650 to be a dirt bike. "Let's face it," R. S. Griffith wrote in his comments about the F650 in *Motorcyclist* magazine's first full road test of the BMW thumper, "as nice as fantasies of roosting in the Baja 500 or Paris-Dakar may be—where do you *really* spend most of your saddle time?" The answer was, of course, on the street. As a streetbike, the BMW was a featherweight, with nimble handling that let the little thumper run with top-notch sportbikes when the roads turned to spaghetti.

"I don't think I've ever cornered anything harder through the Ortega Highway's canyons than I did with this BMW," Dave Searle wrote in *Motorcycle Consumer News'* test of the F650.

Motorcycle Consumer News editor Lee Parks also praised the F650. "On paper this motorcycle is pretty uninspiring with its one cylinder, quirky styling and 427-lb weight," Parks wrote. "Once out in its element, however, I was a converted man." Parks reserved his highest praise for the bike's handling: "Perhaps the most impressive aspect of the ST (Strada) is its ability to straighten

RIGHT: The head that gave the Oilhead its name. Notice the scars on the valve covers. While the new Oilhead was narrower than the old Airhead, the excellent handling of the new Oilheads made incredible lean angles possible.

FAR RIGHT: Over the years BMW has refined its Paralever suspension nearly to the point of perfection.

tight roads as well as many top-line sportbikes, and to do so with less physical and mental effort."

Like the 30,000 Europeans who had bought F650s prior to the model's trek across the Atlantic, *Motorcyclist* magazine gave the bike "a big, ol' Siskel-and-Ebert thumbs up. It's a great motorcycle that need not confine itself to the entry-level ranks. Many a grizzled vet could have quite a romp on this thumper."

BUILDING A BETTER BOXER

Bikes like the F650 and the various Airhead boxers proved strong sellers for BMW. Sales of the R80RT and R100GS remained strong, and the new boxer models added more to BMW's bottom line. BMW sold almost 21,000 copies of the various R100R versions, but BMW's management knew the company couldn't bank on its 70-year-old Airhead design forever. People wanted boxers, but various environmental and noise regulations meant that BMW could only produce the existing design for a finite amount of time.

Designing a new boxer was a difficult proposition. The technology itself wasn't that daunting. The problem facing BMW was that it had to design a new boxer engine that maintained a link to the company's 70-year history while at the same time using technology every bit as modern as that used by the company's Japanese competition. Harley-Davidson had faced a similar dilemma when designing a replacement for its ancient Shovelhead V-twin engine. Harley's answer had been to build a virtual replica of the old cast-iron powerplant, only using modern materials and manufacturing techniques. BMW had already gone that route when it introduced the /5 series in 1969.

What few people realized at the time was that BMW had been working on a new generation boxer for years. In 1984, one year after introducing the K series, BMW engineers began working in earnest on an engine that would later be given the code R259. The original parameters of the project were that the engine would be a longitudinal boxer with the cylinders stuck out in the cooling air stream, just as God and Max Friz intended. This would eliminate the need for a heavy and bulky liquid cooling system. Instead, the new engine relied on a combination of air and oil to keep operating temperatures within reason. BMW used two separate oil pumps, one to circulate lubricating oil, and a second to circulate cooling oil through cooling passages around engine hot spots like the exhaust valves. This system led to the new engine earning the nickname "Oilhead." The engine would be connected to the transmission through an automotive-type dry clutch, like every motorcycle BMW had ever built, and like all other Beemers, it would pass its power to the rear wheel via a driveshaft.

K-bike engine designer Stefan Pachernegg, who was BMW's chief of motorcycle development at the time, headed

a developmental team working on the new engine design. The main problem the team encountered involved creating a four-valve cylinder head that adhered to state-of-the-art cylinder filling theories without being overly wide and cumbersome. The system also had to be reasonably economical to manufacture. Using a conventional double-overhead-camshaft design would lead to an engine that was far too wide for adequate ground clearance, regardless of how oversquare the bore-and-stroke ratio was, so the team had to come up with an alternative design.

In 1986, Georg Emmersberger, one of the engineers on the team, finally developed a valvetrain that met performance, packaging, and manufacturing criteria. This "combined valve actuation" system, as BMW calls it, features a single cam located low in each cylinder head, down by the valve seats. These cams operated forked rocker arms through short lifters, and the rockers in turn each opened two valves. While this cam-in-head system limited ultimate engine redline a bit, it still allowed the engine to rev higher than any pushrod Airhead, and it was suitably compact for the boxer design.

With the R259 powerplant, BMW abandoned the one-piece tunnel engine case, a design that had come to define the look of BMW engines. Instead, the new Oilhead used a pressure die-cast, two-piece, vertically split crankcase that could be produced more efficiently and economically than the old tunnel design. Like the post-1980 Airheads, the Oilhead engine featured a nickel-silicon coating on the cylinder walls.

ABOVE: The Oilhead GS bikes have become favorite motorcycles for riders competing in the grueling Iron Butt Rally.

FAR LEFT: The R1150GS may look like an adventure-tourer capable of conquering far-flung continents, and it is, but it is also an excellent sporting mount.

TELELEVER

The new R259 Oilhead engine was innovative, but the motorcycle that would ultimately bear that engine was far more so. Take, for instance, the frame, a difficult assignment, given there was no frame of which to speak. The stout aluminum drivetrain composed the frame, with a modern rendition of the Paralever rear suspension pivoting in the transmission case. BMW motorcycle designer Wolfgang Seehaus devised this clever and effective system. A steel subframe supporting the seat bolted to the top of the engine and transmission cases, and another subframe bolted to the front of the engine cases supported the steering head. This front subframe provided little structural support because the front wheel was supported by perhaps the most innovative feature of all: the Telelever front suspension.

BMW had a long history of using alternative front suspension technology. The company had built the world's first production bikes with telescopic forks, the R12 and R17, in 1935. But the telescopic fork had always presented inherent compromises such as dive under braking. The Earles forks of the 1950s and 1960s had been designed to eliminate most of the problems associated with telescopic forks, but they had presented their own set of compromises, namely high unsprung weight and slow, heavy steering.

The Telelever circumvented most compromises associated with either telescopic or Earles-type forks. A conventional telescopic fork performs the combined functions of steering, wheel suspension, springing and damping, transfer of steering forces, and countering of brake movements. To cope with the ever-increasing demands of ever higher performing motorcycles, telescopic forks steadily increased in size and weight. The Telelever design removed all the functions except steering from the fork tubes. As a result, BMW ceased calling the tubes a "fork," and instead began referring to it as a "front wheel alignment system."

RIGHT: Many people consider the Roadster versions of the Oilhead series some of the best all-around motorcycles BMW has ever built. Shown here is a 2002 R1150R.

FAR RIGHT: Although aimed at the luxury-touring market, the R1100RT Oilhead handled so well it was compared favorably to sport-touring bikes.

The heart of the Telelever suspension consisted of an A frame attached to a ball joint above the front fender. This A frame becomes the central load-bearing structure. At the base of the A frame, a single central shock absorber handles the remaining fork functions. This has the potential of eliminating brake dive entirely, just as the old Earles fork design had done, though BMW engineered in some brake dive just to make the bike feel more like a traditional motorcycle under braking. And rather than adding extra unsprung weight, as the Earles fork had done, this system actually eliminated unsprung weight.

Thinking the K bikes would cover the big-bike range, BMW originally intended to make the new boxer a midlevel 800-cc-class machine, but as development progressed, it became apparent that, while relatively popular, the K bikes' appeal would always be somewhat limited. Many BMW fans wanted boxers, and only boxers, and they wanted the top-of-the-line models to be boxers, so early in the design process BMW reconfigured the R259 design with an oversquare bore-and-stroke ratio of 99 millimeters by 70.5 millimeters, giving a displacement of 1,085 cc.

BMW introduced the R1100RS, the first of the Oilhead models, to the motorcycle press in early 1993, 70 years after the company had first displayed Max Friz' R32. For years BMW motorcycles had impressed the press, but never before had the company created this much excitement. From its unique suspension to its unique chassis to its adjustable seat, windshield, footpegs, and handlebar, this was a motorcycle unlike any the assembled editors had ever witnessed. When the bike reached production the following year, *Motorcyclist* magazine gave the R1100RS its "Bike of the Year" award.

The magazine's assessment of the bike generally mirrored the views of the world's collective motorcycling press:

"When it's all bolted together, the new hardware results in a motorcycle so excruciatingly well balanced that it just had to be our Bike of the Year. There's power there to push the bike up to 136 miles per hour and sprint a quarter-mile in 12.48 seconds at 108.9 miles per hour. There's precise handling, sportbike steering quickness, excellent suspension—so anyone who can't get comfortable on the ergonomically adjustable boxer should stay home on the BarcaLounger. There is good fairing protection and hard saddlebags that lock with the same key as the ignition. Excellent ABS II is available for a few dollars more, too—all in a beautifully wrapped package weighing only 520 pounds."

GELÄNDSTRASSE, TAKE THREE

BMW quickly followed up the success of the R1100RS with other Oilhead models. For the 1995 model year, the company introduced a *Geländstrasse* version, the R1100GS. With its juxtaposition of graceful, sweeping lines and rugged angles, the new GS looked unlike anything the motorcycling world had ever seen. The bike looked all the more peculiar thanks to the fact that its advanced Telelever front suspension was exposed rather than hidden by bodywork, as on the R1100RS model. Add to that a large beak-like fender mounted high, as on a dirt bike, and the look became even more interesting. *Motorcyclist* magazine described the bike as "a visually high-impact motorcycle." In his personal comments on the bike, former editor Art Friedman echoed the sentiment of many observers and called the bike "ugly."

Most observers were more charitable in their opinion of the bike, preferring the adjective "purposeful" to describe the bike's appearance. Purposeful it was. The world may have still been acclimating itself to the appearance of the Telelever suspension, but no one quibbled with its effectiveness. Every aspect of the bike had been designed with functional considerations overriding aesthetic concerns. "The design statement as a whole underlies its functionality," BMW designer David Robb told *Motorcyclist* when it first tested the new GS. "This model should communicate its function and its personality through its look. It would be inappropriate if it looked cute. I think of this bike as a very handsome, well-functioning tool." Robb used the above-mentioned duck-bill front fender to illustrate the form-follows-function approach his team took when designing the GS. He said the fender was mounted where it was to protect the oil cooler, which was mounted below the headlight. It was shaped the way it was to provide clean airflow to the cooler. The shape also applied downforce on the front tire at high speeds. "Definitely not just cosmetic," Robb said.

Robb's vision of the BMW proved to be more prophetic than Friedman's view. The sheer purposefulness of the machine grew on even its most vocal critics, and after a while the inner beauty of the design overpowered its initial strangeness. In a 1998 test of the bike, *Motorcycle Consumer News* editor Lee Parks

summed up this progression of opinion toward the big GS: "When the GS came out in '94, I thought it was one of the ugliest bikes ever made, but my strange eccentric nature now finds it … I can't believe I'm saying this … beautiful."

If ever there was an adventure-tourer that a rider did not want to take on a Supercross track, the 572-pound R1100GS was that bike. "Sliding around on this behemoth has much in common with rattlesnake ranching, hanging out with Jeffrey Dahmer or dating Lorena Bobbitt," John Burns wrote in *Motorcyclist*'s September 1984 road test of the R1100GS. Of course, the weight of the big bike included 6.6 gallons of gas, which meant the remarkable new GS had a range of more than 300 miles per tank, just the ticket for serious adventure touring.

The R1100GS might not have been capable of tackling the triple jumps on a Supercross track, but it was more than sturdy enough to tackle mountain fire roads or the most rugged, unpaved sections of the Trans Alaskan Highway. "It's a very sturdy bike, engineered to take on a lot," Robb told *Motorcyclist*. "It won't let you down."

BMW may have built the ultimate adventurer-tourer in the R1100GS, but what surprised many people was that the bike handled stretches of twisty pavement as well as many top-notch sport bikes. Burns' fellow *Motorcyclist* staffer Tim Carrithers was one of the first journalists to catch on to this aspect of the machine. Carrithers wrote: "You'd never know to look at it, but BMW's newest GS is as close as I've come to the ultimate sport-bike. Huh? What? Granted, your average fully faired, race-replica ego massage unit carves up curvy pavement amazingly well. But so does the GS; up to 300 miles per sitting. And it's even more fun on bumpy pavement or broken pavement or no pavement at all."

ROADSTERS

BMW also introduced unfaired roadster versions of the Oilhead in 1995. The R1100R and its sibling, the R850R, an 848-cc version of the bike created by retaining the 70.5-millimeter stroke but using an 87.8-millimeter bore, were basically just R1100GS models stripped of all superfluous bodywork.

Magazine testers raved about the R1100R. *Motorcyclist* called it "one of the easiest bikes out there to ride quickly." The magazine began its March 1995 road test of the new Oilhead roadster by asking, "Does the spinning propeller logo and lack of paint-splashed plastic conjure up the 'b' word? Boring? A bike for old guys? Good. That's just the way us 'old guys' like it, and when one of us riding an R-bike grows big in your mirrors on some twisty mountain road and leaves your neon-pink crotch rocket for dead, then you may begin the journey to enlightenment."

The editors' individual comments were even more enthusiastic. Kent Kunitsugo called the bike "pure fun," and Art Friedman wrote that he was "dazzled."

"This is the best-handling BMW ever—by a significant margin," Friedman wrote. "It works fabulously. Everybody should have one."

Perhaps John Burns best summed up the new roadsters appeal: "This bike combines everything there is to like about motorcycles in a simple package capable of embarrassing most 'sportbikes' on a curvy road."

The 848-cc version of the roadster wasn't as well received as its bigger brother. While BMW priced the R850 at $1,000 less than the base 1,085-cc R1100R, the only real difference between producing the two was the size of the holes in the cylinder barrels (87.8-millimeter versus 99-millimeter). Which meant the cost of producing both bikes was almost identical, so that $1,000 savings had to come straight from the profit margin.

For 1,000 fewer U.S. dollars the buyer received a bike that weighed exactly the same as the R1100R, with exactly the same chassis measurements, but one producing 11 fewer horsepower and almost 17 foot-pounds less torque. While the R850R could make short work of the quarter mile (12.62 seconds at 102.8 miles per hour), doing so required revving the engine to within a millimeter of its life. "The baby boxer never feels happy revved up where it needs to be for recognizable acceleration," Tim Carrithers wrote in *Motorcyclist's* road test of the 850.

While hard core sport riders like *Motorcyclist* staffers Kent Kunitsugu and John Burns raved about the sporting capabilities of the R1100R, comparing it to Ducati's Monster, they were at best lukewarm to the R850R, as were most motorcyclists. It seemed people would rather pay $10,000 for a great motorcycle than pay $9,000 for a mediocre motorcycle. The model sold poorly and was withdrawn from the market after just two years of production.

The year 1995 saw not only the introduction of the R1100GS, R1100R, and R850R, but the end of the road for the old airhead boxers, and it was for real this time. BMW dropped all airhead models except the R80GS Basic, an updated version of the original R80G/S, which remained in production for the German market for a couple of years more. When the biggest boxers originally disappeared in 1984, a huge public outcry had brought them back to life. This time airhead boxer fans remained dead silent. The new Oilheads were that good.

NO K85?

Another BMW motorcycle series that bought the farm in the mid-1990s was the K75 triple family. After producing a small production run of K75 models in 1996, the triple faded away after an 11-year production run. On the surface, the decision to cancel the popular triples seemed odd. BMW had sold 64,577 of the various K75 versions since the introduction of the

BUILDING A CHEAPER BEEMER

BMW created the R850R as a motorcycle for the masses, a less expensive Beemer for people who couldn't afford the 1,085-cc Oilhead boxers. Yet the more expensive bikes sold extremely well while the less expensive—and less capable—848-cc model languished on showroom floors. BMW soon dropped the model from its line-up.

Such had been the fate with almost all decontented motorcycles produced by the German firm over its long history. The R850R illustrated a problem that had long plagued BMW: the problem of building affordable entry-level motorcycles. Even when BMW had produced its shaft-driven single-cylinder motorcycles, those motorcycles were basically replicas of the company's twins with one cylinder lopped off. If BMW was ever to provide a truly entry-level bike that had something unique to offer, it would have to rethink its long-held entry level strategy.

This is what the company did with the F650 series. The F650 was indeed the least expensive motorcycle in BMW's line-up, thanks to the innovative cost-sharing system with Aprilia, but the little BMW thumper could not be considered inexpensive by any standard. When introduced to the U.S. market in 1997, the F650 cost $7,490. By comparison, Kawasaki's KLR650, a dual-sport single with specifications similar to BMW's F650, sold for $4,999. In 2002, the F650GS started at $8,190. Adding ABS to the option list brought the price up to $8,690. The street-only F650CS topped out at $9,190 with ABS. The 2002 Kawasaki—admittedly unchanged since the 1997 model year—still listed for $4,999. BMW, it seems, will never be able to produce a truly inexpensive entry-level machine for the price-conscious novice rider.

series in 1986. The K75RT, a model that featured a larger touring fairing, had proven especially popular, selling 18,878 units since its introduction for the 1991 model year.

BMW's triple still held its own against the Japanese competition. In a 1995 comparison test between the K75S, Honda's VFR750, and Suzuki's Katana 750, *Motorcyclist* magazine gave the old K bike generally positive reviews. As would be expected, the BMW was the best touring mount of the bunch. Staffer Tim Carrithers wrote, "The BMW is the smoothest, most comfortable mount for crossing a few state lines before nightfall."

But the BMW also fared well in the sport part of the sport-touring equation. "[The K75S] can be thrown into corners with almost as much (w)reckless abandon as the others, with full confidence," the magazine reported. "You're not going to get there *ahead* of the Katana or VFR unless you're truly talented, but you're not going to be embarrassed by them, either. None of that really matters anyway, does it, because you'll be a beautiful Wagnerian goddess in a helmet with horns when you arrive and they never will."

It may have still been a competent motorcycle, but the decision to cancel the three-cylinder K bikes made perfect sense

The police version of the R1100RT sports a few unusual standard features including a Billy club, ticket book, and an on-board police radio.

155

The most successful of BMW's first eight decades occurred during the 1990s, and much of that success can be traced to one man: David Robb. Robb became BMW's chief motorcycle designer in 1993 at the ripe old age of 37. The aesthetic sensibilities he brought to the job helped shape some of the most popular motorcycles in the company's history.

Born in Boston, Robb spent his childhood living with his missionary parents in Kobe, Japan. At the age of 13, he returned to the United States, eventually graduating from high school in Texas. He earned a degree in transportation design from Pasadena's Art Center College, the same school where Ducati Monster designer Miguel Angel Galluzzi earned his degree.

Robb graduated in 1979 and went to work for Chrysler, where he was immediately laid off by the financially troubled company. His next job was with Germany's Audi. He jumped ship to BMW in 1984, where he worked on BMW's successful 3-series, 5-series, and 7-series cars. While working on BMW automobiles, Robb became heavily involved in bringing computer-aided design to the German company. It was during his time working on BMW automobiles that Robb became interested in motorcycles. When he went over to BMW's motorcycle operations in 1993, he brought his computer-aided design expertise with him.

Robb's greatest contribution to BMW design has been his integrated approach. All the motorcycles he's worked on—the R1100RT, the K1200RS, the R1200C, the R1100S, the K1200LT, and all their derivatives—have been characterized by a unity of design. Previous BMW's, like the original four-cylinder K bikes, began by designing a basic platform, then adding on parts as needed. Robb explained this approach in a May 1999 *Motorcyclist* article: "The K1100LT was something that was added onto. We wanted more comfort so we put another box [pannier] on, put some more wind protection on, added a radio." Robb said his preferred approach was to go back to the basics, ask the customer, "What would you like? What do you expect?" then design a motorcycle where every part works together to meet those expectations.

As his first decade as BMW's chief designer drew to a close, Robb elaborated on this philosophy: "When we start a project, we try to look at the big picture. For example, we ask ourselves, 'What does luxury mean? Are we offering that? Should we offer that?'" Robb says the key to answering such questions depends on the people who will ride the motorcycle. "A lot of motorcycle design only happens when you add the human interface." To understand how the bike and rider interact requires lots of what Robb calls "the three R's: riding, riding, riding."

from a marketing standpoint. The success of and potential for the Oilhead boxers meant that an updated triple would have created too much overlap in BMW's model line-up. Such a K bike would likely have cannibalized more sales from the popular Oilheads than it would have brought in new sales. Even so, fans of the smallest K bikes (of which there are many) mourn what might have been: an 820-cc, 12-valve triple with Paralever rear suspension and Telelever front suspension.

AN OILHEAD FOR THE LONG HAUL

Throughout the rest of the 1990s, BMW introduced new models at an almost Japanese pace. Next in line for the Oilhead treatment was the RT touring concept. The resulting R1100RT, introduced for the 1996 model year, was long expected. Fans assumed BMW would take the basic RS version, enlarge the fairing, give the bike a more upright riding position, and call it a day. They were partly right. The new RT was based on the R1100RS chassis and engine, as expected. The reason it took so long to get to market was because of the revolutionary way in which the motorcycle was packaged. The R1100RT design team, led by David Robb, had no intention of simply designing a new fairing around the basic R1100RS. "Design, in this case, is not something you put on top of the fairing," Robb told *Motorcyclist* magazine when it tested the RT for its February 1996 issue. "It *is* the fairing." Robb and his Teutonic posse had sculpted the RT as a solid piece.

Other manufacturers had tried the integrated bodywork concept. Honda's ST1100, PC800 Pacific Coast, and original CBR models all featured encompassing bodywork that blended together. Ducati tried the concept with its Paso series designed in the 1980s. Vincent had tried it back with the fully enclosed Black Knights and Black Princes from 1954 to 1955. With the possible exception of Honda's ST1100, the concept of a fully enclosed shrink-wrapped motorcycle hadn't been terribly successful. In fact, the Vincents had been such devastating failures that they helped drive the company into receivership. Thanks to its carefully sculpted organic lines that pleased on an aesthetic and a functional level, Robb's design worked. "The David Robb-led design team burned a lot of midnight oil arriving at this engaging blend of svelte organic curves and taut creases," *Motorcyclist* wrote in its first full road test of the new R1100RT.

Clever design touches abounded on the Oilhead interpretation of the RT concept. "It takes people who actually ride to figure out that a little row of 'teeth' under each mirror will divert jet-propelled raindrops before they end up in your lap," *Motorcyclist* noted. Add such seemingly minor details to the bike's major features, like adjustable ergonomics, adjustable windshield, and the very best hard luggage ever mounted on a motorcycle, and BMW had created one of the world's greatest long-distance motorcycles.

"This thing is possibly the most comfortable bike I've ever sat buns upon," *Motorcyclist*'s John Burns reported.

The mechanics of the bike worked too. Although the RT outweighed the R1100RS model, it masked the extra weight well, and only gave up a small penalty in overall performance for quite a bit of comfort in return. "There's enough usable power spread across the tach face from 2,000 to 7,000 rpm to roost triumphantly past the Anti-Destination Society with precious little shifting," *Motorcyclist* reported.

The R1100RS-based chassis meant that this was one of the best-handling touring bikes ever built. "The torque pump engine and stone-stable chassis put the latest RT near the top of the heavyweight sporty-touring class—and light years ahead of its forefathers—down any twisted road," *Motorcyclist* wrote.

The K1200RS addressed most of the complaints about the original Compact Drive System K series.

BMW's hard luggage continued to set the industry standard into the 21st century.

TOP RIGHT: The elegant detailing of the C model helped make it BMW's best-selling model in the U.S. market for 1998.

BOTTOM RIGHT: Perhaps the most controversial of all modern BMWs is the R1200C cruiser. Those who dislike the bike really hate it, while the people who like the bike really love it.

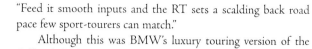

"Feed it smooth inputs and the RT sets a scalding back road pace few sport-tourers can match."

Although this was BMW's luxury touring version of the Oilhead platform, the R1100RT was compared to sport-touring bikes more often than it was compared to other touring bikes. To make matters worse for competition like Honda's ST1100, the R1100RT won those comparison tests as often as not. In a five-bike sport-touring comparison, *Motorcycle Consumer News* awarded the R1100RT first place. "For me, there's only one choice in this group—BMW's marvelous R1100RT," editor Lee Parks wrote. "The adjustable windscreen and seat, heated grips and incredible front end put the Beemer in a league of its own when it comes to versatility… and versatility is the key in the sport-touring world."

"When you're hard-pressed on a rough and twisty road," senior editor Fred Rau reported, "you don't want anything under you but BMW's Telelever suspension."

Contributor Marry Sorensen seconded Rau's assessment of BMW's Telelever system: "The incredibly stable front end on this motorcycle makes it handle like a much smaller bike through the twistiest mountain roads."

Motorcyclist even went as far as comparing the R1100RT with an all-out sportbike, Yamaha's YZF600R, in a four-bike comparison test that also included Honda's VFR800F Interceptor and Suzuki's Bandit 1200S. While putting the RT in such sporty company might seem like a set up for a sucker punch, the big BMW held its own, even when the road turned twisty. "As you begin to turn up the pace," the magazine reported, "the RT acts the willing partner. Those tall polished-aluminum handlebars exert tremendous leverage on BMW's trademark Telelever front suspension and cause the bike to heel over with just a whiff of grip effort. Better yet, the bike has neutral steering response; once leaned it tends to hold the lean angle without trying to stand up or fall in."

With the new RT, it seemed BMW had finally perfected the sport-touring formula, at least for a lot of riders. *Motorcyclist*'s Tim Carrithers explained the bike to the magazine's readers: "Think of the R1100RT as an all-day (or all-week or all-month) sportbike that lets you pack your jammies and sleep overnight."

BMW'S NEW BEHEMOTH

BMW surprised everyone with its next new model, which wasn't even based on the R259 Oilhead concept. Rather, for 1997 BMW introduced a completely revamped four-cylinder K bike. By October 1996, when BMW introduced the new K1200RS at the Cologne motorcycle show, the Oilhead had eclipsed the flying brick for so long that many people forgot BMW was even still making them. The striking new K1200RS brought to the K family all the technological advances BMW had made over the decade. In addition to featuring the latest iterations of the Paralever rear suspension and ABS system, the K1200RS brought BMW's Telelever design to the K bikes. This marked the first time the technology had been used outside the Oilhead family.

The new K bike was physically large, huge, really, weighing in at 643 pounds with its 5.5-gallon tank filled, but the new engine was more than up to the task of propelling all that bulk. It was the fastest motorcycle BMW had ever produced with its 111 rear-wheel horsepower and 79.1 foot-pounds of torque, which were transmitted to the rear wheel through a new Getrag-designed six-speed transmission. The K1200RS turned in a quarter-mile time of 11.77 seconds at a blistering 118 miles per hour, making it the

GERMANY'S GLASS HORSEPOWER CEILING

Building a 100-plus horsepower motorcycle meant BMW had to do more than just break technical barriers. It also had to break social barriers. In Germany, motorcycles were "voluntarily" restricted to 100PS (98.6 horsepower) in a sort of self-imposed censorship by motorcycle manufacturers. While there were never any provisions to enforce this glass horsepower ceiling, BMW always adhered to it. It seemed the firm agreed with the philosophy behind the limit. "We consider 57 hp sufficient for the majority of riders," Wilfried Kramm told *Motorcyclist* in October 1972.

When the magazine visited BMW's Berlin factory nine years later, that philosophy hadn't changed much. At the time, BMW management had decided a commitment to join the horsepower race raging in Japan was "counterproductive." This rationale still held sway over the powers that be at BMW when the new K series was designed. Part of the reason for the decision to go with an 8-valve cylinder head in the original K100 instead of a 16-valve cylinder head was because the 8-valve version met Germany's 100-horsepower limit. Anything more was deemed unnecessary.

The 1997 K1200RS, with its claimed 130 crankshaft horsepower, signified that BMW was finally abandoning its slavish adherence to horsepower self-censorship.

fastest sport-tourer on the market at the time. "The K12 puts out the kind of mid-range passing power the flashy BMW K-1 promised, but didn't deliver," *Motorcycle Consumer News* reported in its first full test of the new K1200RS.

The 1,171-cc engine received its displacement not through the normal process of boring the cylinders, because at 70.5-millimeters the cylinders were already bored to their limit. Instead, BMW engineers gave the crankshaft an additional 5 millimeters of stroke, making it once again unfashionably undersquare. Other than the increased stroke, the additional power came from the same-old same-old hot-rodding tricks BMW usually used, like steeper cams, increased compression, and lighter pistons.

One thing the engine didn't receive was a counterbalancer. Instead, BMW came up with a different solution for taming the buzz of its four-cylinder brick, one that meant abandoning the company's patented Compact Drive System. Unlike all the other new bikes BMW had introduced during the modern era, the new K1200RS had a frame. This consisted of a massive aluminum backbone section that ran from the steering head back to the transmission, where it split and ran around the transmission down to the swingarm pivot. This allowed the use of rubber engine mounts while retaining a stiff chassis. It also accounted for much of the extra weight of the new model.

The system worked as promised when it came to quelling engine vibes. "Fire up the RS and the first thing you notice is an absence of vibration," *Motorcycle Consumer News* noted. "We're

ABOVE: The C model sported the most unusual front suspension ever mounted on a cruiser. This unfaired Cruiser shows BMW's unique front suspension better than any other model. Note the aluminum frame tying the steering head to the engine.

RIGHT: BMW revived the S concept in 1998 when R1100S was introduced.

not talking just improved or fixed, we're talking Gold Wing country here."

When *Motorcyclist* tested the new K1200RS, the magazine questioned the use of the heavy frame to control engine vibration: "It makes you wonder if maybe a pair of counterbalancers inside the crankcases—as used in the comparably-sized-yet-90-pounds-lighter, ultra-smooth-running new CBR1100XX Honda—wouldn't work just as well?" The bike's weight became less of an issue when moving. "The K works surprisingly well in tight-road sport use," *Motorcyclist* noted. "But it's a bear when it comes time to turn the thing around in your garage or driveway." Many hot-shot sportbike riders have looked in their mirrors to see a whale of a BMW looming large and find they are unable to shake the beast, no matter how hard they push their own bikes. "For all its 643 pounds," *Motorcyclist* reported, "the thing is solid and sure-footed when thrown into bump-riddled, high-speed corners."

The K1200RS was one of the most difficult of all modern BMW motorcycles to categorize. "The K1200RS clearly suffers from an identity crisis," *Motorcycle Consumer News* concluded after testing the bike. "From the factory, everything you put your eyes on screams 'sportbike,' and sitting on it confirms that feeling. The K12 loves to go fast, but it is just too heavy to keep up with current open-class rocketships." Comparisons with the sportbikes of the time were inevitable because of the ergonomics of the K1200RS, which placed the rider in an almost race bike-like crouch. Although the

ergonomics were adjustable, *Motorcyclist* wrote they were adjustable in the way that the IRS offers various payment plans: "None are really comforting."

The machine's performance seemed to back up its sportbike intentions, but its bulk combined with the unusual ergonomics made the riding experience decidedly odd. *Motorcyclist* compared riding the K1200RS to "straddling some road-hugging cruise missile," like Slim Pickens in *Dr. Strangelove*.

But some people like a bike that is different. *Motorcycle Consumer News* editor Lee Parks wrote that the only real flaw in the K1200RS was "the uncharacteristically radical seating position," which, as he also noted, was fixable. And BMW has consistently worked to make the ergonomics of the K1200RS more humane. Over the years the most-sporting K bike has developed a dedicated following. Many riders agree with Fred Rau's personal opinion of the K1200RS published in *Motorcycle Consumer News'* first full road test: "I think this is one of the most perfect motorcycles I have ever ridden."

CRUISING

Next up on BMW's seemingly never-ending parade of new motorcycles was the R1200C. The "C" stood for "Cruiser," and the bike represented BMW's attempt to cash in on the lucrative U.S. market for cruiser-styled motorcycles. Harley-Davidson owns this market, and most companies seriously attempting to break into it do so by building a motorcycle that is as Harley-like as is possible without incurring the wrath of the H-D legal department. The U.S. market was historically unkind to cruisers that did not look like the Big Twins from Milwaukee.

BMW seemed an unlikely candidate to enter the cruiser wars. "When rumors first began circulating that BMW would enter the cruiser market, many of us in the industry refused to believe it," Fred Rau wrote in *Motorcycle Consumer News*. "A BMW cruiser? Isn't that an oxymoron? Could German engineers actually be coerced into intentionally 'dumbing down' one of their products? Would they castrate the revolutionary Type 259 engine and prostitute the vaunted Paralever and Telelever suspensions in the name of fashion?"

The answer to Fred's questions were, in order, yes, maybe, yes, yes, and sort of, but regarding the most important part of the question, BMW most definitely intended to enter the cruiser market. The move made sense. Cruisers comprised the largest category in the lucrative U.S. market, accounting for 33 percent of all motorcycles sold in 1996. The bike would, to a small degree, be technologically "dumbed down," as Rau feared, it's engine slightly "castrated" and its shaft-taming Paralever rear suspension, if not prostituted, at least gone

BMW borrowed a bit of style from its Italian neighbor, Ducati, when it designed the underseat exhaust system for the S model.

AWOL. The Paralever looked too busy for a cruiser, BMW engineers rationalized, and using it meant that the exhaust system would not fit. But the cruiser would, like all BMW motorcycles, follow its own path in pursuit of fashion. BMW's David Robb approached the cruiser problem in his usual existential fashion: by questioning the very nature of cruisers and the nature of BMW itself. "What is a cruiser?" he wondered, "and what is a BMW?"

Introduced in the summer of 1997 in, appropriately enough, the American West, BMW's R1200C definitely looked like nothing Harley-Davidson had ever built. Nor did it look like anything anyone else had ever built. For starters, the result of Robb's "I-cruise-therefore-I-am-a-BMW-motorcycle" styling exercise was powered by a version of the Oilhead boxer. Add to

that the Telelever front suspension and Monolever rear suspension, all of which was hung in plain view for the entire world to see, and you had a motorcycle that *Motorcyclist* magazine called "a weird-looking rig." Still, the magazine admitted that the R1200C's avant-garde techno-rockabilly styling had its own urban-punk charm.

The bike's appearance polarized people. As Art Friedman wrote in *Motorcycle Cruiser*, "Not everyone likes the lines of the suspension components but everyone has an opinion about the looks." If the job of a cruiser is to attract attention to its rider, the new BMW succeeded and then some. "No one walks past it without at least a slight break in their stride," Friedman wrote, "and most folks have to stop and say something."

The K1200LT was the motorcycle that finally dethroned Honda's Gold Wing as the top-rated touring motorcycle.

The folks who liked the C model really liked it. "The R1200C is the most tactile object I have ever encountered," gushed Jenny Han in *Motorcycle Cruiser*. "Even the key screams 'touch me!' It is a veritable feast for the senses. From the moment I walked up to the beast I was intoxicated. Visually, the BMW is one sexy piece of work."

In addition to abandoning the Paralever rear suspension for the old-tech Monolever system, the C broke with its Oilhead brethren by using a small aluminum frame to tie the engine to the steering head. Rather than hiding this frame, which also housed a pair of oil coolers, behind bodywork, BMW hung it out in plain view, using it as a design element. The steel subframe was also more substantial, and ran down to the rear of the transmission to form the pivots for the Monolever rear end. The engine attained its 1,170-cc displacement through a 101-millimeter bore and a 73-millimeter stroke, up from the original 99-millimeter-by-70.5-millimeter bore and stroke of the 1,085-cc R259 Oilhead.

Even though it used the older Monolever rear suspension, the BMW handled relatively well, much better than most of the motorcycles populating the hot-selling cruiser market. "We're quite certain we could chap a few sportbike hotshoes if we were to rumble upon them during a Sunday ride," *Motorcyclist* observed. The magazine rated the C as the best handling cruiser on the market.

The biggest gripes with the new cruiser centered around the bike's sound, about which *Motorcyclist* wrote, "The family Vanagon had a ballsier exhaust note." Otherwise, testers were generally pleased with BMW's rendition of the peculiarly American genre known as the cruiser. "It sure ain't no Hog," *Motorcyclist* concluded, "and it certainly isn't a Japanese knockoff.

The K1200LT comes standard with a huge top case (not shown here).

chrome trim. All models came standard with electronically adjusted windshields, ABS, four-speaker AM/FM cassette stereos, electronic reverse drives, adjustable ergonomics, electronically heated hand grips, cruise control, intercom systems, and many, many more features.

While it used the same basic backbone frame as the K1200RS, the swingarm was 3 inches longer than the swingarm on the RS and the subframe was beefier to handle the extra weight of the LT's standard luggage. And there was plenty of extra weight. The LT tipped the scales at a mind-boggling 851 pounds with its 6.3-gallon tank topped off. But when compared to other luxury-touring motorcycles, its weight was just average, and excessive weight really isn't considered a handicap in this market anyway.

Heavy or not, the LT retained the RS models' good handling characteristics and threw in huge quantities of comfort and luxury in the process. "Off the highway," *Motorcyclist* reported, "the LT becomes less luxoboat and more sport-tourer: firmer suspension, lighter weight, and Telelever front suspension combine with superior ABS stopping power for a sporty ride that doesn't feel as counter-intuitive as it does on the 'Wing." That was the perfect formula for success in an American-style touring bike, and the K1200LT became BMW's best-selling model in the U.S. market, despite having a price tag that started right around $17,000 for the base model.

The magazines liked the new BMW at least as much as the touring crowd did, and the biggest BMW ever won every touring comparison it entered. After the bike won the magazine's 10-bike touring comparison in early 1999, *Motorcycle Consumer News* wrote, "What you've got here is simply the best-handling, best-equipped, largest load carrying, only ABS-equipped, most aerodynamic full-dress touring rig ever invented."

Like all the BMW motorcycles designed under David Robb's watch, the new LT's mission statement was to present an integrated motorcycle that met the rider's need. The unstated goal of the bike was to dethrone Honda's mighty Gold Wing and become the world's new ultimate touring bike. "Unlike previous K-LTs, which offered a uniquely European and slightly Spartan view of Grand Touring, this new and biggest BMW has Honda's sybaritic Gold Wing dancing in its cross hairs," *Cycle World's* Steve Anderson wrote. It was a lofty goal. Many had tried, but in nearly 25 years, none had succeeded in knocking the Gold Wing off the top of the luxury-touring food chain. The then-current version of the Gold Wing, the six-cylinder 1500, had been around since 1987, and it still remained the standard against which all other touring bikes were measured. Lofty goal or not, with the new K1200LT, BMW succeeded in dethroning the Wing.

It's funky and odd and most definitely different, all rolled up in one nicely chromed package."

Weird or not, the R1200C proved popular and became BMW's best-selling bike in the U.S. market for the 1998 model year. *Motorcycle Consumer News* identified the appeal of BMW's new cruiser: "If you're sick of cookie-cutter clones, this could be the bike for you."

BMW'S ULTIMATE BEHEMOTH

The cruiser would only retain its best-seller rating for a single year, not because it became less popular, but because BMW introduced a new bike for the 1999 model year that outsold the C model. The long-expected new K1200LT replaced the K1100LT, the last of the original Compact Drive System flying bricks. By 1998, the K1100LT had become superfluous. While an impressive bike when it debuted at the beginning of the decade, it was even then outclassed by Honda's six-cylinder Gold Wing. In *Motorcycle Consumer News'* four-bike comparison test of 1998-model luxury touring bikes, the K1100LT came in dead last, losing out even to Harley-Davidson's Electra Glide. The magazine called the K1100LT a "half-hearted effort."

The K1200RS served as the basis for the new LT model, or rather, models. The bike was offered in three distinct trim packages: Standard, which was the base model; Icon, the midlevel model; and, Custom, the top-of-the-line model. The base model had pretty much every luxury a rider—even a touring rider—could imagine. The Icon had everything and then some. The Custom model had all that along with additional splashes of

Like the other magazines, *Cycle World* gave the new BMW the nod over Honda's Gold Wing. "Because the BMW hauls longer and harder," journalist Allan Girdler wrote, "the BMW wins."

Motorcyclist concluded its comparison between the K1200LT and the Honda Gold Wing: "Get the Beemer. And if you call it a car again, we'll have to kill you." The magazine even entered its long-term K1200LT test bike in the grueling Iron Butt Rally, an 11,000-mile, 11-day torture test of both rider and machine. While the magazine's test bike only finished in 55th place, a total of five of the new LT models finished the event, including the bikes piloted by rally winner George Barnes and second-place finisher Rick Morrison. Barnes set a new Iron Butt record by riding 13,346 miles over the 11-day event.

RETURN OF THE S

By the end of the 1990s, BMW was feeling its oats. Just to prove its string of successes weren't just flukes, and that the company would not be returning to its historical dormant state any time soon, the company introduced a second important new model for the 1999 model year: the R1100S.

The new S model used the same basic engine from the R1100RS and R1100RT, but thanks to a free-flowing and sexy under-seat exhaust system, as well as some traditional hot rod tweaks, the bike pumped out an additional 5.6 horsepower. "Engine power is excellent," *Motorcycle Consumer News* reported, "with abundant *umph* available from 2,000 rpm and continuing in a linear manner to its peak at 7,500 rpm."

The new S model was more than a mere styling exercise. It introduced an important new feature to the Oilhead line: the six-speed Getrag-built transmission from the K1200RS. It also featured an aluminum frame, whereas the rest of the Oilhead family featured no frame at all. BMW cloaked the new machine in stunning bodywork that could only have come from a design studio headed by David Robb.

The R1100S proved to be a very good motorcycle, though contrary to its racy looks it was still a sport-tourer rather than an all-out sportbike. It was, however, the sportiest sport-tourer BMW had ever built. "Cornering clearance was remarkable," *Cycle World* reported, "and the Telelever suspension gave excellent feedback, with very little front-end dive under braking. The bike was dead-stable at speed, and even fitted with Dunlop's less-than-gummy D205 sport-touring rubber, the chassis allowed remarkable cornering speeds for a bike of this weight." There was the caveat: "*For a bike of this weight.*" "In slower, really tight corners, the 1100S's mass became more noticeable, and the bike more of a handful," the magazine continued. Like all BMWs, the S was a versatile machine. It was easily comfortable enough for cross-country trips, at least if such trips were taken solo, but with a wet weight of 540 pounds, it was just a little too heavy to be taken seriously as a pure sportbike.

But it was never meant to be a single-purpose sportbike. "The BMW is farthest in this group from a pure sportbike," *Cycle World* concluded after a multibike comparison test between the BMW, Ducati's ST4, Honda's VFR800F Interceptor, and Triumph's Sprint ST, "but it is a fantastic all-around sporting machine. The dividend is exceptional long-haul comfort, with options that include fine hard luggage ($754), heated handgrips and the aforementioned ABS."

Motorcycle Consumer News elaborated on this point even further: "Superior performance can be had from the likes of the Ducati ST4, TL Suzukis, or even a Honda VFR or Superhawk. But none of those bikes offer factory heated grips, antilock brakes, shaft drive, Telelever suspension, or other options of the S-bike, and only Ducati matches the 1100S with available factory hard bags."

It was *Motorcyclist* that best explained the new S: "Have the Legendary Engineers of Germany gone and built a Superbike? No. It's not a racer-replica—not a replica of anything, really. What it looks like from here is exactly what the R90S was back in 1973: a BMW that plays nasty on the weekend without forgetting its all-around manners during the week."

BMW IN THE NEXT MILLENNIUM

The R1100S was a fine motorcycle to serve as the closing chapter of BMW's most successful decade ever, but it was the last really new motorcycle BMW would introduce for the next several years. After a decade of introducing innovative new motorcycles, BMW returned to its process of refining existing products.

The company introduced an upgraded *Geländstrasse* Oilhead for the 2000 model year, the R1150GS. Unlike the R1100S, this bike retained the original frameless R259 design, but added the six-speed Getrag transmission from the S and K1200RS. This bike retained the original 70.5-millimeter stroke from the R259 engine, but used the 101-millimeter bore from the cruiser to achieve a displacement of 1,130-cc. These upgrades made an already excellent machine even better.

The price of the big GS had risen to $14,190 for the 2000 model year, but no one expected a BMW to be inexpensive. Besides, the latest iteration of BMW's adventure-tourer performed extremely well in a variety of functions. It was a terrific sportbike, a competent touring bike, a practical commuter bike, and even a passable trail bike, provided the trail in question was very well groomed. As *Cycle World*'s sports editor Mark Hoyer pointed out, "It *is* kind of like getting two bikes for the price of one." Actually it was more like getting four bikes for the price of two, but he had the right idea.

Bill Stermer summed up the appeal of the expensive GS in his *Rider* road test:

" In its latest incarnation the R1150GS remains one of the most versatile machines available. Its riders can venture into places that are functionally off-limits to all but a handful of other two-wheelers, and it's surprisingly quick on the road too. It can still take you more places than nearly any other big streetbike on the planet, with features and amenities most machines still only dream about.

In 2000, BMW took production of its single-cylinder bikes in house. Rather than having Aprilia construct the bikes in Italy, BMW moved production to its Berlin plant. For 2001 BMW introduced a restyled version of the F650, the F650GS. This bike featured a fuel-injected version of the four-valve thumper, along with a new steel parameter-type frame that carried its fuel under the seat. BMW also offered a more radically styled Paris-Dakar version of the bike. This bike was in many ways improved over the original, but BMW didn't get the fuel injection right on the earliest models.

For 2002, BMW introduced the F650CS, a slick roadster version of the GS, one that abandoned all off-road trappings and accepted itself for what it was—a neat little road bike. That abandonment of dirt pretense is reflected in the bike's name: "CS" stands for "City Sports." The most innovative feature of the new CS is its single-sided swingarm and belt-drive system. The coolest feature of the CS is the fake gas tank that houses a portable storage compartment. This compartment is really a backpack, once removed from the housing.

For 2002 BMW brought the same upgrades to the rest of the Oilhead line-up that it had given to the GS model two years prior. The three updated models—the R1150RS, R1150RT, and R1150R—featured the Getrag six-speed transmission, larger 1,130-cc engine, and revised styling. The R1150R roadster was perhaps the most dramatically restyled motorcycle of the bunch. "The classic roadster has always been about fun, and we wanted to build on that quality," David Robb says. "The art is in the subtle nuances. It looks a little different from each angle. From behind it has a sensual look with a slim waist for a raw, natural quality. A side view reveals a more muscular feel with the integrated oil coolers. And the front looks even meatier, like it will gobble up whatever is in its path."

When *Motorcycle Consumer News* tested the 2002 R1150R, test rider L. T. Snyder thought Robb's styling looked "kinda bulky," but when it came to the way the bike worked, he had no qualms: "If you have a hankering to stuff Yamaha R1s, this bike can do it."

Some 2002 BMW models also featured BMW's new Integral ABS system that links the front and rear brakes, along with the company's radical new EVO braking system that uses large (but extremely light) brake rotors and redesigned master cylinders. This system produces phenomenally short stopping distances, but it has received mixed reviews. More experienced riders sometimes find it distracting. "I never thought a jock strap would make my list of required touring equipment," Brian Catterson wrote in his personal comments regarding Cycle World's R1150RT test bike, "but then, I never thought motorcycles would come with power brakes, either."

END OF THE CENTURY

In the past, BMW has entered periods of steady, quiet upgrades when the motorcycle division has been strapped for cash, but that would not seem to be the case at the turn of the 21st century, given the record run of success the company's motorcycles had throughout the 1990s.

But in a strange turn of events, BMW did find itself in a dire financial position at the dawn of the new millennium. In the past, it had been BMW's automotive division that had bailed out the struggling motorcycle division. By the year 2001 those tables had turned. BMW automobiles were selling as well as ever, but the automotive division was in deep trouble due to an ill-advised buyout of the Rover automobile company in the mid-1990s. The ailing Rover proved a tremendous drain on BMW's resources, and in 2001 BMW sold most of the struggling company to Ford for a paltry $4.77 billion in U.S. dollars. Just arranging the sale itself cost BMW $3 billion. Thanks to the tens of billions of dollars BMW lost trying to revive Rover, the Munich-based firm found itself cash poor heading into the new century.

The motorcycle division was one of the few bright spots on the company's balance sheet. Thanks to its innovative new bikes, particularly the popular Oilhead models, the hot-selling F650 singles, and the K1200LT series, BMW motorcycle sales continued to break records year after year, especially in the U.S. market. On February 15, 2002, BMWNA announced it had just posted its 10th consecutive year of record sales, charting an 8 percent growth over the year 2000. North America was BMW's single largest market, and the $16,290 R1150RT was

POWER BRAKES

Historically, braking has been one of the least well developed skills among the average motorcyclist. In Harry Hurt's ground-breaking study on motorcycle safety, the Hurt Report, the greatest number of rider control errors in emergency situations involved the use of the brakes. The study found that 62 percent of riders involved in the accidents studied failed to use their brakes effectively.

Such research led BMW to become the staunchest proponents of antilock braking systems in the entire motorcycle industry. In 1988, the company developed the first ABS system for motorcycle use. For 2002 the company introduced another technological breakthrough: power brakes.

The system features a pair of electro-hydraulic servo-assist pumps that are activated when the rider touches the brake levers. These pumps reduce pressure needed on the levers by 50 percent, according to BMW. The EVO system, as BMW calls it, is available in fully-integrated form, which applies a greater amount of power to the brake receiving the greatest force from the lever, and partially integrated form, which only applies power braking to the front rotor. The fully integrated system is standard on the R1150RT as well as the K1200LT, and the partially integrated system is available on the R1150R, the R1100S, and R1150RS.

the company's best-selling model in that market for 2001. What makes this all the more impressive is that the R1150RT was an early-release 2002 model.

Worldwide, BMW's motorcycle division also posted its best sales year ever. The best-selling model worldwide was the F650GS. BMW sold 17,445 of its smallest model. Overall, BMW sold 90,478 motorcycles in 2001.

While the parent automobile company was experiencing financial hard times in the early years of the new millennium, it had some important assets waiting in the wings. In particular, BMW had retained rights to the new Mini when unloading the rest of its British portfolio onto Ford. Because BMW had been forced to design the new Mini twice (the original British design had been completely unacceptable, forcing BMW's German engineers to redesign the car from scratch), the company had too much invested in the Mini to unload it in its fire sale to Ford. In the meantime, the motorcycle division thrived as never before. The fabled German bikes that were once rare became everyday sights on the world's highways. In some urban areas of the United States, places like San Francisco, BMWs outnumbered even Japanese and American motorcycles on the city streets. And the situation on the motorcycle front would only improve throughout the first decade of the twenty-first century.

The naked 2002 R1150R shows off BMW's latest iteration of the Telelever front suspension. The A arm is now much lighter than the original version. The sleek scoop below the tank funnels air to the oil cooler.

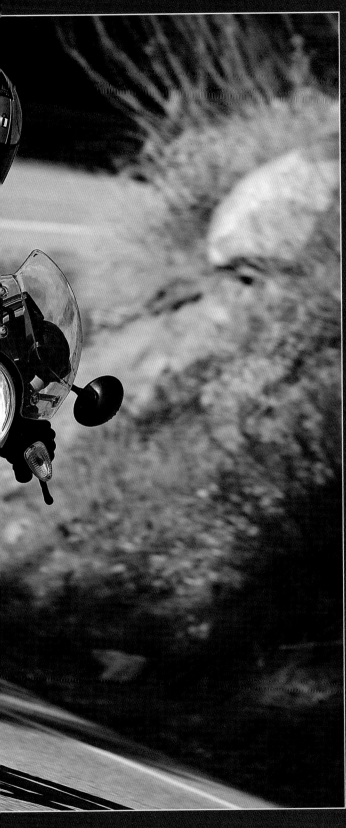

CHAPTER 8

NEW LIFE
IN A NEW MILLENNIUM

If BMW had followed historical precedent after the sale of its British holdings, it would have withdrawn into a period of quiet product evolution. But as the first decade of the new millennium wore on, BMW made it abundantly clear that it had thrown historical precedent to the curb. Christopher Bangle, director of BMW group design, flipped an upturned middle finger in history's direction and plowed head on into so many uncharted design waters that the only people who seemed to understand all the changes were the descendents of Herbert Quandt, who retained ownership of 46 percent of the company.

In some cases the pioneering spirit Bangle brought to BMW design wasn't always appreciated. His "flame surfacing" design esthetic, which characterized BMW automobiles throughout the decade, met with mixed reviews at best, and the iDrive driver interface system he championed was universally hated (though other companies have adopted both with greater success).

But without a doubt Bangle's love of innovation gave David Robb, who remained in charge of design at BMW Motorrad, license to pursue his wildest and most whimsical fantasies. And with a notable exception or two, Robb's visions meshed perfectly with changing public tastes, a fortuitous nexus of motorcycle design and public demand that set up BMW Motorrad for the most successful decade in the company's history. Seldom does a motorcycle designer emerge from nameless, faceless bureaucratic obscurity (quick—who designed the latest Honda CBR1000RR or

ABOVE: The large hole in the R1200R's hollow rear axle shows the lengths to which BMW engineers went in an attempt to shave weight from their motorcycles.

LEFT: BMW's R1200R is as basic a motorcycle as one can buy today—two wheels, an engine, a frame, a place to put fuel, a place for the rider to sit— but the associated bits that make it all work (the suspension, the electronics, the overall engineering) are as high-tech as the basic concept is simple.

In the relatively anonymous world of motorcycle designers, BMW's David Robb, shown here aboard a 2006 F800S, is the equivalent of a rock star. *BMW AG*

Yamaha R1?), but Robb's designs throughout the 1990s and 2000s were so innovative that he became something of a celebrity in the motorcycle world. In an August 2002 test of the BMW F650CS, Motorcycle.com wrote:

> Ever heard of David Robb? Well, now you have. This bespectacled chap stands behind all of the controversial two-wheeled stuff that's been coming out of Munich lately, prompting the established Beemer fraternity to wonder where it's all going to end.

ROCKSTER

The R1150R had caused quite a stir with its unconventional design mated to thoroughly unconventional styling, but that styling was sedate compared to the next iteration of the R-model Oilhead, the R1150R Rockster, unveiled in Munich in September 2002. Robb's design team blacked out just about every part of the bike, including the engine and chassis, mounted a vestigial wind deflector over a headlight nacelle lifted from the R1150GS, then covered much of the bodywork in brightly colored strobe stripes that could give small children and other rudimentary primates epileptic seizures if they stared at the thing too long. Finishing the wheels in the same color as the strobe stripes made the Rockster even more striking.

The Rockster featured dual-spark-plug heads, a first for a BMW boxer twin. This design improved fuel mileage and reduced emissions by promoting more uniform combustion. BMW claimed the engine produced 85.0 horsepower and 73.0 pounds of torque, though dyno tests showed the actual numbers to be 74.9 horsepower at 8,250 rpm and 66.0 pounds of torque at 5,250 rpm. While this wouldn't scare a Yamaha R1 rider, or even an R6 rider, it was more than enough power for an unfaired motorcycle.

The mechanical improvements and visual trickery made what was already an extremely competent and desirable motorcycle even more desirable. Factor in a relatively low (for BMW) price of $10,790 for the non–ABS-equipped version (buyers wishing to spend more could add just about every amenity BMW offered, including ABS, which set a buyer back a whopping $2,200), and BMW had another popular model on its hands. More importantly, the Rockster sold to a desirable market demographic with which BMW hadn't previously made many inroads: younger buyers. For the first time BMW had a motorcycle that was not only competent and elegant but also cool.

The press didn't quite know how to react to a cool BMW motorcycle. In a test of the 2003 Rockster for Motorcycle.com, Jason Roberts wrote:

> To me, BMW motorcycles have always seemed like old-fart bikes, kinda fuddy-duddy, boring, something my grandfather would ride. . . . Even their sportiest offerings, such as the R1100S, are hardly seen in the trendy sportbike circles and hangin' at the usual rider roadhouses. Neither hip nor cool.

Roberts concludes that the rockster was indeed hip and cool—cool enough, in fact, that he would purchase one with his own money. He wasn't the only one who felt this way; with its bad-ass looks (which BMW described as "predatory" in its literature) and all-around basic greatness, the new Rockster sold in huge numbers, especially in the style-conscious U.S. market, helping to make 2003 BMW's best year ever when it came to U.S. sales. In 2002, BMWNA had sold 13,232 motorcycles in the United States. In 2003 that number jumped to 15,412, thanks in part to innovative new products like the Rockster.

THE MISSTEP

Building a cruiser had always been a controversial move for BMW because, by the genre's very nature, a cruiser is something of an anti-BMW. The defining characteristic of a cruiser is the elevation of form over function; the defining characteristic of a BMW has always been the emphasis of function over form. The R1200C had sold well at first, but BMW didn't do much with the model after its introduction. The company added some saddlebags and a windshield to the basic cruiser package and called it the Montana, and for the 2001 model year engineers mounted a pair of flashy three-spoke rims and splashed on a healthy dollop of chrome plating to create the Phoenix version. The company also sold a blacked-out Stiletto version as well as a sport-touring version with small bags and a

BMW celebrated its 80th anniversary with a special edition 2004 R1150R Rockster. The Alpine White and Sapphire Black Metallic bike came with heated grips, ABS, and a blue badge with "80 Years" in script lettering. *BMW Motorrad USA*

With its asymmetrical headlights, Telelever front suspension, and opposed-twin engine, BMW's 80th anniversary R1150R Rockster couldn't be confused with any other bike on the planet. *BMW Motorrad USA*

The riders on this BMW R1200CL look happy enough, probably because they can't see the bike's insect-like face from the saddle. This bike represented a rare misstep for BMW's motorcycle division. *BMW Motorrad USA*

café-racer-type windscreen, but these "new models" simply amounted to Robb's designers raiding BMW's accessories catalog in an attempt to spruce up an aging platform that BMW's core audience had never embraced in the first place. After half a decade without a major update, sales had virtually stopped by the time the 2003 models were introduced.

The C model's first significant update would prove to be its last. In a last-ditch attempt to revive C-model sales, Robb's team mounted hard saddlebags and a top box, oil-cooler covers/fairing lowers, and a handlebar-mounted fairing to the basic Cruiser. This formula had been used with great success by Harley-Davidson, which had invented the touring motorcycle by mounting hard bags and a handlebar-mounted fairing on its full-sized FL model decades earlier.

Copying the template created by rival Harley-Davidson did not sit especially well with Robb's team of visionaries, so in an attempt to differentiate BMW's touring cruiser from the scores of other such bikes on the market at the time (as if the BMW C model, with its funky Telelever front suspension and in-frame oil coolers, wasn't already differentiated enough), they squeezed four lights into the space usually occupied by one on a traditional handlebar-mounted fairing. Two side-by-side-mounted outboard headlights flanked a pair of vertically stacked driving lights. The resulting motorcycle looked much like the compound lenses of an insect's eyes.

Other than a tweak to the fuel-injection system that eliminated the manually operated fast-idle circuit, the engine was unchanged from the standard C model's engine, retaining that bike's claimed 61 horsepower and 72 pounds of torque. BMW did fit its new touring rig with the same six-speed transmission that had been used on all the Oilheads for the 2003 model year except for the remaining C models. While 61 horsepower might have been adequate for the naked Cruiser (*Motorcycle Cruiser's* dyno testing put the rear-wheel horsepower closer to 52 horsepower), it was on the low side for a heavy touring bike (BMW claimed a dry weight of 679 pounds, but *Motorcycle Cruiser's* test bike weighed in at 724 pounds). The more polite testers described acceleration as "leisurely." Others were less charitable.

As bad as the combination of anemic engine and excessive weight was, other aspects of the R1200CL measured up even worse compared to BMW's competition in the touring-bike market. In particular the low-speed handling drew intense criticism from the motorcycling press. Once moving, the bike's handling improved thanks to relatively stiff springing. Motorcycle-USA.com compared the bike to "a chunky ballerina," writing: "the CL has some surprisingly good moves as long as the going doesn't get too tight. Keep the speed above 30 mph, and the CL has neutral steering that allows for pavement carving beyond expectations."

By all accounts the R1200CL wasn't a very good motorcycle. Nor was it a cheap one; the basic bike retailed for $15,990, and the Classic version with radio, CD player, and heated seat ran $16,490.

The buying public seemed no more impressed with the genuinely weird-looking R1200CL than was the motorcycling press, and this lack of love was reflected in abysmal sales. By the 2005 model year, the 1200CL was but a bad memory. The basic C model itself also disappeared from BMW's lineup following the 2004 model year, ending the firm's foray into building function-following-form motorcycles.

THE LAST FLYING BRICK

If the R1200CL was a misstep for BMW, another new bike introduced for the 2003 model year—the K1200GT— proved to be exactly what the market wanted.

The four-cylinder K1200LT introduced for the 1999 model year had been a hit, giving Honda's Gold Wing the stiffest competition the Japanese bike had ever encountered in the luxury-touring market. It remains popular as of this writing; in 2009 it began its second decade of production virtually unchanged from the original 1999 model, indicating that BMW got the basic bike right from the start.

The original K1200 model, the K1200RS, didn't fare quite as well, especially in the U.S. market. That wasn't because there was anything wrong with the bike. As anyone fortunate enough to have spent time in the saddle of the sportiest version of the 1,170cc flying bricks will tell you, the K1200RS was a superb motorcycle—handsome, smooth-running, and remarkably agile for such a large machine. Compared to hard-core sportbikes, it was comfortable, too.

The problem was that many American riders did not care for the bike's riding position: Although well suited to flat-out running down Germany's autobahns, it was a bit too sporting for America's slower-paced roads. Most of the sport-touring motorcycles sold in the U.S. market had higher bars and lower, more forward-placed footpegs than did the big Beemer. American buyers and journalists alike didn't know how to categorize the K1200RS. It was too big and too heavy to be a sportbike, but the riding position was too extreme for the thing to be a sport-tourer; in other words, it was a bit of a t'ain't, to use the vernacular of our time. *Motorcyclist* magazine described the situation:

From where we sit, the K1200RS has always been something of a jackalope. You know, the beast immortalized on wacky roadside postcards: a composite creature with a jackrabbit chassis grafted to the top half of a puzzled antelope.

For 2003 BMW introduced the bike that many had thought the K1200RS should have been: the K1200GT. Very little changed in the conversion from RS to GT—the 1,170cc engine was still of the laid-down flying-brick variety, still generated a claimed 130 horsepower at the crankshaft, and was still rubber-mounted in the same aluminum frame found on the RS. The only substantial changes involved the bodywork and riding position. With more upright ergonomics, a more comfortable (and electrically heated) seat, and more protection from the elements provided by a larger fairing—which included an electrically adjusted windshield and color-matched saddlebags as standard equipment—the K1200GT hit the sweet spot for a lot of U.S. sport-touring fans.

The GT earned much praise in period road tests. *Rider* magazine called its four-cylinder engine "a marvel of automotive smoothness" and felt "its endless stream of power" made the big Beemer "great fun on smooth, fast sweepers."

Though the GT clearly represented a step forward for BMW's K series, it came to the market at a time when there was more competition in the sport-touring market than there had ever been. By 2003 just about every motorcycle manufacturer was building a competent (and in some cases extraordinary) sport-touring motorcycle. In particular, Yamaha and Honda were building shaft-driven sport-touring bikes that competed directly with BMW's K bikes—the FJR1300 and ST1300, respectively. Both of these bikes were clean-sheet designs using the latest technology; by contrast the BMW was a mildly updated version of a bike that had originally been introduced in

The K1200RS had been a bit of a 't'ain't ('t'ain't a sportbike and 't'ain't a sport-touring bike) and never really caught on in the U.S. market. For 2003 BMW gave the bike a roomier riding position, better weather protection, and larger luggage to create the K1200GT. *BMW Motorrad USA*

the fall of 1996, and it suffered in comparison to the newer designs. In his comments for Motorcycle.com's first ride of the K1200GT, John Burns wrote:

"It works, sort of, but it strikes me as a band-aid fix you'd expect to find on a K-car or something." In particular, Burns singled out the flying-brick engine for his most scathing criticism: "The engine BMW says was new five years ago was, in fact, a stroked version of the original inline-four flying brick that—I'm sure you'll correct me if I'm wrong—originated in the late '80s [he was wrong—it originated in the early 1980s]."

What most journalists didn't know was that BMW considered the K1200GT a placeholder. When the K1200GT hit the market, BMW was putting the final touches on a completely new line of four-cylinder bikes with completely new engines. The only things these new four-cylinder motorcycles would share with the flying bricks would be a blue-and-white BMW badge. The K1200LT would remain in the lineup, but within a couple of years after the introduction of the K1200GT, the LT model would be the last remaining example of the original flying bricks introduced in September 1983. BMW was about to abandon its laid-down, longitudinal four-cylinder engine.

The heart of BMW's modern K-bike series: the 1,157cc, inline, four-cylinder engine canted forward 55 degrees.

A COMPLETELY NEW ENGINE

At the 2004 Intermot Motorcycle and Scooter Fair in Cologne, Germany, BMW introduced a new motorcycle powered by a completely new engine design. This was big news. If you consider the Oilhead an evolution of the original boxer design, and if you consider the original single as simply a boxer cut in half (which is what it was), and if you consider the K-series triple to be simply an abbreviated version of the original K-series flying brick (which is exactly what it was), then for its first 80 years BMW had only brought two completely new, clean-sheet engine designs to the market. (The F-series singles aren't included in this count because that engine was developed by Rotax instead of BMW.) The new K1200S introduced for the 2005 model year raised that number to three.

Given that BMW introduces completely new engine designs only slightly more often than Halley's Comet cycles past the earth, this introduction warranted a great deal of attention. With the company's long history of using unique engine configurations, many BMW fans wondered what sort of a design would follow the longitudinal, inline four. Would it have more or less than four cylinders? Given that BMW had built one-, two-, three-, and four-cylinder engines, an engine with five or more cylinders wasn't completely out of the question. Would it use conventional valves, or would BMW mine its Formula 1 auto racing heritage and use pneumatic valves?

Instead of reinventing the internal combustion engine, BMW surprised everyone by introducing a motorcycle with an engine that used thoroughly conventional transverse, inline-four architecture. The transverse, inline, four-cylinder engine design was so closely associated with Japanese motorcycles that the design defined what became known as the UJM (universal Japanese motorcycle). After generations of refusing to follow the patterns set by the Japanese, BMW finally seemed to be marching in lock step with its Asian competition.

Closer inspection revealed that while the basic engine layout might be the same as that found on a Yamaha R1 (or Honda CBR or Suzuki GSX-R or just about every other sportbike that ever left a Japanese factory), BMW did indeed dip into

With the 1200S, BMW introduced the most sporting motorcycle in the company's 80-plus-year history. But it was still a sport-touring motorcycle. When the bike was enlarged to 1,293cc for the 2009 model year, the company had already announced plans to build a full-on sportbike.

its bag of Formula 1 tricks to make the new powerplant as unique as fans expected a BMW motorcycle engine to be.

BMW claimed the new 1,157cc engine put out an astounding 167 horsepower at 10,250 rpm and generated 96 pounds of torque at 8,250 rpm. The engine was light, weighing a claimed 179.3 pounds, and compact, thanks to the arrangement of the auxiliary systems. Like most Japanese motorcycles built since the 1950s, the engine featured an integrated gearbox, allowing the engine and cassette-type transmission to share lubricating oil. By tilting the cylinder axis on the engine of the K1200S to the front by 55 degrees, BMW engineers allowed the use of a downdraft intake system while also enhancing the overall weight distribution. It also allowed the valves to be set at

very narrow angles, enhancing combustion efficiency. Yamaha had long championed this design, originally using it on the company's FZ750 introduced for the 1985 model year, but with its new engine BMW took this concept to the extreme.

The crankshaft of the new four-cylinder engine was forged out of one piece of heat-treated steel. It ran in anti-friction bearings, using a method of supplying oil to the crankshaft and bearings originally developed for BMW's Formula 1 engines. This, in turn, allowed for a very short stroke—with a 1.33:1 bore-to-stroke ratio, the engine was extremely over-square—leading to lower piston speeds, which allowed the engine to run at higher rpm. BMW limited the production engine to 11,000 rpm, but conceivably the potential existed for a much higher redline. In addition to a high redline, the compression ratio of 13:1 contributed to the engine's prodigious horsepower output.

Rather than rubber-mounting the engine to control vibration, as BMW had done on the last versions of the flying brick, the company used a pair of counter-rotating balance shafts that ran at twice the speed of the crankshaft.

One area in which the new BMW engine broke with Japanese orthodoxy was in its oil supply. The new K1200S engine used dry-sump lubrication similar to that used on racing engines. This allowed steady oil flow even under extreme conditions and helped to centralize mass. The oil reservoir was in the frame right behind the engine. An oil cooler in the front fairing was also part of the system.

To keep the high-compression engine from knocking, BMW used an advanced digital engine management system. Though the new BMW required premium fuel, the new engine management system could handle lower-octane fuels, lowering horsepower output in the process.

A NEW CHASSIS

Anyone who feared that BMW was turning too Japanese with its new K1200S was disabused of such a notion when confronted with the radical new chassis housing the surprisingly conventional engine.

The basic frame of the K1200S followed standard Japanese sportbike practice, utilizing a pair of aluminum spars wrapped over the engine, which was a stressed member of the frame. The extreme forward cant of the engine allowed BMW engineers to place the main frame members lower in the motorcycle than they were on a typical Japanese sportbike. This further contributed to centralizing the mass of the motorcycle, which, in turn, made the relatively heavy machine (BMW claimed a dry weight of 547 pounds) feel much lighter when changing direction.

BMW introduced yet another new front suspension design on the K1200S: the Duolever. The company credited the design to a Scot named Norman Hossack, a self-taught engineer who had cut his teeth with Bruce McLaren Motor Racing. In the 1980s Hossack applied the lessons he'd learned designing Formula 1 chassis components to a motorcycle suspension design he called the Hossack System. This was the basis for the Duolever system.

The Duolever used hollow, rigid, cast-aluminum tubes in place of a traditional telescopic front fork. The tubes pivoted on a pair of A-arms that worked like a double-wishbone suspension on an automobile. The arms were connected to a single shock, and the steering was stabilized with the help of an oil-filled steering damper. The system resembled an enormous pair of scissors connecting the front wheel to the frame via what

seemed to be an impossibly complex system of levers, bearings, and joints. Under cornering, the suspension compressed without affecting the bike's steering. Under braking, the suspension did not dive, allowing the bike to be trail-braked into a corner. This system was lighter than the Telelever system, and it provided improved feedback to the rider.

The system was an innovative departure from existing suspension designs, but innovation was nothing new for BMW. The important thing was that it lived up to BMW's expectations. After riding the new K1200S, *Motorcyclist* magazine wrote:

Though it has an inline, four-cylinder engine like the sportbikes from Japan, the K1300S also has a shaft final drive and unique Duolever front suspension that make it better suited for use on the open road than on the tight, twisty confines of a racetrack.

Steering is a little sluggish at parking-lot speeds, especially on cold tires first thing in the morning. But for going fast, it's a significant step forward for BMW. You get more chassis pitch under hard braking than on a Telelever-equipped bike, along with a better feel for what the front tire is doing in any situation. Step off a GSX-R1000 or CBR1000RR and the S's chassis isn't exactly nimble. No surprise there, but Duolever steering effort is more linear than a telescopic fork, on or off the brakes. Steering around an ugly patch of midcorner goose sushi seems easier as well. [The K1200S] feels planted and confidence-inspiring at speed, largely because of its wonderfully compliant suspension.

KEEPING THE SHAFT

Another system in which BMW broke ranks with its Japanese competition was the final drive. The German company considered shaft final drive "absolutely indispensable on a large BMW motorcycle," according to BMW's press release announcing the K1200S; Japanese sportbikes invariably used chain final drives. BMW had introduced a new, lighter, stiffer Paralever design on the 2005 R1200GS and adopted that system for its new four-cylinder sports machine.

Adjustable suspension components had become standard equipment on Japanese sportbikes by the time BMW introduced the K1200S. The typical Japanese system required riders to get off their motorcycles and adjust the shocks manually, but BMW took the concept one step further, creating an optional system that allowed the rider to adjust the springs and dampers electronically at the touch of a handlebar-mounted button. The rider entered the bike's load condition ("solo," "solo with luggage," or "rider with passenger and luggage"), then selected from "comfort," "normal," or "sports" modes. Taking this input, the electronic control unit then selected the appropriate damper rates based on optimum parameters preset in the motorcycle's central electronic system (CES).

BMW's EVO braking system came as standard equipment on the K1200S, as did the company's ABS system. On the K1200S the system was partially integrated, which meant that both front and rear brakes were activated when the rider pulled the handbrake lever, while the footbrake lever acted only on the rear-wheel brake.

EXPANDING THE LINE

For 2006 BMW brought out an entire line of motorcycles based on the new K-bike platform. An all-new K1200GT, based on the K1200S, replaced the older model with the same name. As it had done when converting the K1200RS to the original K1200GT, BMW added saddlebags and a fairing with more weather protection to the basic package. Another improvement came from adjusting the ergonomics for a roomier riding position. The result was a more comfortable and capable long-distance mount. When retuned for sport-touring duty, the engine produced 152 horsepower at 9,500 rpm and 96 pounds of torque at 7,750 rpm.

These simple changes made an already good motorcycle even better. *Cycle World*, which had been one of the few magazines to give the 2005 K1200S a lukewarm reception, named the 2006 K1200GT its sport-touring bike of the year:

> The strengths and capabilities of a sport-touring bike should be as varied and rich as the roads and destinations in this world. Further, the best bikes in the class should suggest such promise and adventure on even the shortest ride. . . . From electronic suspension adjustment to heated grips and seat to electrically adjustable windscreen to capacious saddlebags to the incredible urge of its 152-horsepower inline-four, the BMW K1200GT is a leap forward in swift comfort and cornering composure. All the bikes in this class promise a lot in terms of how far you can go and how much fun you can have getting there. The BMW K1200GT promises more.

NAKED K

When BMW introduced its first four-cylinder motorcycle back in the fall of 1983, a motorcycle without bodywork was the norm. Such bikes weren't even called "standards" back then; they were simply called "motorcycles." The few motorcycles available with fairings, saddlebags, or any other plastic bodywork were the aberrations. A quarter of a century later bikes without such accoutrements were the aberrations, a fact driven home by the term used to describe these machines: "naked bikes."

BMW kept up its long-running tradition of building eccentric-looking motorcycles with the K1200R. Engineers for the naked R version of BMW's four-cylinder platform flaunted its unusual suspension components by surrounding them with an equally unique motorcycle. *BMW Motorrad USA*

BMW hadn't offered a naked four-cylinder motorcycle since the end of the 1986 model year, when the original K100 had disappeared from the lineup. That bike had disappeared due to lack of public interest in bikes without bodywork, but in the years that followed, naked bikes had begun to make a comeback, thanks to the success of machines like Ducati's Monster series. By the time BMW introduced the K1200RS in the late 1990s, naked bikes were once again in vogue, but with its Telelever front suspension, the K-bike platform of the late 1990s was deemed too weird-looking to be seen naked in public.

With its Hossack-type Duolever front suspension, the new K1200S was even odder looking underneath its clothing than the K1200RS had been. It seemed an unlikely candidate for the naked-bike treatment, but the same could have been said of the original Oilhead models, and the naked R version of the Oilhead had proven a popular model. In particular the Rockster, a bike that had successfully exploited BMW's unusual engine and suspension systems as part of its overall in-your-face design, had been well-received by the motorcycle-buying public. The members of Robb's design team had proven they were more than up to the challenge of designing a naked version of the new four-cylinder platform.

BMW made few mechanical changes to the basic platform in the transition from K1200S to K1200R. The new R's engine, which featured a single ram-air intake snorkel as opposed to the twin intakes hidden in the fairing of the S model, was tuned to produce 163 horsepower and 77 pounds of torque. In keeping with its urban-assault-vehicle mission, BMW gave the K1200R comfortable, upright ergonomics with high, wide handlebars. The gearing was a little shorter for enhanced urban trolling (and also for hooliganistic wheelies), and the steering geometry was a bit more aggressive to enable the R to dart through tight traffic, making the K1200R an urban street fighter without peer.

Not only was the K1200R a new kind of motorcycle for BMW, it was one of a number of bikes that were showing BMW to be a new kind of motorcycle company. BMWs had always been about quality, competence, value, and exclusivity. Now BMW was adding an ingredient not previously associated with its brand: exuberant fun.

For 2009 BMW updated the entire line of K bikes (with the exception of the K1200LT, which still utilized the older flying-brick design). BMW bored and stroked the engine to 1,293cc. In addition to necessitating an update of model names to K1300S, K1300R, and K1300GT, this bump in displacement, along with

RIGHT: To create the sport-touring version of the K-bike line, the K1300GT, BMW took the basic sporting K bike and added hard saddlebags, a more comfortable seat with a more upright riding position, and a fairing that provided more comprehensive weather protection.

When upgrading its best-selling model, the R1150GS, BMW didn't veer far from the proven GS formula. Robb's team kept what worked—which was basically the entire bike—but upgraded the engine and suspension, then trimmed off the excess weight that was one of the original bike's few drawbacks.

twins, it had neglected its multi-cylinder bikes. Apparently the company had learned some lessons from this because even while it was developing a new line of four-cylinder motorcycles, it continued to update and improve its bread-and-butter boxer-twin models.

The first boxer to receive a major makeover was the popular GS model. In mid-2004 BMW debuted the R1200GS as an early-release 2005 model. When revising its best-selling motorcycle, Robb's team focused on more power and less weight. BMW coaxed 18 percent more horsepower from the boxer engine through traditional hot-rodding techniques—namely increasing the stroke—leading to a displacement of 1,170cc. The new engine also had larger valves opened by more aggressive camshafts, and lighter, higher-compression pistons also contributed to the bump in horsepower. The engine was the biggest, most powerful boxer engine yet. It was also the smoothest, thanks to a cleverly packaged counterbalancer that quelled the rocking under acceleration that had plagued boxer twins since the very beginning.

To reduce weight by nearly 60 pounds, BMW's engineers reexamined every part of the bike, from the Telelever front suspension to the Paralever rear end. Evidence of this weight saving could be seen in such parts as the rear axle, which was hollow with a beer-can-sized hole through its center. The redesigned rear end also featured a sealed-for-life gear system that never needed its oil changed.

The new, improved GS received so many awards that it was almost embarrassing. *Cycle World* named it the world's best streetbike, *Motorcyclist* made it the magazine's bike of the year, the Industrial Design Society gave it a gold medal in the group's International Design Excellence Awards, and it was awarded the prestigious International Bike of the Year trophy in an annual contest decided through ballots cast by the world's top motorcycle magazines. About voting for the GS as International Bike of the Year, a writer for *Cycle World* said: "This is a motorcycle almost without limits—part standard, part sport-tourer, part backroad bomber, part dual-purpose bike—at home anywhere from the Interstate to the outback, ready for anything."

The public agreed with the magazine's assessment. From the spring of 2004 through August 2007, BMW produced 100,000 copies of the R1200GS and R1200GS Adventure (a version of the bike with an enlarged fuel tank and various adventure-touring styling cues), making it BMW's best-selling motorcycle ever. The success of the model required BMW to add additional work shifts at the Berlin factory to meet worldwide demand. As we enter the second decade of the twenty-first century, the R1200GS continues to be the best-selling motorcycle in BMW's lineup.

some tweaks in the cam profiles, raised claimed power output to 175 horsepower in the K1300S, 173 horsepower in the K1300R, and 160 horsepower in the K1300GT. BMW instituted a Jenny Craig–like program to reduce weight, shaving off pounds wherever possible, replacing, for example, the steel lower A-arm in the Duolever front suspension with a lighter aluminum unit. The result was a claimed 44-pound reduction in dry weight. These alterations improved the bikes' performance, but all of this was overshadowed by one seemingly small change that was universally celebrated: the use of normal turn signal switches.

BIGGER BOXERS

In the past, BMW had tended to focus on one line of bikes at a time. For example, when the company had invested in developing its multi-cylinder lines, the boxer twins had languished without major updates; when the company focused on the boxer

Within months of introducing the R1200GS, BMW brought out a new R1200RT and R1200ST. The RT was an updated version of the popular R1150RT with the same basic upgrades as the R1200GS, namely more power and less weight. BMW had also made dramatic improvements to the linked EVO braking system, addressing the complaints its power brakes had generated over the years. As the result of more power, more comfort, more user-friendly brakes, and less weight, the R1200RT represented a significant improvement over the R1150RT.

The R1200ST replaced the R1150RS and featured the same improvements as the other 1,170cc models. The bike was attractive, comfortable, and, with a claimed 452-pound dry weight, relatively light for a BMW. It was also fast, with a claimed 110 horsepower at the crankshaft (dyno testing showed the bike to be generating an extremely healthy 102 horsepower at the rear wheel), but it never really caught on with the public, and the model lasted just three model years before disappearing from BMW's lineup.

Next, BMW updated its remaining boxer twins, the R1100S and the R1150R. The R1200R was exactly what one would expect—a lighter, faster R1150R with better brakes. The R1200S received a more thorough makeover, in part because the R1100S had skipped all the improvements the rest of the line had received when they were upgraded to 1150 status. The S model lost more flab than the rest of the line, weighing in at a claimed 419 pounds dry, a whopping 111 pounds less than the claimed dry weight of the R1100S it replaced. The new model generated a claimed 122 horsepower at the crankshaft, making it the most powerful twin-cylinder BMW had ever sold to the public. But it was still a traditional BMW, more of a sporty all-around motorcycle than a balls-to-the-wall sportbike. That would come later.

HP2

Even though BMW had achieved terrific success in off-road racing events like the infamous Dakar Rally, the bike that had won the Dakar—the R900R—had been so highly modified that it bore virtually no resemblance to the motorcycles BMW

BMW took the HP2 concept to the street with the HP2 Sport. This bike took Boxer twin performance to unheard of levels.

The HP2 Sport followed the same basic principle established for all of BMW's HP2 motorcycles—to strip away all excess weight, as evidenced by the carbon-fiber-and-Kevlar valve covers. But for the Sport version BMW reengineered the engine, using double-overhead camshafts for the first time on a Boxer twin.

sold to the general public. No one had ever considered BMW's gigantic production dual-sports to be real off-road motorcycles; rather, they were extremely capable road bikes with mild off-road abilities. In 2005 BMW announced a new motorcycle that would replicate the company's Dakar racing bikes as closely as possible: the HP2 Enduro.

For fans of BMW's R900R, the HP2 was a dream come true: an uncompromising, sporting, and exceptionally light off-road boxer. The basic concept was simple; take a standard R1200GS and strip off every nonessential component until all that remains is an engine, a fuel supply, and a small seat and subframe to hold the rider in place, then add top-shelf off-road suspension components. Doing the latter meant abandoning the Telelever front suspension in favor of a traditional hydraulically damped fork, since the heavy Telelever design was never meant for serious off-road use. The end result was a motorcycle that weighed a claimed 386 pounds, still heavy for a true off-road bike, but feather-light by BMW standards.

To promote the new HP2, BMW fielded a semi-factory racing team fronted by Finnish enduro racing champion Simo

Kirssi to compete in various events and series around the world, including both the Baja 500 and the Baja 1000.

All this off-road capability didn't come cheap; the new HP2 Enduro had a price tag on the far side of $20,000, but with about 90 horsepower at the rear wheel and a top speed north of 125 miles per hour, there really wasn't another production vehicle in its league. Everyone who had the opportunity to ride this over-the-top dirtbike was blown away. *Cycle World* wrote: "Of course that begs the question, impressive as this dirty boxer is, can a 400-plus-pound (fully gassed), $20,000 motorcycle be taken seriously as an off-roader? In HP2's case, amazingly, yes."

After introducing the Enduro version of the HP2, BMW followed up with the HP2 Megamoto. For this, Robb's designers simply added mirrors, turn signals, a street-legal exhaust system, and a sticky set of 17-inch road-racing tires to the basic HP2. Though this brought weight up to 440 pounds, it also exponentially increased the potential for serious antisocial behavior. The suspension had to be stiffened for street use. Up front BMW mounted a fully adjustable, fine-response, upside-down Marzocchi fork with fat 45-millimeter sliding

After decades of building off-road racing motorcycles based on the company's road-going machines, BMW got serious about building a real off-road racer and introduced the G450X for the 2009 model year.

tubes. In the back an adjustable Öhlins shock with over seven inches of travel kept the race rubber planted to the pavement.

For the company's next version of the HP2, BMW applied the same high-performance trickery to a pure street version of the concept, the $23,375 HP2 Sport. This race bike for the street utilized the lessons BMW had learned from building the R1200S that won its class at the 24 Hours of Le Mans in 2007. Like its HP2 brethren, the HP2 Sport relied on light weight for improved performance, but it also featured a redesigned engine that used double overhead camshafts, a first for a production BMW boxer engine. BMW claimed the HP2 Sport produced 130 horsepower at 8,750 rpm and 84.8 pounds of torque at 6,000 rpm, with a redline of 9,500 rpm. To emphasize the unique nature of the engine, the valve covers were made of carbon fiber and Kevlar, with each side having a built-in slider puck.

A REAL OFF-ROAD MOTORCYCLE

With all the focus on its twins and four-cylinders, it would have been easy for BMW to forget about its single-cylinder motorcycles, but the BMW Motorrad of the twenty-first century had the resources to update all of its product lines. For 2007 it unveiled a completely revised line of singles with a new alphanumeric designation—the letter G now replaced the letter F. (The reason for this switch will be discussed below.) This line consisted of the G650Xmoto, the G650Xchallenge, and the G650Xcountry. (BMW tried to get people to pronounce the "X" as "Cross"—the "Crossmoto," the "Crosschallenge," and the "Crosscountry"—but since BMW couldn't send out a marketing intern with every bike to explain this esoteric naming system, most people just pronounced the X as "ex.")

The $8,675 G650Xcountry was the most direct descendant of the previous F650GS, a lightweight streetbike with dual-sport tires and modest off-road capabilities. The $9,575 Xmoto was a lightweight machine with 17-inch race tires, sort of like a miniature version of the HP2 Megamoto, and the $9,075 Xchallenge was a more focused off-road machine. All three continued to use Rotax-designed engines, though once again BMW farmed out production to Aprilia. All of these bikes were competitive with the bikes from other European and Japanese manufacturers, though their price tags were a bit on

The most innovative part of the G450X's stainless-steel tube frame was its extremely forward-mounted swingarm pivot that allowed for an extra-long swingarm.

the steep side. The one exception was the Xchallenge, which was still too heavy and too street-oriented to compete with the enduro bikes offered by manufacturers like KTM.

But BMW never intended the Xchallenge to be a serious off-road motorcycle; the company was developing a completely new motorcycle to fill that niche: the G450X. For the 2009 model year BMW got serious about tapping into the lucrative off-road market and introduced a full-on, race-ready, 450cc enduro.

As could be expected from BMW, the new off-road machine was not a simple copy of the dirtbikes from Asia and Europe. To build a clone of an existing bike, BMW would simply have had to raid its parts bin. The company had purchased the off-road motorcycle manufacturer Husqvarna in July 2007, giving BMW engineers ready access to Husqvarna's well-respected line of off-road motorcycles, but the German company chose to develop the G450X in-house without Husqvarna input, though the two companies did share some technology. The result was a completely unique motorcycle. For example, the bridge-type frame, which was constructed of side plates and stainless-steel tubing that wrapped around the sides of the engine and featured an extremely forward-mounted swingarm pivot, bore absolutely no resemblance to any other dirtbike on the market. The forward-mounted pivot allowed BMW to use a long aluminum swingarm while retaining a fairly standard 58.1-inch wheelbase. By using a concentric mount

between the pivot and the countershaft sprocket, BMW created a system that kept constant chain tension throughout the suspension's stroke. The downside of this system was that changing the front sprocket required removal of the swingarm, but BMW claimed that an experienced mechanic could do the job in about 15 minutes.

To create space for the swingarm pivot, BMW moved the clutch to the end of the crankshaft. The frame design and compact engine allowed BMW engineers to cant the cylinder forward 30 degrees, creating enough room to allow the airbox to be mounted above the powerplant. This also freed up room for BMW to install dual-throttle-valve fuel injection, making the 450X the first off-road bike to have such a system. This closed-loop system used an oxygen sensor and three-way catalytic converter to allow the 450X to pass Euro III on-road emissions standards. Because the airbox occupied the area normally reserved for the fuel tank, BMW moved the 2.1-gallon fuel cell to an area under the saddle.

By building a serious off-road motorcycle, BMW dove headfirst into one of the most competitive motorcycle markets of all. Did it succeed? As of this writing the answer to that remains unknown, but initial impressions indicate that, at the very least, it didn't fail. After its correspondent's first ride aboard the bike, *Cycle World* reported: "In its current state, though, it doesn't work any better than the conventional offerings, so the G450X's defining factor is its uniqueness, a trait that will make people stare, question and converse. But make no mistake, the BMW dirtbike has arrived!"

A NEW KIND OF TWIN

In the spring of 2006, BMW unveiled the F800 series, yet another new line of motorcycles with yet another completely new engine design, this one a parallel twin. The advent of the twin-cylinder F series had been the reason BMW renamed its single-cylinder line the G series. Like the F650/G650 machines, the new middleweights used an engine jointly designed by BMW and BRP-Rotax. Rotax built the engines and shipped the completed units to BMW's Berlin facility for assembly. BMW experimented with a number of different engine designs, including V-twins, but selected the parallel twin because of its compact dimensions.

The F800 series consisted of three models: the F800S sportbike, the F800ST sport-tourer, and the F800GS adventure-tourer. Displacing 798cc, the liquid-cooled engine powering these models featured a four-valve cylinder head operated by a pair of camshafts mounted atop the cylinders. The oversquare pistons had a 12:1 compression ratio, requiring premium fuel to prevent detonation. The pistons used a 360-

degree firing sequence, meaning that they traveled in tandem. This necessitated some sort of counterbalancing system to quell the vibrations inherent in a parallel twin with a 360-degree crankshaft. As could be expected, BMW engineers shuffled to the beat of their own drummers when designing the counterbalancing system. Rather than using the counter-rotating shafts used in most other counterbalancer systems, they attached a dummy connecting rod to the crank, offsetting it 180 degrees from the pistons' rods, producing the same effect as a separate counterbalancer but without the noise normally associated with a counterbalancer.

The F800 series used an aluminum chassis that located the fuel tank beneath the seat, making room for a tall airbox above the engine. BMW used a conventional telescopic fork rather than one of the complex (and expensive) Telelever or Duolever designs. Things got a bit more interesting at the rear; instead of the traditional shaft, BMW attached a toothed-belt final drive to the single-sided Monolever swingarm for all models except the GS versions, which used chains instead of belts.

WHEN IS A 650 NOT A 650?

The nomenclature of the F800-series models followed the traditional BMW formula: the F800S was the sporty version, with the most extreme riding position; the F800ST was the sport-touring version, with more upright ergonomics and a more comprehensive touring fairing; the F800GS was the dual-sport

One didn't need to predict the future by reading the carbon deposits on a spark plug to guess that BMW would build a GS version of its F800 vertical-twin platform.

BMW's liquid-cooled, 798cc, parallel twin engine, with its double-overhead cams and four valves per cylinder, made an ideal powerplant for the company's midsized GS model.

version, with dual-purpose tires, higher fenders, more ground clearance and a wider handlebar. On August 19, 2008, BMW announced a fourth member of the F800 series: the F650GS. The motorcycle world responded with a collective: "What the . . . ?"

Given the nomenclature, a rational person would expect the new F650GS to be a revised version of the slow-selling F650GS single cylinder machine. That rational person would be wrong. The new F650GS was really a version of the twin-cylinder F800GS. A rational person would expect that, given the "650" in the F650GS name, the bike would feature a smaller version of the twin-cylinder engine. Again that rational person would be wrong. For reasons known only to the marketing brain trust at BMW, the F650GS displaced the same 798cc of the

F800GS. BMW intended the F650GS to be an affordable entré into the F800 lineup. Its 798cc engine was slightly detuned to a claimed 71 horsepower (the more upscale bikes cranked out a claimed 85 horsepower). A lower seat height made the (we can't call it smaller so we have to call it cheaper) GS more accessible to the inseam-challenged rider.

The basic idea of the F650GS was sound—a lightweight, inexpensive middleweight with a comfortable seat height—and the execution of the bike was superb. When testing it for Motorcycle.com, Dustin Wood called it "a fabulous little bike that exceeded my expectations," but the bizarre marketing decision to call it an F650GS confused many potential buyers. Because its bodywork was intentionally designed to resemble the previous single-cylinder F650GS, many people assumed it was a single-cylinder descendant of that bike and ignored it. Those potential buyers who realized that the bike had a twin-cylinder engine assumed that it was sleeved down to 650cc and again ignored it. A few people did realize what this bike actually was—one of the best all-around motorcycles on the market. At $8,255, the bike was also one of the best values the German company had ever offered. It just had a confusing name.

SUPERBIKE

For years BMW had been rumored to be developing a racing motorcycle. Many people expected the company to compete in the popular MotoGP series, which pitted pure racing proto-types against one another, in contrast to the World Superbike Championship (SBK), which featured production-based machines that had to be homologated by having the company build a certain number of corresponding road bikes. Entering the series required an incredible commitment on the part of BMW, which never before had built—and presumably never would build—something as irresponsible as a sportbike. Or would they? On April 17, 2008, BMW officially announced the 2009 S1000RR race bike, which would compete in the World Superbike series beginning with the 2009 season. To meet homologation requirements, BMW committed to building at least 1,000 units per year.

From the outside, there was nothing about the S1000RR (the street version of the proposed racing bike) to indicate a departure from the standard liter-class sportbike formula. Like the competition from Japan, the bike wrapped a perimeter aluminum frame around a 1,000cc inline-four powerplant. There was no evidence of alternative systems like the Duolever or Telelever front ends, and power was transmitted to the rear wheel by a chain rather than a belt or a shaft. In this ultra-competitive racing series, BMW couldn't afford to be different for the sake of being different; any deviation from the norm would have to be justified by a measurable increase in performance. But the S1000RR did include some examples of technologies that deviated from the norm, including a standard traction-control system. The benefits of such systems had long been proven in MotoGP, but they were not used on production bikes and therefore had yet to be used (legally) in production-based Superbike racing.

Though many people expected an alternative system of valve actuation, such as the pneumatic system used on BMW's Formula 1 racing engines, the valves were activated by means of very small and light cam followers. This system allowed the engine to run at extremely high revs, but it was hardly revolutionary.

GETTING THE SHAFT

By the time BMW introduced the F800 series of motorcycles, belt final-drive systems were well proven. Harley-Davidson had used a belt-drive system for decades, and BMW had been using belt final drives successfully on its single-cylinder models for the better part of a decade. Belt systems have many advantages over chain systems or shaft systems; belts are lighter than either chains or shafts, they don't upset the chassis like a shaft system, and they are as reliable as either chains or shafts. In the case of BMW's Paralever design, a belt system may even be more reliable; as riders logged tens of thousands of miles on their Paralever-equipped BMWs, a disturbing number of them began to experience catastrophic driveshaft failures. This problem seemed to affect BMW's popular GS models the most, perhaps because the tall GS chassis imposes the most extreme bends in the Paralever's articulating joints. The situation didn't improve much with the redesigned system introduced on the 2005 R1200GS. By the end of the decade shaft failures were beginning to take a bite out of BMW sales, which had declined every year after peaking in 2003. Even though BMW was intricately associated with shaft-driven motorcycles, given the problems with the Paralever system, the move to a belt system on the F800 series made sense.

Evidence of how serious BMW was about competing in SBK came when BMW announced it had hired two-time world champion Troy Corser as well as proven winner Ruben Xaus to pilot its new racebikes.

Although BMW didn't expect the new bike to be competitive until at least the third or fourth round of the series, Corser piloted the S1000RR to an impressive eighth-place finish in its very first race at Philip Island in Australia, and as of this writing BMW has earned an impressive 43 points in the series.

On February 8, 2009, BMW Motorrad announced that it had begun building the first batch of street-going S1000RR production bikes. These closely followed the template set by the race version. BMW claimed it had extracted 175 horsepower from the street version of the 999cc, inline, four-cylinder engine (the firm claimed the engine generated 200-plus horsepower in full race trim). With a claimed dry weight of 403 pounds, this most extreme of Beemers was definitely in the hunt with its Asian competition, at least on paper. As of this writing, BMW had yet to announce North American pricing, but the German version was being sold for 15,150 euros.

THE FUTURE OF BMW

On April 18, 2008, BMW Motorrad's new president, Hendrik von Kuenheim, addressed the press for the first time. Von Kuenheim announced his intention to expand the motorcycle business significantly in the coming years. He said that, in particular, the company's boxer-powered bikes would play a key role in future product development, in spite of the fact that

BMW felt the best way to gain credibility in the hotly contested sportbike market was through racing success. Hence the company developed the Superbike racing version of the S1000RR before the road going version. Here, former world champion Troy Corser puts the bike through its paces at Miller Motorsports Park in Tooele, Utah.

BMW had invested so much money and time in developing its four-cylinder K bikes and the new S1000RR sportbike model.

He also announced an ambitious plan to increase global sales by 50 percent within four years. To achieve this, von Kuenheim said BMW would have to focus on the dual-sport, off-road, and sportbike markets because the company had reached a saturation point in its traditional touring and sport-touring markets. This is why the company had invested in its SBK racing program. This is also why BMW had purchased Husqvarna, which was, he said, "the second-oldest motorcycle manufacturer still building motorcycles today." Von Kuenheim said that over the years, Husqvarna had won more than 70 world championships, mostly in off-road racing.

He acknowledged that market conditions at the time were deteriorating, but he still believed that the company's ambitious goals were attainable. He believed that BMW could continue to increase its volume through expansion into different markets. He also acknowledged the difficulties in competing head-to-head with the Japanese in the sportbike class, but he believed BMW was up to the challenge.

Von Kuenheim couldn't have possibly seen the worldwide economic chaos that would erupt in the months after his speech. An international banking crisis plunged the world's economies into turmoil not seen since the 1930s. Automobile sales would plummet by up to 50 percent before the end of 2008 and continue to deteriorate into the following year. Volatile oil prices kept motorcycle sales relatively stable compared to automobile

sales, but for the most part companies were selling small-displacement economy bikes with low profit margins. By the end of 2008, most of the world's motorcycle manufacturers were hurting, and several companies curtailed their racing efforts.

All of this made von Kuenheim's predictions of a 50 percent increase in unit sales by 2012 seem unlikely, the quaint dreams from a previous era. But unlike most manufacturers, BMW Motorrad's sales in the U.S. market—the market hit hardest by the international banking crisis—actually were up

for 2008. True, they increased by just 71 units over 2007, but in the genuinely awful economy of 2008, any increase amounted to an astounding success. This situation carried into the new year. BMW's U.S. sales were up 1 percent in January 2009 over January 2008. This was at a time when automakers were reporting sales declines of 50 percent or more over the previous year. Clearly BMW is doing something right, and that something is building bikes that people want to buy, even in a bad economy.

BMW finally released the details of its entrant into the sportbike market in the late spring of 2009. On paper the new S1000RR appears to have what it takes to compete with its Japanese rivals. *An Neidermeyer, BMW AG*

1924 German 500-cc championship, 19
1948 Geneva Motor Show, 55
1953 German Grand Prix, 62
1979 ISDT, 102
Adjustable suspension, 32, 178
Aldana, Dave, 84, 85
Allach plant, 49, 51, 54
Anderson, Steve, 112
Antilock braking systems (ABS), 128, 171, 179
Auriol, Hubert, 129
Austrian Gran Prix, 62
Baja 500, 184
Baja 1000, 184
Bangle, Christopher, 169
Bayeische Motoren Werke GmbH, 12
Bayerische Flugzeugwerke GmbH (BFW, or Bavarian Airplane Works), 12
Beiber, Franz, 14, 19
Berlin Wall, 146
BMW AG, 12
BMW Nomenclature, 22
Boehm, Mitch, 128
Boening, Alfred, 35
Bruce McLaren Motor Racing, 177
Butler & Smith, Inc., 65, 84, 85, 89
Castiglioni, Camillo, 13
Chandler, Otis, 13
Compact Drive System (CDS), 109, 113, 155, 164, 166
Corser, Troy, 189, 190
Curtiss, Glenn, 15
Cycle World, 67, 69, 79, 81, 82, 86, 87, 89, 112, 179, 182, 184, 186
Czechoslovakian Gran Prix, 62
Dale, Dickey, 62
Das Motorrad, 58
Daytona Orange, 90
Duolever front suspension, 177, 178, 180, 182, 187, 189
Dutch TT, 45
Earles, Ernie, 64, 70
Earles Fork, 62, 64, 65
Eisenach factory, 54
Eisenach Motoren Werke (EMW), 54
Emmersberger, George, 149
Engines
247 cc, 69
450cc, 186
798cc, 186, 188
999cc, 189
1,000cc, 189
1,157cc, 175, 176
1,170cc, 173, 182, 183
1,293cc, 176, 181
M2B15, 13, 14
M2B32, 16, 38
M43, 19
Model 255, 45
Oilhead, 140–167, 170, 172, 175, 180
Otto cycle four-stoke engine, 12

R259, 148, 150, 154, 164, 167
R80GS, 32
EVO braking system, 179, 183
Falkenhausen, Alex von, 35
Federation Internationale Motorcycliste (FIM), 60
"Flame Surfacing" design
Ford, Dexter, 112, 120
Forstner, Josef, 45
Fritzenwenger, Josef, 107
Friz, Max, 12, 14, 18, 27, 48, 49
Gall, Karl, 45
German Grand Prix, 45
Greene, Bob, 89, 91
Gutsche, Rudiger, 102
Hand-shifted transmissions, 18
Hanfland, Curt, 13
Harley-Davidson Tariff and BMW, 107
Henne, Ernst, 27
"High Tension Ignition", 15
Hiller, Ernst, 62
Hitler, Adolph, 34, 45
Hossack, Norman, 177, 180
Hungarian Grand Prix, 45
Husqvarna, 186, 190
iDrive driver interface system, 169
Improvements, 83, 84, 171, 179, 183
Indian Motocycle Company, 16
Intermot Motorcycle and Scooter Fair, 175
International Six Days Trials, 19, 70
Iron Butt Rally, 149
Isle of Man TT, 45, 87
Japanese competition, 98, 173, 175, 178, 185, 190, 191
Kirssi, Simo, 184
Kramm, Wilfried, 83, 86
Kraus, Wiggerl "Ludwig", 45
Ley, Otto, 45
Lindhardt, Fritz, 45
Mann, Dick, 84, 85
Marketing, 117, 185, 188
McLaughlin, Steve, 90
Meier, George, 45, 55, 60
Miller Motorsports Park, 190
Models
5 Series, 52, 53
Airheads, 117
Bison, 13
Corona, 13
Cruisers, 160, 161
F650, 14, 142-146, 186
F650CS, 170
F650GS, 185, 188–189
F800 series, 170, 186, 187, 188, 189
F800GS, 186, 187, 188
F800S, 186, 187
F800ST, 186, 187
Flink, 13
Flying Bricks, 98, 106–108, 173-174, 175, 177
G450X, 186, 189
G650, 185, 186

Geländstrasse, 101, 102, 152–154
Helios, 13, 15
Heller, 13
Heninger, 13
HP2 series, 183–185
K1, 125–129, 134
K75 series, 110
K75C, 115, 116
K75RT, 97, 111
K75S, 112, 115
K75T, 115
K85, 155
K100 series, 106, 180
K100RS, 109, 113, 115
K100RT, 106, 113
K1100LT, 139, 156, 167, 173
K1100RS, 134, 139
K1200GT, 173, 174, 179
K1200LT, 163, 164, 173, 174, 181
K1200R, 180, 181
K1200RS, 157, 159, 160, 173, 174, 179, 180
K1200S, 175, 176, 177, 178, 179, 180, 181
K1300GT, 181, 182
K1300R, 181, 182
K1300S, 177, 178, 181, 182
Kompressors, 27, 28, 36, 38, 45
M2B32, 14
Paralevers, 119–139, 178, 182, 189
Paris-Dakar, 129, 130, 184
Police version of R1100RT, 155
Proletarian singles, 22
R2, 30–33
R4, 31
R5, 36, 38
R6, 38, 46, 170
R7, 35
R11, 30, 31
R12, 31, 33, 34
R16, 29, 30, 31
R17, 31, 34, 35
R20, 46
R24, 55, 57
R25, 57
R25/2, 59
R25/3, 65
R27, 67, 69
R32, 13–20, 48
R35, 46, 54
R37, 19, 20
R39, 20, 22
R42, 17, 19, 24, 26
R50, 64
R50/2, 67
R50S, 67–69
R50US, 70
R51/2, 51, 52, 57, 58
R51/3, 52, 58
R60, 65
R60/2, 67
R60US, 70, 82
R61, 41, 42, 46

R62, 27
R63, 27
R65, 92
R65LS, 104
R66, 46
R67, 58
R68, 54, 55, 59, 60, 62
R69, 64, 67
R69S, 67, 68, 70
R69US, 70
R71, 42, 48
R75, 35, 48, 49, 79
R75/5, 73–80, 82, 83, 86
R75/7, 89
R80/7, 89
R80G/S, 101–103, 120, 122, 129
R80RT, 105, 120, 122
R80ST, 104, 105
R90/6, 87
R90S, 73, 81–83, 86, 87, 91, 95
R100/7, 89
R100GS, 119–121, 124, 129
R100RS, 91, 92, 94, 95, 98, 99, 101, 103
R100RT, 92, 98, 115
R900R, 183
R1100GS, 154,
R1100RS, 141, 154, 160, 167
R1100RT, 150, 152
R1100S in 1999, 165
R1100S, 143, 160, 171, 183
R1150GS, 149, 170, 182
R1150R, 150, 167, 170, 182, 183
R1150RS, 167, 183
R1150RT, 167, 183
R1200C, 158, 171
R1200CL, 172, 173
R1200GS, 178, 182, 183, 184, 189
R1200R, 169, 183
R1200RT, 183
R1200S, 183, 185
R1200ST, 183
Rennsports, 60, 61, 62
Roadsters, 154, 155
RS54 Rennsport, 58, 60–62
Rubber Cow, 93
S1000RR, 189, 190, 191
Scheid, 13
Series 1 R2, 29
SMW, 13
Special K, 134–138
Sporting models, 22
Star bikes, 30
Three-Wheeled Rennsports, 62
Touring models, 22
Ural Motorcycles, 52
Victoria, 13
Monolever rear suspension, 103
Monolever swingarm, 187
Motor Cycle, 58, 65
Motorcycle.com, 170, 171, 174, 188
Motorcyle-USA.com, 173
Motorcycle of the Year, 113–115
Motorcyclist, 89, 91, 112, 173, 177, 182

Muth, Hans, 92, 103
North, Rob, 84, 85
Otto factory, 13
Otto, Gustav, 12
Otto, Nikolaus, 12
Paralever suspension, 146, 147
Paris-Dakar rally, 132, 183
Parkhurst, Joe, 82
Penton, John, 65, 70
Plunger-type rear suspension, 56
Popp, Franz Josef "Karl", 12, 14, 49
Postwar Racing, 60
Power Brakes, 167, 183
Pridemore, Reg, 84, 85
Probst, Martin, 109
Quandt, Herbert, 67, 169
Rahier, Gaston, 129
Rapp, Karl, 12
Rear suspension, 20, 46
Rider, 173
Robb, David, 109, 137, 156, 169, 170, 172, 180, 182, 184
Roberts, Jason, 171
Romero, Gene, 84, 85
Sarossy, Tibor, 70
Saxtorp circuit, 45
Schleicher, Rudolph, 14, 18, 19
Smoke, 80, 87
Spandau, 83
"Star-Frame" concept, 29
Stermer, Bill, 123
Stolle, Martin, 13
Sunnqvist, Ragnar, 45
Swinging arm rear suspension, 56
Swiss Grand Prix, 45
Targa Florio, 27
Telelever front suspension, 14, 141, 150, 151, 167, 171, 172, 177, 178, 180, 182, 184, 187, 189
Telescopic fork, 34, 45, 177, 178, 187
Third Reich, 34
"Toaster Tank", 76
Total-loss oiling systems, 15
U. S. market, 69, 70, 171, 173, 174, 191
Ulster Grand Prix, 45
Versailles Treaty, 11, 12, 18
Von Kuenheim, Hendrik, 189, 190, 191
Wehrmacht, 34
West, Jock, 45
Wet-sump recirculating oiling system, 14
Witzel, Fritz, 102
Wood, Dustin, 188
World Championship Series, 60
World Superbike Championship, 90, 189
World War I, 11
Xaus, Ruben, 189
Zeller, Walter, 62
Zoller, 27